Finding Amy

Finding Amy

A TRUE STORY OF MURDER IN MAINE

Captain Joseph K. Loughlin

Kate Clark Flora

University Press of New England

HANOVER AND LONDON

Published by University Press of New England,
One Court Street, Lebanon, NH 03766
www.upne.com

LIBRARY OF CONGRESS CATALOGING-IN-PUBLICATION DATA
Loughlin, Joseph K.
Finding Amy : a true story of murder in Maine / Joseph K. Loughlin,
Kate Clark Flora.—1st ed.
     p.   cm.
Includes bibliographical references.
ISBN-13: 978–1–58465–533–6 (cloth : alk. paper)
ISBN-10: 1–58465–533–x (cloth : alk. paper)
ISBN-13: 978–1–58465–563–3 (pbk. : alk. paper)
ISBN-10: 1–58465–563–1 (pbk. : alk. paper)
1. Murder—Maine—Portland—Case studies. 2. Murder—Investigation
—Maine—Portland—Case studies. I. Flora, Kate Clark. II. Title.
HV6534.P67L68   2006
364.152′30974191—dc22   2005035369

To Amy Elizabeth St. Laurent

And to all those officers out there who believe

*

When night darkens the streets, then
wander forth the sons of Belial, flown
with insolence and wine.

—JOHN MILTON, *Paradise Lost*

Contents

xi Acknowledgments

1 Prologue: Welcome to the Cop's Life

4 Chapter 1

17 Chapter 2

24 Chapter 3

34 Chapter 4

45 Chapter 5

55 Chapter 6

68 Chapter 7

84 Chapter 8

93 Chapter 9

102 Chapter 10

113 Chapter 11

124 Chapter 12

141 Chapter 13

155 Chapter 14

170 Chapter 15

177 Chapter 16

195 Chapter 17

211 Chapter 18

220 Chapter 19

232 Chapter 20

245 Epilogue: Amy's Legacy

257 Notes

Acknowledgments

First and foremost, our gratitude to Amy's family, for raising the special woman who inspired this book and for their courage in keeping her in the public's eye during such a painful time.

This book would not have been possible without the generous help of the many people who took time from their busy schedules to explain procedure and discuss their role in the investigation. Special thanks to Sgt. Daniel Young, Sgt. Thomas Joyce, and Sgt. Bruce Coffin of the Portland Police Department; Sgt. Matthew Stewart and Detective Scott Harakles of the Maine State Police; Lt. Patrick Dorian and Warden Kevin Adam of the Maine Warden Service; Assistant Attorney General Fernand LaRochelle, Deputy Attorney General William Stokes and Assistant Attorney General Donald Macomber from the Office of the Attorney General; Detective Gerard "Bill" Brady from the Cumberland County Sheriff's Department; and Landon Fake from the Mahoosic Mountain Search and Rescue organization.

To all our readers who gave us feedback and advice on our early drafts: Diane Woods Englund, Elizabeth Armstrong, Esq., Nancy McJennett, Brad Lovette, Andree Buckley, and the most erudite Thomas Yellen of Keio University, Tokyo, Japan.

To our agent, Eve Bridburg, and our editor, John Landrigan, for believing in the book and helping us share Amy's story.

From Kate: Special thanks to my husband, Kenneth Cohen, who put up with my endless trips to Portland—it's not every man who is comfortable with a wife who hangs out at the police department—and to my writing partner, Captain Joe, who kept the faith when I lost it, reminding me that Amy's story mattered. To Lt. Thomas LeMin, of the Newark, Delaware, Police Department, who briefed me on buried bodies; to Lt. Joe Brooks and the Waltham, Massachusetts, Police Department for letting me attend their Citizens' Police Academy; and to Concord,

Massachusetts, police chief Len Wetherbee for answering a million questions.

From Joe: Special thanks to Jennifer True Webber for her love and patience; to Chief Michael Chitwood for his energy and passion; and to Lucille Holt for her faith and friendship. Thanks to Detective Brian Keller and Richard VonVoight, Riverhead, NY, PD (retired) for starting it all by introducing me to the job; and to my neighbor Helene Albert for her insight into the first manuscript.

Finding Amy

Prologue

Welcome to the Cop's Life

I can still recall clearly some of my first days and years on the street after I graduated from the academy. I remember physically shaking on my first call at a domestic disturbance. Training, films, instructor warnings, and danger signals raced through my mind as we made our way up the dark, cold, urine-stained stairwell. A man was screaming, a woman sobbing, and neighbors pointing as glass showered down on us from the third floor.

The senior officer I was assigned to, Cleo Kelly, made it all look so easy. He was more interested in talking about the Celtics than concentrating on our task. I was thinking we were about to be killed. We ended up arresting the man after a brief struggle and counseling the bruised woman as she begged us not to take him away.

The scene at the booking room was just as disturbing. One man was rocking back and forth crying; another spitting and cursing at everyone; tough guys stared ahead and right through me; shouts and curses echoed down the hall from the "tanks" where violent offenders were placed. A man smashed his head against the wall. Metal doors slammed shut; electric buzzers rang out amidst the shouting and screaming. I thought this was what hell must be like.

After a while it all runs together and you forget most of what you are exposed to on the job. By the end of my first year, one of my colleagues was shot in the face, my partner had a breakdown and left the job, and a short while later another officer committed suicide. Yet, I couldn't leave.

It was too interesting, too challenging, and a place where I could do good for the world. It was in my blood, as they say.

One day in the summer I had a fairly busy shift involving some routine and some disturbance calls. One call was for an infant in distress at an apartment. The baby was not breathing. Paramedics and I worked on the baby as the parents tugged and howled at us to help. The apartment was filthy. The man had broken bones from a fall and both legs were in casts. And the baby died in our arms. I distinctly remember that smell and how white the infant looked. After all the reports, I moved on to the next call for service, and the next, adjusting my emotions each time to meet the situation.

Later, taking a break at a Dunkin' Donuts to get a large fruit punch, which I paid for, a man called over to me, "Hey, you guys have it made, doncha. Drive around all day and get free food." I returned to my car, thinking about all I had seen that day alone, then drove behind a building to drink my drink, hoping not to be disturbed by another run, and started sobbing about the baby.

It's eighteen years later. I'm the lieutenant in charge of CID, the Criminal Investigations Division. I've been to hundreds of deaths and horrible crime scenes. It's easier now. Almost routine. Now I sit with other detectives in a hotel conference room, passing around photos with casual indifference, speculation, and study, like people passing around a report or stats at a board meeting. Different conversations float in the air. "Now, that's bullshit!" "She was dead before he tied her up." "Look here, look at her hands, the lividity."

I'm distracted by another detective, as he nudges and points to the Polaroid. God knows what happened to this poor girl. These are not ordinary photos; these are horrible death scenes involving torture and rape. One girl, her nostrils flared, mouth agape, sucking down her last breath in panic. Nice white teeth, lips curled back like an angry dog's. All sorts of emotions running through her last thoughts. Beautiful long brown hair. Yup, she fits the profile all right.

Different agencies are trying to match up the work of a serial killer we think worked in our area. As the meeting goes on, some are even bored with the routine of it. We've witnessed so much tragedy over the years we can view these victims without emotion. I pause and think, God, if "normal" people saw this stuff, they'd be asking for counseling and wouldn't sleep for weeks. Our "board meeting" continues as photos are tossed around like trading cards.

Ironically, we can often see through the horror. "Hey, look at this one," somebody says. "She's good looking." Early twenties, her pretty eyes rolled up with a panicked look. Amazed at what is happening to her. This girl is all tied up neatly by a monster with an eye for detail. Anger wells up toward the suspected perpetrator of these despicable acts, a killer who trained others to follow in his footsteps. Talk about the death penalty. Easy when you see this kind of stuff. What about the families, friends, children? Juries and citizens will never see these pictures. Never be exposed to the whole truth.

We discuss the details with words like *positioning, stains, fibers, hair, DNA, petechia, ligature marks*. Detectives Dumas and Krier are arguing. "Look, you moron, it's Investigation 101! You should know that." "Hey, John, look at this. What's up with the red lividity? That's odd." The voices merge together until they sound like one noise.

After the meeting, I stop on the way home for a steak dinner. I want to be alone, sitting at the bar enjoying a few beers. Mellow feelings wash over me as I wait for my food, dim voices blending with the music. I listen to simple talk and regular lives. People who aren't exposed to the extremes of life's underside. I hear someone talk about a "big problem," something about her nails, and think, lady, you don't know what problems are.

This is what it's like for cops. Day and night. Night and day. Year after year, the unimaginable things pile up. At the academy and on the job, they teach us objectivity. Keep an emotional distance. Separate yourself. After a while, we can see things like today's crime-scene pictures without much emotional response. Mostly it works, but sometimes things get stuck in your head, haunting your dreams and interrupting your thoughts because they matter so goddamned much. A case involving a beautiful girl named Amy St. Laurent was one of those.

I

It is every parent's nightmare—your child goes out one Saturday night and vanishes off the face of the earth. It is also, sadly, something that happens far too often—a sensible and independent young woman who thinks she knows how to take care of herself crosses paths with a predator. The bad guy doesn't look evil. He is charming, charismatic, lively, and fun. It is only when he has his victim alone that his true self— his violent, explosive, self-indulgent, and remorseless side—emerges. Suddenly, a lifetime of striving toward maturity and self-awareness, of good decisions and generous acts, is changed by one bad choice. This is one of those stories.

On Saturday night, October 20, 2001, a lovely blonde woman with a generous heart and a happy disposition set out to show a new acquaintance from Florida the night life in the Old Port area of Portland, Maine. After an evening shooting pool and dancing, twenty-five-year-old Amy St. Laurent disappeared.

This is the story of how a group of tenacious detectives solved the case. From the start, it was an unusual situation. They had no body. No crime scene. No witnesses. Only their certainty, based on years of experience, about what the circumstances suggested and an ever deepening determination to find the young woman they had never known when she was alive but who became, over the course of the investigation, "Our Amy."

They had a complex tangle of lies and half-truths to unravel. A cocky young suspect partying under their noses, shielded by the inaccurate stories, fuzzy or false recall, and inaction of friends and relatives who couldn't believe someone they knew could be a killer. They had difficult jurisdictional and territorial issues to resolve. Personal style differences. Crushing workloads. Weeks of sixteen- to twenty-hour workdays ticked by with no resolution as a Maine winter came relentlessly toward them, the holidays approached, and the family's agony of uncertainty pressed them on.

This is a story about the way real-world investigation works, from the first phone call and the intensity of the first week through the long, miserable grind of many more weeks, then months. It details the way detectives collect information, evaluate that information, formulate theories, and continuously test and retest their theories as new facts become known; how they work under pressure from a desperate family, a worried public, the media, the command staff, and city government, knowing that haste truly can make waste and that a good investigation must be detailed, careful, and methodical. The whole enterprise is informed by their knowledge of the ways they'll be tested when a case comes to court.

This is a story of good, old-fashioned police work. Not the sexy, solve-it-in-an-hour forensics of *CSI* or the intense, sweat 'em in a box psychological manipulations of David Simon's *Homicide.* In the real world, the investigation, arrest, and trial don't happen neatly in an hour, as they do on *Law and Order.* They happen piece by slow, determined, painstaking piece, through a complex interweaving of different detectives' skills. The investigation took thousands of hours of legwork, phone calls, interviewing, and report writing. Careful listening informed by instinct and experience. Meetings and arguments and a continuous reassessment of the story. Patience and taking chances, overcoming legal hurdles, refusing to take no for an answer, and coming to know the victim and the suspect extremely well.

The investigators weighed a number of suspects, testing the veracity of their often incredible stories, until they fixed on a young man devoid of empathy and self-discipline whose goal in life was to have sex with as many women as possible; who regarded women solely as objects for his satisfaction, believing he had a right to be satisfied no matter what the cost. A young man who would prove, even to experienced detectives, to be shockingly coldblooded in the lengths he would go to to hide his crime.

This is also a story of unusual interagency cooperation, of strong bonds formed where territorialism and suspicion normally reigned. Of a case that might never have been successfully resolved, a body that should never have been found, of dark dreams and psychics' maps and divine intervention. This is the story of how some good and dedicated cops relentlessly tested the evidence—and the suspect—until the false stories unraveled, waiting for the missteps that would give them their breaks, and, in the way of the best homicide investigators, did not give up until they had found their Amy and brought her killer to justice.

*

Portland is Maine's largest city. With a residential population of around 70,000, it is one of the largest cities north of Boston. During business and entertainment hours, the population swells to 150,000. The population of the surrounding area is about 300,000. The city's old downtown sits atop a hill on a boot-shaped peninsula surrounded by the Fore River, Back Cove, Portland Harbor, and Casco Bay. At the East End and West End, the toe and heel of the boot, there are lovely vistas. Daily ferry service carries residents to the city from the many inhabited islands that rise from the sparkling waters of the bay.

Like many anchor cities in predominantly rural states, Portland is a city in transition. Once a charming port of old brick storefronts, warehouses, and wharf buildings, thriving department stores and businesses, overwhelmingly white and homogenized, by the midsixties it was hit hard by the decline of small manufacturing. Many of the warehouse buildings near the waterfront were abandoned or became decrepit. In the streets near the projects on Munjoy Hill, disgruntled residents partied and battled and lit bonfires in the streets.

A few people with vision, seeing what urban revivals had done for other cities, bought buildings and started to restore the Old Port area, streets of fine brick buildings and old warehouses leading down to a working waterfront. Today, the Old Port is a mecca for tourists, who come by car, Amtrak, and off cruise ships and flock to the interesting shops and restaurants. Urban and suburban couples come to enjoy theater and music and the Old Port's fine restaurants.

At night, it also becomes a destination for another crowd. Young people from as far away as Boston come to enjoy the restaurants, bars, and clubs that line the brick and cobbled streets. Underage teens looking for life beyond the empty streets of their small towns rub elbows with bikers, college students, drug dealers, gangsters, and young professionals. Fights are common. Crowd control is a perennial problem, especially late in the evening as the bars and clubs close, releasing thousands of patrons who are drunk, rowdy, and uninhibited onto the narrow old streets. At closing time, the swarm of bodies on Wharf Street can become so dense in the summer months that uniformed cops find it difficult to see each other when they're only ten to fifteen feet apart.

The same years that have seen Portland's Old Port revival have also seen the city transformed in other ways. Increasingly, the city has had to deal with sharp rises in two populations that require a lot of police intervention—the homeless and the mentally ill, drawn from other cities, small towns, and rural areas to the shelters, the community service agencies, and cheap rooming houses the city offers. Portland also has seen a rise in drug use, bringing with it the associated drug-related violence, overdoses, and deaths. Heroin is rampant, as is cocaine. In 2001, there were twenty deaths from drug overdoses, along with hundreds of close calls suffered by users who were saved because of the city's fine medical facilities.

Added to this are the complexities of dealing with new immigrant populations. In particular, Portland has seen an influx of Vietnamese and Cambodians and, more recently, many refugees from Africa and eastern Europe. All these populations have brought added language and cultural difficulties to the usual challenges of policing an urban area.

The city is served by a 165-person police department headquartered at 109 Middle Street, on the edge of the Old Port area. Each year, Portland police respond to approximately seventy-five thousand calls for service, mostly 911 calls. They are dispatched to over two thousand domestic violence cases and over a hundred death scenes, including suicides, homicides, and drug overdose deaths, as well as to burglaries, rapes, terrible child abuse, and vicious assaults.

For seventeen years, the department was presided over by Chief Michael Chitwood, a former Philadelphia detective. In Philadelphia, his flamboyant style and controversial record led critics to call him "Dirty Harry." In Portland, his outspoken style and strong public stands on issues such as concealed weapons permits, children in horrendous home situations where the Department of Human Services wouldn't act, and district attorneys who settled too many cases, earned him the nickname "Media Mike." Chitwood was a strong and controversial leader in a department recently under fire for alleged police brutality. Despite these controversies, he was very popular with a public who felt he was making the city safer, and he forged good relationships with the media.

However controversial he might have been on many fronts—an article in the *Boston Globe Sunday Magazine* called him both a smooth operator and a loose cannon[1]—Chief Chitwood had a passionate concern for crime victims. Throughout his career, his press conferences, often held with victims and their families, helped the media and the public understand the true impact of crime on ordinary people.

Portland is a microcosm of any large U.S. city, and its troubles are a microcosm of any big city's woes. But even for Portland police, who see stabbings, beatings, child abuse, drug overdoses, pedophiles, rapes, and suicides on a regular basis, a murder is still a big deal. In an average year, there are between twenty-five and thirty murders in the entire state of Maine. A genuine whodunit, as opposed to a domestic murder, a drunken dispute settled by violence, or a drug deal gone bad, is rare. The challenge of solving a murder triggers all the hardwired investigative responses trained into a personal-crimes detective. For the best detectives, it immediately becomes a contest that they *must* win.

✳

Police involvement in the Amy St. Laurent case began with one of those informal cop-to-cop phone calls the public rarely hears about. At 7:30 p.m. on Monday, October 22, 2001, Cumberland County deputy sheriff James Estabrook called his friend Danny Young, a Portland police detective, at home, and asked if he could speak about a missing South Berwick woman. The young woman, Amy St. Laurent, was the daughter of a friend of Estabrook's girlfriend. She had gone out on Saturday night to show a visitor from Florida the nightlife in Portland's Old Port district. She never came home.

Estabrook made his call to the right receptive ear. Danny Young, a tenacious investigator with finely honed cop's instincts and twenty-one years on the job, had a daughter the same age as the missing woman, and her name was Amy. Detective Young himself defines stable and decent. He's married to the high school sweetheart he met at age fifteen and is a devoted father and grandfather. A heavyset man with a comfortable fatherly, engaging manner, Danny Young exudes the kind of warmth and amiability that make him deceptively easy to talk to. But behind that genial exterior is a dedicated homicide detective.

Young is known for his encyclopedic grasp of the details of a case, as well as an anal-retentive's compulsion for order and filing. Along with his charm, Young has the naturally competitive pit-bull quality of the true detective. He will work tirelessly because he's not going to let the bad guys win, leaving victims and their families to suffer a double set of losses and betrayals.[2] Supervisors say Young is the detective they'd want on the case if something happened to one of their family members.

Estabrook had been lucky to find him at home. Since the events of September 11, Young had been working seven days a week. Along with his detective duties, he was also a bomb investigator. As part of the post-9/11 heightened security, he and his bomb dog, Karla, had been patrolling the *Scotia Prince*, the ferry that provided service between Portland and Nova Scotia, every evening. He was also regularly called out for patrols at the airport and other locations. The night of Estabrook's call was his first Monday night at home in more than a month. He was half an hour into *Monday Night Football* when the phone rang.

Young listened carefully to Estabrook's information about the missing woman and asked some questions. He then followed up with phone calls to the woman's mother, Diane Jenkins, and to the South Berwick police. Good cops are adept at applying their investigative instincts to the facts. Danny Young had spent a lot of years of assessing situations and sorting out facts, and the story he was hearing didn't feel right.

Normally, when an adult goes missing, it is not an immediate cause for alarm. In any given year, the Portland police get reports of around two hundred missing persons. The reasons people disappear are usually related to drugs, alcohol, financial or relationship problems, mental health issues, or general irresponsibility. Most of those reported missing eventually turn up, often expressing surprise or even annoyance that anyone bothered to worry.[3]

It wasn't unusual for an attractive, single, twenty-five-year-old woman to go out on Saturday night and not come home. But it was unusual for *this* missing woman—Amy St. Laurent, a caring owner who was devoted to her cat—not to return on Sunday or Monday to feed it. Because of the cat, she rarely stayed at her mother's South Portland house late in the evening or overnight. If she did stay overnight somewhere else, she always went home in the morning to check on the cat or arranged for someone else to feed it.

It was also unusual for this woman to let days go by without a call to her mother or her younger sister, Julie. Amy St. Laurent belonged to the cell phone generation. She was regularly in touch with people by phone and e-mail, and she was close to her mother and her younger sister. She was also close to her father, Dennis, who lived nearby in South Berwick. If she needed help with the cat, or a ride because her car was in the shop, she would give him a call. But Amy St. Laurent hadn't been home or called anyone for two days.

It was more unusual still for St. Laurent, an ambitious young woman who had worked her way from the third-shift assembly line at the Pratt & Whitney aircraft engine assembly plant to a responsible administrative position, not to show up at work on Monday. Plenty of young adults are haphazard about their jobs, or work only to get the money to go out and party, but St. Laurent was not one of them. When she had to miss a day and knew in advance, she would let someone know. If she was sick, she would always call in or e-mail, but no one at Pratt & Whitney had heard from her.

Although she had been an honors student in high school, she had chosen not to go to college; perhaps in part to compensate for that, she had taken a very professional approach to her work. She had been employed at P & W for several years, moving from the Portland area to South Berwick, forty miles away, to be closer to her job. She was pleased by her promotion to an administrative assistant position, enjoyed her increasing responsibilities, and was saving to buy a house. There was an important presentation on Tuesday she had to help prepare for, the sort of project she enjoyed, yet she hadn't shown up at work.

Police investigations are rarely the stuff of high drama seen on TV. Often, it's the small details that tell the story. For Detective Young, who'd

seen at least a thousand missing person cases in his career, all those ab-
errations from St. Laurent's normal routines were significant. Everyone
had said the same things about Amy St. Laurent—with respect to her
responsibilities, she was regular, she was faithful. She was close to her
family and would not behave in a manner that would alarm them. She
would not neglect a helpless animal to go off and have fun.

Detective Young relayed his concerns to his supervisor in the Criminal
Investigation Division, Detective Sergeant Tommy Joyce, who was also at
home. Joyce, like Young, felt that the sudden changes in St. Laurent's behavior were a cause for concern. Although neither of them was scheduled
to work that evening, they decided to drive back into Portland to see what
they could do about finding the missing woman. Sergeant Joyce called his
lieutenant, Joseph Loughlin, for permission.

"Ahh . . . c'mon, Tommy. It's bullshit and you know it."

"I'm telling you, Joe . . . I mean Lieutenant *. . . this is the real deal."*

*Tommy has got my attention now as I prepare my dinner. It's Monday
night, October 22, 2001, and it's been a long day. When he calls me "Lieutenant" instead of Joe, I know he's serious, but I'm the boss and I have to worry
about the bottom line. "Tom, look. I can't do the overtime. I'm maxed! What's
the girl's problem? Drugs? Boyfriend? Finances? Or did she just plain take off
for a day?"*

"Okay, Lieutenant. You talk to the mom then and tell her we're not *going to
look for her daughter that went missing from* Portland*!"*

*We continue with another spirited argument, one of several a week we have
about cases and crime scenes. Tom and I have known each other for twenty
years, professionally and personally. We can have some intense exchanges.*

*"Look, Dan talked to Estabrook, that's how we got it and it really doesn't
look right."*

*I give in. I'm still skeptical but Tom and Dan both have good instincts.
"Okay, okay. But just you and Dan, Tom. Just you two. See you tomorrow,
Tom, and let me know when you find her nursing a hangover and I paid all of
this OT for squat as usual with missings!!"*

*"Hey, Joe," Tommy shoots back, "remember—all the actors aren't just in
Hollywood."*

I recognize the quote from Tom's dad, Thomas, Senior, a now deceased

Portland police detective from the 1960s. The craft of being a good detective is passed down from the guys who came before us. And Tommy's dad was right. Some of our criminals are really great actors.

Despite their lieutenant's misgivings, the two detectives, who at that time lived about three hundred yards apart, met and drove back into Portland. At that point, they had the following information: that St. Laurent had called her mother sometime between 10:00 and 10:30 p.m. on Saturday night the twentieth, stating that she was on her way to the Old Port area of Portland; that she was traveling in a car driven by Eric Rubright, a man from Florida she had met three weeks previously while visiting a friend in Ft. Myers, Florida; and that Rubright had flown into Portland on Thursday night and rented a car before going to meet St. Laurent.

Before he left for Portland, Young called the Portland Jetport and asked Melissa Sargent, a Portland officer on duty there, to check car rental agencies to see if Rubright had rented a car at the airport. She called back to report that Rubright had rented a maroon GMC Envoy with an OnStar system. Through the South Berwick Police Department, which was already involved in searching for Ms. St. Laurent, OnStar was contacted. The vehicle was located parked in downtown Portland. Young assigned a patrol unit to watch the car until he could get to Portland and try to locate Mr. Rubright.

By the time Detective Young got the call on Monday night, St. Laurent's parents, concerned about their inability to reach their daughter on Sunday, had already contacted the South Berwick police. They were so alarmed by her continued absence that her mother, Diane Jenkins; her younger sister, Julie; St. Laurent's ex-boyfriend, Richard Sparrow; and worried friends had spent Monday tacking up posters with her picture, description, and the information that she was missing all around the city.

Under the dramatic heading MISSING since *Saturday* night 10/20/01, pictures of blonde, blue-eyed St. Laurent, smiling her vibrant smile, had appeared on posts and poles and in storefronts all over Portland, asking anyone who had seen her to contact her family or the South Berwick police.

At 10:30 Monday night, Eric Rubright walked up to the police officers waiting by his rental car. He readily identified himself, said he'd just seen

MISSING PERSON

Amy St. Laurent, Age 25
White female, 5'5", 120#
Lt. brown/blonde hair
Blue eyes

Last seen October 21, 2001 at
1:45 AM at a Brighton Avenue,
Portland apartment.

Last seen wearing blue jeans,
a gray sweatshirt with the logo
"Pratt-Whitney" on the front,
and sneakers.

She was carrying her driver's
license at the time of her
disappearance.

Missing poster given to police personnel searching for Amy St. Laurent. Similar fliers were posted in store windows throughout Portland and southern Maine. (Photo, Stewart Smith Photographers)

a flyer with St. Laurent's picture and the information that she was missing, and had just called the South Berwick police and offered to tell them what he knew about her whereabouts on Saturday night and early Sunday morning. Rubright, who had been drinking, then agreed to come to the Portland Police Department and talk about Amy St. Laurent, rather than driving the forty miles to South Berwick.

Back at the department, he was interviewed by Sergeant Joyce and Detective Young. Sergeant Joyce, a 22-year veteran of the department, was in charge of the crimes against persons section of the Criminal Investigations

Division, as well as supervising the crime lab and evidence technicians. A former evidence tech himself, Joyce was an adept personnel manager but readily admitted that evidence was his first love. Evidence, he would say, just sits there and tells the story. It doesn't lie. Officers who have worked with him describe him as a brilliant and instinctive reader of crime scenes.

At six foot one, Sergeant Joyce is a lean, spare man who is rarely still. He's got dark, unruly hair and glacial blue eyes. Colleagues tease him about being sartorially stuck in the sixties, but the style suits him. He has an air of being perpetually overworked, which he is, and an abrupt, physical impatience (colleagues call his jerky style of pacing when he wants your attention "parakeeting"), which hides a storyteller's knack and a subtle Irish charm. He is territorial and argumentative and runs at 78 rpm when everyone else is at 33. Even at 3:00 a.m. on a cold February night when his people are up to their asses in crime scenes, he's got a smart remark or quick bit of banter. He functions calmly in the controlled chaos of a detective bureau and thrives on it.

In a recorded interview, Rubright told Joyce and Young he had met Amy St. Laurent three weeks earlier in Florida through Jason Kolias, a mutual friend she was visiting, and had decided to come to Maine and see St. Laurent, with her permission, when he was coming to New York to visit his grandmother. He told the detectives that Amy St. Laurent had been "a totally cool girl, a totally cool human being," and he had wanted to see her again.

He had arrived on Thursday. On Saturday they had gone to Boston to the Museum of Fine Arts. They had had dinner in Boston, and later in the evening they had decided to visit the Old Port section of Portland, driving directly from Boston to Portland without stopping at St. Laurent's house in South Berwick. On the way, St. Laurent had called her mother in South Portland and invited her to join them. Her mother had declined.

Once in Portland, they had gone first to the Fore Play Sports Bar, where Rubright, who didn't play pool, had drunk beer and St. Laurent had played pool with some men she didn't appear to have known. Another guy had come up, described by Rubright as having dyed blond hair with brown roots, heavily gelled, maybe five foot eight or five foot nine and maybe 160 pounds. This new guy, according to Rubright, "played pool like a shark." The man had been with a chubbier friend Rubright hadn't paid much attention to.

St. Laurent had chatted with the men, and the guy with gelled hair had given her his phone number. Later, after Rubright and St. Laurent had stopped at a pizza place where she bought him two slices of pizza, they met up with the men again at the Pavilion, a smart, high-ceiling dance club renovated from an old bank building. Rubright, who didn't dance, again hung around and drank beer in the pulsating noise of the dance club while St. Laurent said she was going to find someone to dance with. He had leaned against the wall and watched as St. Laurent talked and danced with the two men she had met earlier at the Fore Play bar.

He told the officers that shortly after last call, between 12:45 and 1:00, he went to the men's room before his trip back to South Berwick. There was a long line. When he came out of the bathroom, St. Laurent and the two men had disappeared. He looked around for her inside, then went outside to see if she was waiting for him; he stood outside the door until 1:20 a.m. but could not find her. At that time, the staff began asking people to move away and leave, a policy Old Port drinking establishments had adopted to cut down on the rowdy crowds that led to vandalism and fights.

Everyone had left the club, so he assumed that St. Laurent had left with the two men. He returned to the garage and got into his car. St. Laurent's cell phone, coat, purse, and backpack were still in his car where she had left them. All that she had taken with her were her driver's license and some money. He stated that he might have driven around the block once looking for St. Laurent but didn't see her. Then, figuring she'd find her own way home, he drove back to St. Laurent's house in South Berwick.

According to Rubright, he followed the compass in his car and went south, stopping in South Portland to buy gas. Somewhat incoherently, during his interview with the detectives, he produced a sheaf of receipts from his wallet, trying to re-create his spending that night. Eventually he found some receipts, which he gave the detectives, including a credit card receipt for the gas. After he bought gas, he told them, he continued south, got on the turnpike, and drove to the Wells exit. From there, he followed the route he knew to her house.

Rubright also told the detectives that at the turnpike tolls he had discovered he didn't have any money. He told the toll taker that he only had fifteen cents and asked if he could please use the highway anyway because it was the only route he knew back to South Berwick, which the toll taker allowed him to do.

When he got back to St. Laurent's house, she wasn't there. He checked her phone and cell phone for messages, but there were none. He said he was uneasy about spending the night in her house when she wasn't there, so he slept in his car.

In the morning, he used the key she had given him to enter her house and take a shower. There was still no sign of her. He left a note on her door, asking what had happened to her and thanking her for the visit, left her purse and backpack inside, and placed her coat on the hood of her car. Remembering he still had her house key, he put it on a tire of her car. Then he left without ever hearing from St. Laurent.

2

Eric Rubright looked like a good suspect. His story of St. Laurent's disappearing while he was in the bathroom seemed suspicious, as did his tale of driving back to her apartment forty miles away with her coat, her purse, her cell phone, and her backpack. His description of leaving her coat on the hood of her car, her housekey on the tire, and the rest of her things inside was strangely detailed, and police officers are trained to notice and suspect an excess of details. As training manuals put it, "Liars lie with specificity."

Nor were police impressed by his claim that he'd run out of money and had to talk his way onto the turnpike, or by the fact that he'd felt uncomfortable in Amy's apartment and slept Saturday night in a car in her driveway. It seemed far more likely that he'd slept in the car because he couldn't face being in her apartment after he'd done her harm and that he had her belongings because she no longer needed them. Both interviewers felt that he merited further scrutiny. They decided to search Rubright's car and ask him to consent to a polygraph.

In the middle of the Rubright interview, Detective Young received a call from Amy St. Laurent's stepfather, Don Jenkins. Jenkins had just heard from a man in the Old Port who had seen the "Missing" poster with the picture of St. Laurent and was calling because he had been with her early on Sunday morning. Jenkins said he had told the caller and the other men he was with to go to the Portland Police Station and ask for Young.

At such an early stage of a disappearance, detectives regard time as "of the essence," in case the missing person is still alive and can be found. Therefore, Detective Young and Sergeant Joyce were eager to speak with anyone who might have information regarding Amy St. Laurent's behavior, whereabouts, and contacts on the night she vanished.

*

Portland police Sergeant Jon Goodman was in his car in the Old Port when he was flagged down by three young men who told him they were supposed to go to headquarters and talk with the police. Sergeant Goodman called the station, asked whether Detective Young wanted to see the three men, and upon receiving an affirmative answer, asked them to get into his car. The three, Jeffrey "Russ" Gorman, Kush Sharma, and Jason Cook, all residents of an apartment at 230 Brighton Avenue, got in willingly, and he drove them to 109 Middle Street, where he escorted them to the Detective Bureau.

The men said that they had been at a bar called Diggers and the bartender had shown them the flyer with St. Laurent's photograph. One of them, Jason Cook, recognized her as the woman Russ Gorman had been with early on Sunday morning. At their urging, Gorman had called the contact number on the flyer, had spoken with St. Laurent's stepfather, and was told to contact the Portland police.

Two essential principles of investigation came into play here. First, it is important to interview witnesses as soon after an incident as possible, in order to get the freshest possible memories of the events and to lock witnesses in to their stories. Second, since guilty parties frequently coerce or persuade their friends to collaborate on a story, persons with potentially probative information are quickly split up and interviewed separately so that they can't agree on a common version of the story.

Experienced detectives know that it is difficult to maintain a lie. If you didn't live it, it didn't happen, and therefore the details aren't hardwired into your mind. Liars have a hard time keeping a story straight, which is why subsequent versions are often verbatim recitations of the first telling, with very specific details offered to make the story seem truthful, while a truthful version may vary or be more vague. For this reason, it is important to lock in the details early and then keep pressure on suspected liars to see how they behave when telling their stories and how their stories hold up over time.

At this very preliminary stage, however, Joyce and Young were focused primarily on collecting information. The two detectives now had four subjects to interview, so they called in patrol officer Kevin Haley and evidence technician Chris Stearns to assist. Sergeant Joyce interviewed Russ Gorman, Officer Haley took Kush Sharma, and Stearns interviewed Jason Cook, while Detective Young continued to interview Eric Rubright. It was unusual, so early in an investigation, to have so many witnesses turning up, but even at this stage it was clear to the two detectives that things were heating up fast.

Gorman's story was essentially this: He met Amy St. Laurent at Fore Play, a raucous, rowdy bar and pool hall at 436 Fore Street, at around 10:30 p.m. He and his roommate, Kush Sharma, played pool with her and an older man for fifteen or twenty minutes. St. Laurent was with a man from Florida who watched but didn't play. Gorman and Sharma left Fore Play to go to a bar called the Iguana. Around 11:45 p.m., they went to a dance club called the Pavilion.

About an hour later, according to Gorman, Amy St. Laurent came up to him at the Pavilion, pinched him on the side, and told him she couldn't find her friend from Florida. Gorman invited her to come back to his house, where there was going to be an after-hours birthday party for roommate Jason Cook. After St. Laurent had looked around and couldn't find her friend, who had her keys, she agreed to go to the party.

At that point, Gorman was shown a picture of Amy St. Laurent, which he identified as the woman he was speaking about. He said he and Sharma and St. Laurent went in his car from the Old Port to an apartment at 230 Brighton Avenue, where Gorman was staying. Gorman had told St. Laurent that some friends were getting together for a birthday party, but when they arrived around 1:15 a.m., no one else was there. Gorman had some drinks and Sharma had some drinks. Gorman said he couldn't remember whether St. Laurent was drinking. (This statement, from a young hotshot who'd picked up a pretty girl in a bar, struck Sergeant Joyce as odd. Normally, a guy who's interested in having sex with a girl will pay close attention to what, and how much, she drinks.)

At some point, Sharma and St. Laurent went outside to walk Jason Cook's dog and so Sharma could smoke. When no party materialized, she asked to be taken back to the Pavilion, saying she would look for her friend from Florida and, if she didn't find him, would go to her mother's in South Portland. Jason Cook arrived at the house as Gorman was leaving to drive St. Laurent back downtown, around 1:45 p.m.

Gorman stated that he dropped her off in front of the Pavilion just before 2:00 a.m. It appeared that she was walking toward the entrance. He noticed other people standing around outside but didn't see her speak with anyone before he drove off. He went directly home, a trip he estimated took him less than ten minutes, and stayed in for the rest of the night. All told, Gorman stated he had been gone from the Brighton Avenue apartment about twenty minutes.

This early in the process, especially with no victim, no crime scene, and no witnesses to any violence, it was too early to rule anyone in or out as a suspect. Too early, even, to conclude that a crime had taken place, though their instincts told the detectives that this was so. At this point, the detectives needed to talk to as many people as possible who knew St. Laurent or might have seen her that night, trying to test the veracity of the information they'd been given and gathering clues about where to look for the missing woman.

Normally, their experience would have focused the detectives on Russ Gorman, the last person seen with the missing woman. But Eric Rubright had been her companion that evening, and his story needed to be checked out as well. It was strange and elaborate, and his manner and presentation were definitely peculiar. If Gorman had dropped her off at the Pavilion as he said, an angry Rubright might well have come back around and picked her up. And Rubright had still had St. Laurent's personal effects.

Gathering information would mean talking with Gorman's roommates and friends, and with the staff and any witnesses they could locate at Fore Play and the Pavilion who might have observed St. Laurent, Gorman, and Rubright. It would mean trying to locate witnesses who might have been outside in the street when Gorman dropped St. Laurent off. It would mean checking Gorman's and Rubright's criminal histories, if any, to develop profiles of the two men.

It would also mean, since they had to consider the possibility that St. Laurent was the victim of foul play, that they needed to develop a fuller picture of Amy St. Laurent—that detailed assessment of the victim known as *victimology*. Was there anything in her character, for example, to suggest that the picture of a responsible young adult they had been given wasn't the whole story? Anything to suggest that she had simply taken off for a few days? People did. Was she still alive somewhere, perhaps held against her will?

Because in the beginning of any investigation detectives have to keep their minds open to all possibilities, Joyce and Young also needed to determine whether there was anyone else in Amy St. Laurent's life who might have been motivated to harm her, such as an angry ex-boyfriend, current boyfriend, spurned suitor, jealous other woman, or aggrieved co-worker. Could she have met someone else on the street after Gorman had dropped her off?

They knew that anyone they had already spoken with or might speak with could be the person responsible for St. Laurent's disappearance. They had to pay close attention to everything they were told and be diligent about taking notes and producing detailed reports.

Danny Young, describing their investigative approach, said, "we felt we had to follow every lead to its logical conclusion." Sergeant Joyce explained that, from the beginning of an investigation, they would have their eyes on the whole potential trajectory of a case. Failing to follow through with a viable suspect or a promising tip would leave them vulnerable to a "reasonable doubt" attack at trial when the defense asked, "Did you even bother to look at this person?" and they would have to say no, leaving them looking careless, deceptive, or inept before the jury. Sergeant Joyce was diligent in reminding his detectives of the rules underlying all good investigations—don't let your assumptions get ahead of the facts, test all your facts several ways, and keep testing your theories of the case against the known facts. He and his detectives constantly checked and rechecked facts as an investigation proceeded, constantly revising their theories as more facts became known.

Late as it was on the first night of the St. Laurent case, Joyce and Young sat and discussed what they'd learned from their interviews, already arguing, testing out theories, and playing the "what if" game as they began to plan for the following day. Danny Young wanted to focus their efforts on Russ Gorman, quoting the "KISS" rule. KISS is Keep It Simple, Stupid. In this case, their training and experience indicated that the last person known to be with a victim or possible victim was the most logical suspect.

But at this point—who was that? Was it Gorman or Rubright? Plus, despite the family's alarm, the detectives did not know what kind of case they had yet. A crime? A runaway? A hostage?

Sergeant Joyce wanted to focus first on Eric Rubright because Rubright was transient. Unless they had some legally sustainable reason to detain him, he would leave the area soon. If he returned to Florida before they had investigated him thoroughly, it would be very difficult to get to him for forensic evidence or further interviews. Therefore, it made sense to re-interview Rubright and follow up his story before he left town. If Rubright was willing or could be persuaded, they also hoped to do a polygraph test and obtain DNA.

Later that morning, Sergeant Joyce would be adding a major new case to the workloads of his detectives, juggling the resources of his extremely busy bureau to free up Danny Young to be the primary investigator and get Young some supporting detectives. With so many people to be interviewed, the process would require a huge investment of personnel. And since witnesses quickly forget what they've seen, they all needed to be interviewed as soon as possible. Detectives would also need to check on any videotapes or closed-circuit TVs in the Old Port area.

Joyce's first step would be to get his lieutenant on board. Police departments are paramilitary organizations. Even when detectives are given latitude about how they staff and manage a case, progress is constantly monitored by the CID sergeants and the process is governed by written rules called SOPs (standard operating procedures), by department policies, and by internal customs. Information about the investigation needed to be passed up the food chain. The chief needed to be informed. The command staff. The media would need to be briefed. Someone well informed, in this case Joyce's lieutenant, would need to deal with the family.

The "Missing" posters with St. Laurent's picture were already all over town, creating great public concern. A public that is involved and interested in a case in turn cranks up the pressure on the city council and the chief's office. The public asks, in effect, "Okay, cops, let's see what you've got."

By morning, the department would be flooded with calls. Along with calls from the media, worried parents would be asking if their own daughters were at risk. There would be calls from individuals with tips as well as from the nutcases who call whenever there's a big case. Because the first few days of any major investigation are crucial, the Detective Bureau would be assigning as much manpower as possible to the case.

By the time Rubright, Sharma, Cook, and Gorman had been interviewed, it was Tuesday morning. Amy St. Laurent had been missing for nearly forty-eight hours. A regular workday was about to begin, but before they left, the detectives would finalize their notes and start the endless series of "to do" lists that are a vital part of any investigation.

They would begin a records check on all the subjects they had interviewed, with a special focus on Rubright and Gorman, starting to build a personality profile of these two men and determining whether they had any history of arrests and convictions. They would complete a missing person report on Amy St. Laurent so that the information could be entered in the National Crime Information Center (NCIC) system as an "Attempt to Locate" (ATL). Before they left to sleep through the small part of the night that was left to them, they made a plan to meet again later in the morning. Then they left, both feeling strongly that something was wrong.

3

By Tuesday morning, Sergeant Joyce had made Danny Young the primary, and the Portland Police Department's involvement in the case of Amy St. Laurent, missing person, began moving forward in a big way. Joyce's first task was to update his lieutenant and convince him that Amy St. Laurent was not just an irresponsible young adult who'd taken off for a few days and that the case merited major attention.

Mornings at 109 are hectic in the Detective Bureau. Reports are stacked on the detective sergeants' desks as they go through the cases and assign them to the detectives. I have an 8:30 meeting with my sergeants, then a staff meeting with the chief and crew. Sergeant Jones and Sergeant Coffin are waiting to start reviewing last night's activity, but no Sergeant Joyce.

I can feel my head and ears get red as I get pissed and call his extension in the bay. "Tom? Don't make me come out there."

Tom comes into my office, full of energy, bouncing like an awkward daddy longlegs. "What's the holdup?" I ask.

"I told ya. I told ya. The South Berwick thing. The girl is really missing. This is wrong all the way. It feels like the Tevanian case a few years ago."

Hand up, I hold off the other guys for a moment. "Why, Tom?"

"She's totally departed from her normal behavior. Totally. It's very unusual. Very . . ." He goes on about the facts.

My pager is blaring and the loudspeaker is calling for me at the same time my phone is ringing. It's about other crimes, and the chief wants to see me before staff. I rush the crime review and Tom gives us more.

"She's never showed at her work. Never called her mom like she always does.

She never took care of her cat. Hell, never left her cat like that before. This is real and it's heating up fast, Joe! A guy named Rubright was up visiting from Florida and says he slept in her driveway Saturday night. She never came home! He looks wrong, too. Plus, he has her belongings!"

He goes on about the quirks in her behavior as I pull on my jacket and straighten my tie for staff. "How old is this girl, Tom?"

"Twenty-five."

"And what's her name?"

"Amy St. Laurent."

Later that morning, Chief Michael Chitwood and Amy St. Laurent's family members held a news conference in which she was officially declared missing. St. Laurent was described as stable and cheerful, a responsible young woman who was not the type to simply disappear. Family members pleaded with the public for any information they might have and for help in locating the missing woman.

Detectives spent the day gathering information[1] on their most likely suspects, Eric Rubright and Russ Gorman, and beginning the long process of checking out their stories concerning their activities on Saturday night and early Sunday morning. Some detectives worked the phones while others spread out to interview witnesses, setting aside their existing caseloads wherever possible because the early days of an investigation are so crucial. But many other cases were fresh, urgent, and had to be attended to.

Eric Rubright was scheduled to depart that same day on a 4:00 p.m. flight. In response to the police request that he return for a second interview and take a polygraph, he agreed, after some deft cajoling, to delay his flight until Wednesday. Detectives were pleased by his apparent cooperation, but several things they had learned still concerned them. First was the information from Amy St. Laurent's neighbor, Ruth McElaney, provided by the South Berwick Police Department, about Rubright's angry behavior in their shared driveway on Friday night and St. Laurent's statement to McElaney that he was angry because he had hoped to have sex with her and that wasn't going to happen. Other friends of St. Laurent's confirmed that, in the days before Rubright's arrival, she had become increasingly nervous about his visit, worrying about being able to handle him.

Along with some minor drug offenses, detectives learned that Rubright, who was a big guy and a former semiprofessional rugby player, had been given a restraining order after being involved in a domestic incident with a former girlfriend who was also named Amy. They reasoned that a man who flew over a thousand miles to see a girl he hoped to have sex with might well react badly if his plans were thwarted. Especially if that man had a history of reacting violently—even more so if the man had a history of reacting violently toward women named Amy.

It looked like they could make a pretty good case for obsession. If Russ Gorman was telling the truth, and he had dropped off St. Laurent at the Pavilion, it would not be hard to imagine a scenario in which Eric Rubright, already angry at her for leaving with another guy, is cruising the Old Port, sees Amy St. Laurent, and decides he's going to get what he came for. Nor to imagine how badly things could go wrong if she resisted.

On Tuesday evening, with all this information in hand, Portland police borrowed Detective Gerard "Biff" Brady from the Cumberland County sheriff to polygraph Eric Rubright. Rubright didn't do well. Even before he was connected to the machine, while Brady was conducting the cognitive interview, trying to get Rubright comfortable and taking him through the story of the night Amy disappeared, Rubright's body language was strange. He crossed his legs, lowered his eyes, and tried to move away from the interviewer, all suggesting to Brady that Rubright was hiding something. As Brady began the polygraph and took him through the story, just mentioning Amy's name evoked a strong response. Queried about the response, Rubright told Brady about a situation with a woman named Amy in Florida, which resulted in a restraining order. He flagged as deceptive again when Brady queried why Rubright was able to enter Amy's apartment to take a shower but was uncomfortable sleeping there.

The polygraph session lasted for hours, with Brady coming out to consult with the observing detectives several times. Even after being confronted about being evasive and admitting it, Rubright continued to be untruthful, registering a strong response again when Brady asked if he had had anything to do with St. Laurent's disappearance. Sergeant Joyce and Lieutenant Loughlin, observing the interview, both felt that Rubright could be the guy. His behavior was strange and suspicious, he was obviously holding things back, and testing showed his behavior was "consistent with practicing deception."

"For God's sake, of course it's him! It's great. Less than twenty-four and you guys got him. It looks good, Danny! He's establishing his story . . ."

Danny looks at me and says, "I'm not sure, Lieutenant. He does look good but I'm still not sure. I feel funny about a few things."

"Dan, he slept in her driveway. Does that tell you anything? He was disgusted with himself. He went into a jealous rage because of these other guys and probably broke her neck. Then he dumped her somewhere. Look, he couldn't even sleep in her house! Why would you do that unless something else was going on? He stayed there the night before, so why wouldn't he stay again and wait for her return? It's because he killed her and can't stand it. Now, of course he's cooperating. Wanna bet he fails his poly?"

My good buddy Gerard "Biff" Brady is on loan to us to perform a polygraph. Brady is a talented interviewer and has solicited confessions from some of the worst child abuse cases I've ever run across.

"Biff'll get it out outta him." I head back through the bay toward my office.

We all feel confident Rubright has something to do with this girl's disappearance. Tom Joyce and others are in the room watching the closed-circuit videotape of the polygraph.

"Check his history out," I say. "You'll see. He's hot."

It's Tuesday night around 2000. Just twenty-four hours since Danny got the call. We're all still working, but I feel good. They got a guy who looks responsible or certainly knows something. I call the chief and let him know what we got.

Chief Chitwood was involved in over five hundred homicide cases during his career in Philadelphia, including the Ira Einhorn/Holly Maddux murder. He's a cop's cop. I have tremendous respect for the man.

"Yeah, Chief, he's in the poly now and it's not looking good for him. Christ, not only that, he went back to her place Sunday morning with her cell phone, coat, purse, backpack still in his car. He has some BS story about driving around, looking for her, etc. Then he slept in his car in her driveway. There's a whole bunch of crap. I'll keep you up on it. You never know, but yeah, he looks like the guy."

Brady emerges from the room, drained, and tells the huddled detectives that Rubright has failed on a number of parts, plus he seems nutty.

"He has lied to me several times and admitted to that later on. He's real emotional, of course, considering the circumstances, but he's testing deceptive or inconclusive on various categories. You guys know all of the flags, and that he's got all her belongings to boot? Something certainly isn't right."

Tom and I get into it a bit. "Christ, Tom, check it out and you'll find the homicidal triad[2] in his background, personality disorder, history of violence. Should I go on?"

"Oh, you gonna start this up again?" Tommy says.

"Well, Tom, how many times have I been right on this?"

"Oh, okay, Lieutenant. You know. You know."

We banter back and forth, our usual mechanism to work our minds. "Now, Tom, when I was in the FBI academy back in '95 in that criminal psychology course . . ." I go on for fun. "Hey, don't make me go to the box, Tom . . . Don't."

The box is an old cardboard box of my solved cases from the '80s and early '90s that I literally slam down on a detective's desk every now and then as a reminder that I, too, did this job.

"Well, he is cooperating," Tom says.

"Wouldn't you, in a case like this?" But he's right. We still have to be objective. Tom and I like Rubright as a suspect. Sergeant Bruce Coffin likes Rubright. Danny is shifting.

At this point, it's three to one, but Danny pushes on. "Remember, Rubright was mad the night before as well."

"Look," Tommy exclaims, "Rubright is gonna leave. He leaves, gets a lawyer, and then it's back and forth to Florida. We gotta hit it hard now and push this other guy aside. He can wait." Tommy's just doing his job here—prioritizing and being practical.

Brady emerges from the polygraph again, shaking his head wearily, and consults with Coffin. "He's testing deceptive and inconclusive again. Admits he's still lying to me. Plus there's this thing with another girl named Amy. He's got harassment papers against him and this other girl fits your girl's description."

I'm feeling excited because I think we've got our perp. It's a strange, conflicted story, and everything points to him. But Danny is still holding out. He's pushing this other guy, Russ Gorman. Gorman's on probation, which means a criminal history.

"Look," Danny says, "this Gorman was the last one seen with the girl. We can't eliminate him yet."

"Dan, he dropped her off, okay? Then nutbag here picks her up and he's in a jealous rage 'cuz she left him. Plus they had that fight the day before she went missing."

Tom jumps in. "He's leaving tomorrow and we've got nothing on this guy. We have a lot of work to do to check this out."

No one goes home. We're working against the clock on Rubright with a million other things to check. This is what investigation is all about. It's hard, frustrating, and tedious, but we're starting to think maybe we've got a dead girl, and that's what matters.

Danny Young, who was the primary, continued to disagree. He wanted to focus the attention on Gorman. Young, who felt he had a pretty good rapport with Rubright, took over interviewing him, an interview observed by Sergeant Bruce Coffin. (Frequently, significant interviews will be conducted by one detective with a second one observing.)

Sergeant Coffin is a tall man, wide shouldered and lanky with a graying Abe Lincoln beard. He always wears a suit. Coffin has a ready smile and is quick with a joke to ease tension or lighten people's spirits. His impatience, his eagerness to resolve matters quickly, contrasts oddly with the fact that he is a wonderful and patient explainer of police procedure. When he's not fighting crime, Sergeant Coffin is a gifted artist whose paintings are shown in galleries.

Although both the inconclusive polygraph and Rubright's peculiar manner continued to concern the detectives, Rubright was cooperative and forthcoming. He described being unable to find Amy, leaving the Pavilion nightclub, and using his compass to travel south until he reached the turnpike. Young found Rubright's story and demeanor convincing, and was impressed by his continued willingness to speak with them and his openness about his story.[3]

Young's feeling was that Rubright, a former college rugby player who was currently unemployed owing to the effects of a severe concussion sustained in a car accident, was just a down-to-earth, dumb jock who had developed a big thing for Amy St. Laurent, a feeling that she didn't reciprocate. However, at the end of the interview, concerns were raised again when Young and Coffin asked Rubright for hair samples and DNA and he refused. Why balk at this after having been so cooperative, unless the cooperation was just a ploy?

At the same time that they were collecting information about Eric Rubright, the detectives were also focusing on Russ Gorman, the man who, according to the timeline they were developing, appeared to be the last one known to have seen Amy St. Laurent alive. Gorman was twenty-one years old, a five-foot-ninish, 160-pound pretty boy with artificially streaked blond hair fashionably spiked with gel. He had multiple tattoos and a pierced ear. He was a regular in the Old Port bar scene, well known to bartenders and bouncers.

They learned that Gorman had been raised in Troy, Alabama, and Delray Beach, Florida, and had lived in the Portland area for about eighteen months. He had moved up from Florida after his mother, Tammy Westbrook, and her boyfriend, Rick Deveau, had moved to Scarborough.

A state criminal records search revealed that he was on probation in Maine for theft, a piece of information he had neglected to share in his interview with the police. (Individuals on probation are obligated to disclose this information when being questioned by police. They are also supposed to inform their probation officer of any contacts with the police.) The omitted information was significant because probation suggested a serious level of criminal activity. Detectives contacted the Troy and Delray Beach police departments to determine whether Gorman had a record in those states.

On the same Tuesday he interviewed Eric Rubright, Danny Young interviewed Russ Gorman a second time. Gorman said he had worked as a car detailer and was an on-call bouncer at the Iguana bar. He had been crashing at the Brighton Avenue apartment for about two weeks, sleeping on one of the living room couches. The other residents of the apartment were Kush Sharma, Jason Cook, Dave Grazier, and Grazier's fiancée, Dawn Schimrich. Prior to staying at 230 Brighton Avenue, Gorman had stayed at 136 Oxford Street with Matt Despins, another bouncer at the Iguana, and Brent Plummer.

Gorman repeated his version of events: He and St. Laurent and Sharma had left the Pavilion and gone to the apartment on Brighton Avenue. When no party materialized, St. Laurent wanted to go back to the Pavilion

Video monitor photograph of Detectives Danny Young and Mark Teceno interviewing Jeffrey Russell Gorman.

to look for Eric Rubright. Gorman left the apartment at about 1:45 a.m. to drive her back to the Pavilion in his red Pontiac Grand Am. On their way out, they met Jason Cook returning from work.

At the Pavilion, Gorman said, he slowed down in the street to let her off, not even putting his car in park, and there was a group of people hanging around out in front when he dropped her off. He told Young he had reservations about leaving her there alone at that hour, but he insisted this was what she wanted. He then returned directly to 230 Brighton Avenue.

Gorman said that the trip took only about six minutes each way but balked when asked to name the streets he'd taken, refusing to be locked into any specific route. Gorman told Young that St. Laurent did not appear to be drunk.

Gorman said that when he got back to the apartment, Jason Cook was on the computer, sending an e-mail message to his aunt in Florida. Gorman also reported that he made a phone call, although he couldn't recall whom he had phoned. He gave three possible names: his ex-girlfriend Jamie Baillargeon, Matt Despins, and a friend named Kermit Beaulieu. He said he was on the sofa, watching TV, when Dawn and Dave returned.

As they had with Rubright, the detectives told Gorman that they would like him to take a polygraph test, which would help with their investigation and would help to eliminate him as a suspect.[4] Gorman refused to take the test, saying he would want to consult a lawyer first. Police then asked Gorman if he would let them search his car. He indicated that it was an inconvenient time and added, "I'm definitely seeing a lawyer."

Gorman's responses, when he was not in custody or being interrogated but only being interviewed along with many other people, told the police a lot. First, they flagged a familiarity with the criminal justice system. Gorman was not intimidated by police or by being in a police station—behavior that is sometimes unnerving to police officers. Indeed, he started his second interview with a line of chatter about a "guy in a yellow suit acting weird in the Old Port" that the police definitely ought to take a look at. Gorman was also very comfortable asserting his rights. Once they got his records from Florida and Alabama, the detectives would understand why.

Detective Donald Krier, observing Gorman's behavior, remarked, "In my twenty years as a cop, I'd never seen a guy so cocky and arrogant in a police station. He made eye contact and was actually sizing us up."

Second, if the police were not already focusing on him, Gorman's statement that he wanted to consult an attorney would have immediately drawn closer scrutiny. If he was telling the truth and had nothing to hide, why not cooperate? Known in police parlance as "lawyering up," expressing the desire to consult an attorney in a situation where there is both custody and interrogation, and thus a person's Miranda rights apply, automatically brings questioning to an end. But this was not a custodial situation. Gorman knew this was only an interview and he was free to walk out at any time.[5] He was only one of many individuals asked to stop by the department and speak with detectives. With the city stunned by the news of St. Laurent's disappearance, many people wanted to help—but Gorman, apparently, didn't.

Portland detectives also looked at a third potential suspect, Amy St. Laurent's ex-boyfriend, Richard Sparrow. They knew that Sparrow had been at Amy St. Laurent's house on Friday evening, along with Eric Rubright. They had been told that Sparrow was there because St. Laurent was nervous about being alone with Rubright and that Sparrow drank too much and spent the night on her couch.

They had also been told by friends of the couple that Richard Sparrow was unhappy about the breakup and jealous of other men in Amy's life. Witnesses had told them of heated arguments between Sparrow and St. Laurent. Checking out these stories, interviewing Richard Sparrow, and finding witnesses who could establish his whereabouts on Saturday night were added to the detectives' to-do list.

Twenty-four hours into the investigation, Danny Young had already spoken with more than a dozen witnesses and conducted several lengthy interviews. He had been to the Pavilion nightclub to speak with the owner and the manager, obtained lists of employees, and begun those interviews. His phone rang constantly. His desk was buried under a litter of pink message slips as the public, the media, and other police departments reacted to an event that highlighted life's transience and exposed everyone's vulnerabilities—the sudden, unexplained disappearance of a responsible young woman.

In the midst of all this, he had another, and equally pressing, task. He had to develop a detailed profile of the missing woman—Amy St. Laurent.

4

Fundamental to the entire investigation, as it was for any investigation of this type, was for the detectives to come to know the missing woman, Amy St. Laurent. It would be through their understanding of who she was and what was characteristic behavior for her that they could accurately assess and interpret the truthfulness and value of the information they received. They started by talking to the people who knew her best—her parents, stepparents, her sister, friends, and her supervisors and coworkers at Pratt & Whitney.

They had started with some basics. They had her photograph and physical description. Her face stared at them from lampposts and store windows all over town: A pretty, smiling woman with long, reddish blonde hair. They knew that she was five foot five and a slender 120 pounds. She had recently had professional photographs taken and was thinking about putting together a modeling portfolio. They knew that the night she disappeared, she was wearing jeans and sneakers and a gray sweatshirt with the Pratt & Whitney logo on the front, her hair caught back with a scrunchie.

They knew the facts that had triggered their investigative instincts: She was close to her family, especially her mother and her younger sister, Julie, and wouldn't go for days without contact. Her father, Dennis, and his girlfriend, Kathy, lived right around the corner from St. Laurent's apartment in South Berwick. She saw him frequently and worked with Kathy. She was a reliable and responsible employee who would not willingly miss work. She was a devoted pet owner who was crazy about her cat, Alex, and would go to great lengths to ensure that he was never neglected.

Amy St. Laurent. (Stewart Smith Photographers)

Like painters working with a paint-by-numbers canvas, the detectives would gather more and more information about this young woman who, they were increasingly certain, had been the victim of a violent crime.

A great deal of their initial information came from Amy St. Laurent's mother, Diane Jenkins. She created a strong and positive image of her daughter in the minds of the detectives, supplying pictures, background, and stories that illuminated Amy's character. A graceful, thoughtful, attractive, and well-spoken woman, Diane Jenkins provided a powerful visual image for the media when she appeared at press conferences with Chief Chitwood and appealed for help in finding her missing child, reminding people that this could happen to anyone's daughter. Her tragic eyes and trembling courage illuminated for the public something central about the case: that a sudden event like Amy's disappearance exposes everyone's vulnerability.

Valuable as Diane Jenkins's assistance was, the detectives needed to pursue the other traditional avenues for developing a profile of the victim. It is sometimes shocking to realize how little privacy crime victims have. In many crimes, detectives have to scrutinize the victim to determine whether she truly is a victim and whether there has actually been a crime. In the case of a homicide—and from day one, the police proceeded as though this might be one—the perpetrator robs the victim not only of life but also of privacy.

In developing their profile of Amy St. Laurent, detectives would learn about her education. Her work habits. Her relationship history, including her sex life. They would collect information about her lifestyle, including drinking habits and possible drug use. They would talk with her employers and coworkers to form a picture of her as an employee. They would ask questions about her personality, drawing a sense of her from family, friends, and neighbors. They would obtain her medical and dental records. Check her driving record.

Detectives would comb through her past and present, looking for any aggrieved boyfriends or ex-boyfriends, anyone at her workplace who might have shown a special interest in her, any history of arguments or domestic violence, anyone with an obsessive crush, any enemies Amy might have made.

As the inquiry expanded to include a closer look at Amy St. Laurent, her home, her family, and her coworkers, the number of key players on the investigative side also expanded. From the moment Danny Young had received a phone call about the missing South Berwick woman, the Portland detectives had anticipated that another complication would soon arise—the jurisdictional challenges of which police agencies would be involved in conducting the investigation and the question of who would be in charge.

Amy St. Laurent was last seen alive in Portland, but that didn't necessarily make Portland the site of the crime. Her home was forty miles away in South Berwick. Her house and car needed to be searched, along with the area around her house. With no definitive crime scene or confirmation of any actual crime, police would need to spread a wide net. If someone—Rubright, Gorman, or someone not yet identified—took St. Laurent in a car, she could be anywhere.

Maine is a largely rural state. Outside the larger cities and towns, the public safety functions are performed by county sheriffs' departments and the state police. Except in Bangor and Portland, which are authorized by the attorney general's office to conduct their own investigations, the Maine State Police (MSP) handle all homicide investigations.

Police organizations often need to work together to solve crimes, but police are also very territorial and wary about sharing authority, control, and sensitive information. Even in a case like this, where everyone wanted to cooperate, cooperation could be extremely complicated. Different law enforcement organizations participating in the search for Amy St. Laurent would have different command structures and different investigative approaches, different systems for keeping records and writing reports, and different protocols and SOPs for sharing that information. Even their radios couldn't automatically talk to each other.

There were also the natural tensions between police agencies. The edgy rivalry between local police departments and the state police begins at the academy level. For many years, all police officers in Maine trained together at the Maine Police Academy except state police, who trained at their own facility. Their facility had a longer training course, and right from the start there was an assumption that longer must be better. Although both state and local police now train together for part of the time, the traditional sense of inferiority/superiority lingers, often exacerbated by the fact that in most jurisdictions, when the state police arrive, they come to take over.

There was also the practical reality. No cop wanted to put his heart and soul into an investigation that might be jerked out from under him tomorrow, and the best homicide detectives absolutely do put their hearts and souls into their work.

For now, Joyce and Young were cool with the need for cooperation. They could work out the details later. Right now, they had a missing woman, a worried family and friends, and a community on alert. They had one set of priorities, and only one. To find Amy St. Laurent as quickly as possible and, if she had indeed been the victim of foul play, to identify and arrest the person responsible.

The state police arrived in the form of Detective Sergeant Matthew Stewart, Sergeant Joyce's counterpart from MSP Criminal Investigation Division 1, which covers most of southern Maine, including Amy St. Laurent's hometown of South Berwick. Although they were both admitted control freaks and extremely territorial, Stewart and Joyce could hardly have been more different.

Despite hair so closely cropped that its color is undiscernible, Sergeant Stewart, with his smart suits, gold-rimmed glasses, and shiny shoes, looks more like a banker or a lawyer than a cop. Although he is not the tall, hulking presence many state troopers are, Stewart has plenty of that innate, if difficult to describe, quality the police call "command presence." His demeanor is reserved and taciturn, but when he chooses to be, Sergeant Stewart is extremely charming.

Because his job frequently thrusts him in front of the media, and because cops, particularly detectives, are deeply cautious about the careless word or inadvertent slip, Stewart has become an expert wordsmith. He likes to weigh his words before he speaks, and the sentences he finally parts with are masterpieces of verbal construction. He says he has had to acquire the skill of saying something without really saying anything when speaking to the media.

Recognizing that there was much to be done in and around St. Laurent's residence in South Berwick, Portland police cautiously welcomed Stewart's offer to take over part of the investigation. Sergeant Joyce was careful, however, to keep his people involved in any joint efforts to ensure continuity and quick access to new information. After a meeting to update the MSP detectives on the case, it was decided that the state police would concentrate on the South Berwick portion of the investigation. For the first week of the investigation, Sergeant Stewart assigned MSP detective Rick LeClair to work with Danny Young.

MSP detectives, sometimes accompanied by Portland police, conducted forensic searches of Amy St. Laurent's apartment as well as searches of the surrounding area. At that time, police did not know where or under what circumstances she had gone missing. It did not appear that she had made it back home, but until they could rule out that possibility, they had to treat the apartment as a potential crime scene.

On Saturday, when St. Laurent had been missing for a week, her mother, Diane Jenkins, asked if she could go to Amy's apartment to retrieve some personal items. The lock had been changed to control access, and the condition and contents of the house had been documented, photographed and examined, but the police were not yet ready to release the apartment. Although he was supposed to be off that day, Sergeant Stewart agreed to meet Diane Jenkins there. It was the first time he had met Amy St. Laurent's mother.

What followed was an excruciating experience for everyone. Sergeant Stewart, a meticulous and cautious man colleagues describe as the kind of detective who is first to a crime scene and last to leave, was deeply troubled by the dilemma posed by Diane Jenkins's presence, torn between his duty to preserve the scene, because any item might have evidentiary value, and compassion for a desperate mother's desire to touch her daughter's possessions.

The dilemma was vividly played out as Amy's mother went from room to room, reaching out to touch clothes, jewelry, and other items in order to "connect" with Amy, wanting to feel and sometimes take away many of her daughter's things while Sergeant Stewart felt he had to dissuade her from doing that. At one point, Diane Jenkins picked up her daughter's jacket, buried her face in it, and said, "It smells like her."

As they left the apartment, Jenkins asked if anyone had checked the crawl space under the duplex to see if Amy might be there. Stewart assured her that the space had been checked during an earlier search, but recognizing from her forlorn and desperate look that she needed to put that possibility to rest, he crawled underneath with a flashlight.

During searches of the apartment, police carried away Amy St. Laurent's computer and her personal correspondence. Her telephone answering machine. They even collected the bloody tissues from the bathroom wastebasket. Later they would read her letters and her diary, a slender volume designated as the diary of Amy Elizabeth St. Laurent, which charted her struggles to find herself after her breakup with longtime boyfriend Richard Sparrow. Detectives would listen to her phone messages and read the e-mail on her computer. They would contact her correspondents and her callers, checking names, relationships, and stories.

Detectives examined the clothes in Amy's closet, including the pockets. Looked through her dresser drawers. They would check her phone records to see whom she'd been calling. Learn about her spending habits from bank statements and credit card bills.

To an outsider, it sounds terribly intrusive. After all, if something had happened to Amy St. Laurent, she was the one on whose behalf the police were working. But in a potential homicide case the detective stands in the shoes of the victim and becomes her earthly representative. As Vernon Geberth says, "Many times the detective ends up learning more about the deceased than the victim knew about him or herself."[1]

They learned that Amy St. Laurent had spent her earliest years in New Hampshire with her parents, Diane and Dennis St. Laurent. When the marriage broke up, Amy lived briefly with her father, then went to live with her mother. Her mother subsequently married a man named Don Jenkins, and Amy and her younger sister, Julie, lived with them. They moved to South Portland in 1989. She attended South Portland High School. Although she was an honors student, she found high school unchallenging and, perhaps because she feared it would be more of the same, opted not to attend college.

Later, Amy became involved with Richard Sparrow. Amy and Sparrow lived together in various places for about five years, most recently in the apartment in South Berwick. At one point they became engaged, but the engagement was later broken. At the time Amy disappeared, their relationship had been over for several months, but Sparrow was still listed on her credit cards, and they remained close friends.

Part of the reason for the breakup was Amy's feeling that she was too young to settle down. Although she longed for a home and children, she'd always been involved in a relationship and wanted time to find herself before settling into something permanent. She and Sparrow felt that they had grown apart; she had become more career oriented, while he was still content to drink beer and watch TV.

She had long harbored a secret crush on a man named Jason Kolias, whom she had met in high school when they both worked at a Dunkin' Donuts. His wife, who had been a good friend of hers, had died, leaving him with a small son, Jacob, of whom Amy was very fond. It had been on a trip to Florida to visit Jason and Jacob, a few weeks earlier, that Amy had met Jason's neighbor Eric Rubright.

Like many pretty girls in their midtwenties, Amy longed to be taken more seriously for her intelligence and her skills. She was paying more attention to her wardrobe, learning to dress more professionally. She was excited about the challenges and responsibilities of her job. She was saving money toward buying a house where she hoped to live someday with a husband and children. She exercised regularly and did yoga to help her manage stress.

Amy had occasionally smoked pot and was a social drinker. Friends described her as spontaneous but not impulsive. A bouncer in the Old Port who had known Amy since high school described her as the type of girl who could take care of herself. Someone who wouldn't impulsively go off with a stranger. She was careful. She was sensible. She was responsible. She had too much self-respect to take foolish chances. She carried Mace in her purse. She was also good hearted and generous and hated to hurt people's feelings, and she was used to viewing the world, and men, from within the safety of an established relationship.

Although much of the picture they built of her came from other sources, the detectives got closest to Amy through her own words. On the day she broke up with Richard Sparrow, Amy started a diary. She began to chronicle her feelings watching Sparrow's truck disappear after five years together, on a page headed, *"This is the day the Lord has made; let us rejoice and be glad in it."*

The detectives watched her struggle to adjust to the loneliness of an empty house, yet taking pleasure in the way solitude made her more attuned to the world around her. Watching birds at her feeder, working in her flower garden, charting the changes in the summer sky. A summer thunderstorm reminded her of a night when the power went out and Sparrow cooked them noodles over a camp stove. Another storm ended with shimmering rainbows and booming thunder, and Amy mused about nature's way of beauty in destruction, likening it to an "I love Jesus" bumper sticker on a tank.

Reading her diary gave the detectives insight into the caring woman others had described. One day, Amy drove past her high school boyfriend crouched on the lawn beside his baby daughter. She wrote how she was glad she'd moved on but would always retain love for him, how she longed to have a child of her own someday, and wondered how she would feel if Richard Sparrow had a child with someone else.

And there was her diary entry after September 11. After hoping America's response as a nation would not be more hatred and destruction, she asked, "If I died today, what would I regret most? I wish I had noticed all this beauty and tranquility around me before. What the hell was so captivating that I didn't see the spider spinning his web? Didn't hear the crickets every night? Didn't notice all the goodness and beauty around me?"

It might have been her kind heart that got her into trouble on that last Saturday. Detectives knew that Amy had met Eric Rubright on a trip to Florida three weeks earlier. Amy spent some time with Rubright, who took her on a motorcycle ride and showed her places on the Gulf around Ft. Myers, including Sanibel Island. When she returned to Maine, Rubright e-mailed, saying he'd never been to Maine and asking if he could visit her when he came to visit relatives in New York. He sent her roses.

Amy was not romantically interested in Eric Rubright, but she appreciated the attention and didn't want to be unkind, so she agreed that he could come. At first, she was casual about the visit, but as the date approached, she expressed reservations to her mother, McElaney, Sparrow, and others. In her diary, she wrote, "And he's pretty aggressive. Have to keep on my toes when he's around. Keep the defenses up."

Detectives learned from the South Berwick police that they had had a call on the Monday after Amy disappeared from Ruth McElaney, Amy's next-door neighbor and a coworker at Pratt & Whitney. She had contacted the police because Amy's expensive coat was lying on the ground beside her car and had been for some time. McElaney had gotten their landlady to bring the key so that she could enter Amy's apartment and see if everything was all right. Although Amy's backpack was there, Amy clearly wasn't around.

Ruth McElaney told the South Berwick police that she was worried, in part, because Amy had been afraid of a visitor from Florida she'd had over the weekend. On Friday night, McElaney had been turning into their shared driveway when the visitor, Eric Rubright, came peeling out, very angry. Amy, standing outside watching, confided that Rubright was mad because she had dashed his hopes they would have a sexual relationship. McElaney said Amy hadn't wanted Rubright to visit but was too nice to say no. Despite Amy's reservations, after discussions with her friends she had felt she could manage the situation.

The South Berwick officer responding to McElaney's call found a note on Amy's door saying "where the f—— did you go?"

From the description of what Amy St. Laurent had been wearing on the night she disappeared, it appeared that the decision to check out Portland's nightlife must have been spontaneous. In jeans, sweatshirt, and sneakers, Amy wasn't dressed for a night on the town.

Information the detectives gathered suggested that over the course of that Saturday evening, Rubright had been making unwelcome advances to Amy and she might have been worn down, irritated and frustrated with him. She had been drinking, though witnesses varied widely in their views of whether she was intoxicated. They learned that her action in finding a dance partner when Rubright wouldn't dance was not unusual. When Amy had gone to the Pavilion with Sparrow, she would find herself a partner if she wanted to dance and he didn't.

Detectives had Rubright's version of the facts. They had Gorman's version of the facts. They had located witnesses who had observed Amy, Rubright, and Gorman during the course of the evening. Now, their challenge would be to imagine Amy's version. As information was developed, the detectives would do this imagining to develop theories about what had happened, constantly reassessing what they knew, based on their suspects and on their increasingly deep knowledge of who Amy St. Laurent was.

They would picture Amy going through Saturday evening. Playing pool. Buying Rubright pizza. Going to find a dance partner, since he didn't want to dance. Stopping with Gorman and Sharma at the Iguana bar. Amy at the Brighton Avenue apartment, increasingly uncomfortable as no party materialized and her instincts told her she wasn't where she wanted to be. The detectives drove the dark streets she might have traveled, mentally following the car of one suspect or another down those same streets, imagining the clash of wills of a man intent on having sex, who might have became enraged when he was refused, and an independent, capable woman who didn't intend to be anyone's victim.

5

By Wednesday, detectives had checked out Eric Rubright's story more fully. A perfect example of a small thing that tells a big story, Rubright's receipts from the convenience store in South Portland gave them both a location and a time of purchase. That, in turn, led them to a time-stamped surveillance camera tape that put Rubright at the store paying for gas and purchasing food and soda at 1:36 a.m. Neighbors confirmed that Rubright's car was at Amy's apartment on Sunday morning and that her coat, which Rubright said he had left on the hood of her car, was lying on the ground.

The specifics of his suspiciously detailed story were checking out. Police had interviewed him twice, and polygraphed him. With no reason to arrest him or detain him further, they had to let Rubright leave the state. On Wednesday, Rubright agreed to allow police to collect blood for DNA and hair samples. Evidence technician Kevin McDonald went with a detective to the airport and collected these before Rubright left.

In the conference room, watching the videotape from the convenience store, detectives could see that it confirmed Rubright's story. Bruce Coffin, studying the tape, remembered thinking, "Wow, there he is, just like he said. But maybe the girl is still in the car." And questions still remained. Was it possible that, after leaving the store, Rubright had driven back to Portland and reencountered St. Laurent? Detectives drove the route Eric Rubright had taken from the Old Port parking garage to the convenience store, late at night as Rubright had, and back to the Old Port again.

Later in the week, Detective Kevin Curran, an MSP trooper interviewing toll takers on the turnpike, located a female attendant at the Scarborough exchange who remembered a heavyset male matching Rubright's description showing up at her booth early Sunday morning, searching for change and, after coming up with only fifteen cents, asking if he could please use the highway because it was the only route he knew to the house where he'd been staying. She was certain this had happened around 2:00 a.m., as this was when she normally had a snack. Based on this timeline, it would have been practically impossible for him to have returned to Portland and picked up St. Laurent.

Police also contacted the agency from which Rubright had rented the GMC Envoy and arranged to have any trash that had been collected from the vehicle saved. Before the vehicle was cleaned and returned to service, it was towed to police headquarters at 109 Middle Street, where it underwent a forensic examination by Portland evidence technicians. Crazy as it was, Rubright's story was checking out.

Although police had to continue to entertain the outside possibility that Rubright was involved in Amy's disappearance, his timeline didn't mesh with what they knew about Amy's activities after she left the Pavilion. By the time Gorman said he'd dropped Amy off, back in the Old Port, Eric Rubright was talking his way onto the turnpike. Still, while Rubright's story was being checked, investigators searched around the convenience store, South Portland cemeteries, wooded areas, and roadsides along the route that he had taken, looking for Amy or her body, and drove from the Pavilion to the turnpike entrance at night to check the timing.

The detectives also had to check out Richard Sparrow's activities on the night that Amy St. Laurent disappeared. Despite the breakup, he had maintained a presence in St. Laurent's life. They knew he had been sufficiently uncomfortable with the idea of another guy staying at St. Laurent's apartment that he had been there Friday night to check Rubright out.

It was possible that if Amy St. Laurent was stuck without a ride in the Old Port, she might have called him to come and pick her up. It was an outside possibility, since her mother was nearby in South Portland and Sparrow lived more than an hour away in New Hampshire, but a jealous ex-boyfriend known to have been arguing with a missing person could not be ignored.

Sparrow told them he had spent Saturday evening with friends but that the friends had a small child, so it had been an early evening and he had then returned to Newmarket, New Hampshire, where he was sharing an apartment with two female roommates. Detectives interviewed the couple he had spent the evening with, who confirmed Sparrow's version of the story. They then went to New Hampshire and separately interviewed the two roommates, each of whom confirmed his timeline for late Saturday evening and for Sunday. On the basis of the information they had gathered and the timeline they'd made, they felt they could eliminate Richard Sparrow as a suspect.

Just as they were checking the details of Eric Rubright's story, another major focus in this early stage of the investigation would be to test Russ Gorman's story by interviewing the residents of the Brighton Avenue apartment and witnesses such as bartenders, doormen, and customers who might have seen him with Amy St. Laurent at Fore Play, the Pavilion, or the Iguana, another Portland bar where police learned that Gorman, Kush Sharma, and Amy St. Laurent had stopped briefly so St. Laurent and Sharma could use the bathroom before driving to the Brighton Avenue apartment.

On Wednesday, October 24, police reinterviewed Gorman's roommates Jason Cook and Kush Sharma. Sharma's story was essentially the same as Gorman's. He said Gorman had been gone only twenty or twenty-five minutes, then was in for the rest of the night. That he (Sharma) and Jason Cook were sitting on couches watching TV when Gorman returned. That Gorman used the phone and then joined them. Sometime later, the other roommates, Dave Grazier and his fiancée, Dawn Schimrich, returned. Sharma also remembered that Dave Grazier had been at the apartment when Gorman first arrived with Amy, then left to go pick up Dawn.

Jason Cook reported that he had been the manager at the Iguana bar that evening and had left work at approximately 1:45 a.m., arriving back at the apartment between 1:45 and 2:00 a.m. He arrived as Gorman and Amy St. Laurent were leaving. Gorman introduced St. Laurent, and she wished Cook a happy birthday before she and Gorman left in Gorman's car. Cook told detectives that Gorman returned to the apartment about twenty minutes later. Cook stated that he was on the computer sending an e-mail to his aunt in Florida when Gorman returned and that Gorman came in and asked to use the telephone to call his ex-girlfriend, Jamie.

(Gorman was seeking permission to use the phone because he wasn't a rent-paying tenant of the apartment.)

So far, Gorman's story seemed to be corroborated by his roommates. But both Cook and Sharma had described a lifestyle in which nights spent in bars and clubs followed by drinking at home were the norm and details of one day could easily become confused with events of another. Detectives would take none of this at face value without looking for other ways to confirm the stories. It was a basic part of their investigative process—interview, assess, reinterview, check other sources such as witnesses, tapes, or phone records, corroborating and recorroborating information until they felt it was clear. (For example, they would subpoena many witness's cell phone records for the night Amy disappeared.)

Next they interviewed the third roommate, David Grazier. Grazier reported that he lived at the Brighton Avenue address with two roommates, Cook and Sharma, and his fiancée, Dawn Schimrich. Recently a friend of Cook and Sharma, Russ Gorman, had been sleeping on their couch. Grazier stated that when he returned from work on Sunday morning between 12:15 and 12:30 a.m., no one was home. He showered and received a call from his fiancée, asking him to pick her up at the Iguana to go to a restaurant called the Station for breakfast. He left the apartment between 1:00 and 1:30 a.m.

Before he left, Sharma, Gorman, and a girl they introduced as Amy came into the apartment. Grazier identified her from a photograph as Amy St. Laurent. He then picked up his fiancée and they went to the Station. He arrived back at the apartment between 3:00 and 3:15 a.m. His fiancée, Dawn, who had traveled in a different car, arrived at about the same time. At that time, he visited all the rooms on the living floor (there were also two bedrooms upstairs) and did not see Gorman. He stated that Gorman might have been out on the porch, smoking, as smoking wasn't allowed in the apartment.

Grazier told the detectives he had been very tired and had almost immediately gone to bed. When he woke between 4:30 and 5:00 a.m. and came downstairs to use the bathroom, he found Gorman in there, washing. Gorman was fully dressed, did not appear to have been asleep, and wandered restlessly around the apartment after leaving the bathroom. Grazier told police he had later mentioned not seeing Gorman in the house when he returned at 3:00 a.m. to Jason Cook, who had responded, "Well, he was there."

Grazier's fiancée, Dawn Schimrich, told detectives that she had been at the Iguana earlier in the evening and had seen Russ Gorman, Kush Sharma, and a blonde girl in jeans come in around 1:00 a.m. to use the bathroom. Her friend Stacy Rolfe was outside the Iguana and spoke with Sharma, Gorman, and the girl. Schimrich then left to go to breakfast at the Station. When she arrived home a few minutes after 3:00 a.m., Sharma was on one couch and Cook on the other, watching TV. She talked with them for about twenty minutes before going to bed. She did not see Gorman in the apartment.

That same day, Wednesday, October 24, Danny Young got a call from a man who identified himself as Matt Despins. Despins said he had some information he felt compelled to share and asked to meet with Detective Young. Despins came to the police station around 4:00 p.m. He told Young that he was good friends with Cook, Sharma, and Gorman. He was also acquainted with Julie St. Laurent, the missing woman's sister.

Matt Despins told Young that he had been working at the Iguana as a bouncer Saturday night and had seen Sharma, Gorman, and Amy St. Laurent come in sometime after 1:00 a.m. He had been annoyed with Sharma for bringing people into the bar after hours because it violated state liquor laws, which required that all patrons must be off the premises and liquor put away by fifteen minutes after closing time.

Despins told Young that when Sharma and Gorman came in, Gorman immediately went upstairs to speak with Jason Cook. After Gorman had talked to Cook and left the club with Sharma and St. Laurent, Despins went to see Cook, who was acting as manager that evening, to ask if he wanted to go out with a group of them to the Station for breakfast. Cook was usually up for such things, especially if a girl named Shyla Cameron was going, since Cook was interested in Shyla. On this occasion, however, Cook acted weird, said that he wasn't feeling well and that he was going home.

Matt Despins also told Young that he had been in Gorman's car a week earlier and the car was littered with dust, dirt, and trash. Despins had teased Gorman about the fact that although he detailed cars for a living, his own car was filthy. Gorman had told him that the car was a piece of junk and he wasn't going to waste his time cleaning it. Despins reported that he had gotten into Gorman's car the following week, on the Monday or Tuesday after St. Laurent disappeared, and found the car detailed and clean right down to the dashboard and radio knobs, the seats slippery from being so clean.

The interview was being recorded, but Young made a note of this very significant detail—a big flag for the detectives. On Tuesday, Gorman had been "too busy" to let them search his car. Now Young was hearing that the car had been cleaned, most likely by the busy man himself.

Matt Despins also told Young that Gorman had talked to him about polygraph exams. Despins thought his friend seemed overly concerned about polygraphs for someone who insisted he was "innocent." He said that Gorman had also spoken with another friend of theirs, Ryan Campbell, who was a part-time police officer in Old Orchard Beach, and that Campbell and Gorman had used Ryan Campbell's computer to research polygraphs on the Internet and printed out some information for Gorman. Ryan Campbell had told Despins he was missing a handgun and believed that Gorman had taken it.

Beads of sweat dot Danny's forehead as he pokes his face into my office. "Lieutenant, I'm going to talk to Sergeant Joyce and update. You want in?"

"Yeah," I tell him, "get Tom and let's do it in here."

Tom jerks his way into my office, closes the door, and my photo of McSorley's Pub in New York City falls to the floor. "That's your dad, Tom, telling you to slow down." Tom waits impatiently because there is so much going on with this and other cases.

"Go, Dan," I say.

Glasses over his nose, Dan flips the pages of his notepad and goes over all the players. "Eventually, there's flags on this Gorman. This guy is all wrong and I like him for it. He's got background. He's on probation. Tells me, 'I'm definitely seeing a lawyer.' Won't take a poly and is asking his friends about polygraph exams. Won't cooperate and let us see his car. He's real easy with us, used to police, got a real attitude. His timing is all off and that story about dropping the girl off at the Pavilion is bullshit. There's no way."

Danny flips more pages. "He's seen cleaning himself up in the apartment at

4:30 *in the morning, then paces around. He's the last person seen with the girl. I cannot eliminate him at this point."*

"Which one is he, Dan? Oh, yeah, the little guy with the spiky hair? I thought he was a bit arrogant and cocky in a police station." Dan goes on with the other stories of people like Jason Cook, Kush Sharma, Shyla Cameron, Dave Grazier, and others but Gorman is a flag, no doubt. A lot of behavioral indicators.

"Okay, Dan, keep it going and brief me with Tom. I don't want you to have to repeat it all the time."

"You know, Lieutenant, sometimes repeating all of this helps me put it in order, so I don't mind."

"That's what I like about you, Danny." Tom gets up to leave with Dan as we move on to other things. But Dan stops for a moment and says, "One other thing, Lieutenant."

"Yeah, Dan?"

"This guy Gorman detailed his shitbox car right after this girl was missing."

Whoa! Post-offense galore. "You're right, Dan. He is wrong all the way."

Danny Young was focused on trying to find Amy, and on trying to get a straight story about what had happened early Sunday morning, conducting numerous interviews, making dozens of phone calls, and fielding dozens more every day, as well as coordinating information coming in from other detectives. At this stage, as Chief Chitwood told the media, five detectives were working on the case full time. All were going as hard as they could, working against the grim reality that, with every day that passed, evidence was being lost. Tangible, physical evidence can be lost through deliberate destruction but also through natural processes such as weather and temperature. Memory evidence, too, quickly fades or gets distorted over time.

Then, too, the case wasn't taking place in a vacuum. Amy St. Laurent disappeared only six weeks after the events of 9/11, in the middle of hundreds of other cases and a workload significantly increased by the new threat of terrorism. Detectives were constantly called back in from other assignments or after their shifts ended for bomb threats, for suspicious packages, for explosives searches, and for anthrax alerts when people reported the presence of suspicious powders. Everyone was hypervigilant. The department received hundreds of calls about suspicious people. Muslims in Portland were alleging harassment. People were scared, and when people are scared, they look to their police for security. It really cranked up the pressure that two of the 9/11 terrorists who crashed into the World Trade Center, Mohamed Atta and Abdulaziz Alomari, had started their trip in Portland.

People start waving now, saying hello, asking how we are, considering their mortality. It's pro-police all of a sudden, which is refreshing in spite of the horror, but it won't last. The pressure from the media is relentless. Everything in white powder form is anthrax.

There is tension between police and fire personnel. At times, when fire won't go into a building because of a hazardous materials situation, cops end up doing it out of frustration. We are all negotiating through our new world with trepidation, anger, and frustration. Occasionally, when weary police and firefighters try to sort out a scene, it almost comes to blows.

"You freakin' guys have the hazmat [hazardous materials truck]. Who's supposed to go in?"

"Yeah, well, we never dealt with this shit!"

"Well, neither did we."

As we argue, I think: The terrorists have certainly succeeded in further breaking us all down. This is exactly what they want. There are safety and union issues, command and communications issues, masses of emergency personnel gathered around a building trying to determine where to proceed next. These complicated decision processes create tremendous pressure. It's happening everywhere and we have to take each one seriously.

A night I remember distinctly. I'm driving home, planning for a double date with one of the guys' sisters. I leave headquarters at 1800, totally burned out, rushing home to shower and shave, pick up my date, and meet at a great downtown restaurant. I'm partway home when my pager blots out the alternative rock I'm blasting to keep me up.

It's an anthrax scare at the downtown post office. There's powder all over one of the mail-sorting machines. I shout in frustration as I turn and head back in again.

I move through the mass of emergency vehicles and media. News cameras patrol the perimeter. We've got to evacuate the building, decontaminate people, test the materials. My mind's ticking over. How? How? How? Command staff on both sides discuss, plan, argue. Finally, we get buses in to evacuate and quarantine the people. Dozens of them. It's the cops who finally remove the powder and bring it up to the state crime lab.

After hours of waiting, the powder tests out as an unknown industrial cleaning material. Not toxic. We have a note, a potential hoax, connected. We end up prosecuting the perpetrator to send a message — one person's mean or vindictive act is a major drain on emergency resources. It can tie up public safety personnel, putting other people at risk. And break the budget.

The strains on all agencies are unique, new, and absurd. The state lab can't keep up. We're called every day for anthrax scares. Cops end up dealing with it over and over, after a while not even caring if it is anthrax. All these new challenges are added to our workload, because crime doesn't stop. There are new criminal investigations coming at us each day.

My friend and former partner, Sergeant Ted Ross, and I are in the basement of 109 with gas masks on, talking like Darth Vader, as we open potential anthrax letters because it's gotta be done and no one else will do it.

Well, we can't just sit around. We have a job to do. So here we are. Ted and I had worked years together in the early '90s in the drug unit and had been through many precarious and dangerous situations in the past. We had a bond.

"Okay, Ted," I shout through the mask, "gimme the next one. Okay, the address is . . . suspicious because . . . glove up."

A fire truck flies by the station on another run. The city is crazy with post-9/11 fright.

As a New Yorker, I recall with sadness my dad taking me to the Towers many times when I was a child to watch them being built. It was amazing. How could they possibly have come down?

Ted looks up as the fire truck goes past. "Hey," he says, "there goes America's heroes!"

People love firemen. For now, a lot of the time, people love cops, too. It's refreshing. But that will change. Cops are always placed in the middle of societal ills.

"Hey," Ted says. "What about that missing girl?

Through my mask, I sound like I'm speaking underwater. "It's a really weird case. This girl is definitely missing and we think she was murdered and dumped somewhere. We're down to two suspects but there's this guy Gorman who flags up good." *I go on with some of the specifics, the words spooky through the mask.* "Danny's working his ass off. All the guys are. This is a really strange case—really fascinating. This girl is not your typical missing, just boom! Vanished off the face of the earth. This is the real deal, man." *I reach for another letter.*

"Wow, that is strange." *He pauses.* "She's probably dead. What's her name?"

"Amy St. Laurent, Ted. It's Amy St. Laurent."

6

Because their victim was missing, the Amy St. Laurent case was a highly unusual one for the detectives involved. They faced not only the normal challenge of identifying a suspect and gathering enough evidence for an arrest. Every day, every step of the investigation, the detectives had to proceed on two fronts: building a case against the man who was emerging as their prime suspect and trying to find Amy.

There was the obvious reason for finding her—to have definite proof of a crime and a crime scene that could provide evidence to connect the suspect to the crime. There was also the need to calm a public imagination inflamed by the idea of a beautiful young woman vanishing. Most of all, Amy's family needed closure, an end the haunting uncertainty they lived with every day that Amy was still missing.

Without a body, police had no definitive confirmation that Amy St. Laurent was anything but a missing person, but they were convinced, based on experience and training and the responsible person they now knew Amy to be, that they were probably looking at a homicide. They also had no idea where the crime had taken place, other than their suspicion that some part of the crime had involved a car, so they had none of the usual factors for sorting out jurisdiction or narrowing their search area. But for everyone concerned, finding Amy had become the overriding mission.

Although the detectives kept their minds on their job and tried not to let the media pressure affect them, Amy's face and name were on the front page of the daily papers and morning and night on the news, along with Amy's desperate mother standing in the spotlight, pleading for information about her missing daughter. Amy's picture was everywhere. It was inescapable. Everywhere a Portland or MSP detective went, people wanted to know what was happening with the case. Their phones rang not just at work but at home.

For Danny Young, a father with a daughter the same age as Amy, it was impossible not to be moved by the pain and anxiety of a family in limbo. (Ironically, or in a strange coincidence, Danny Young's own daughter, Amy, had met her husband at the Pavilion.)

In the first weeks of the investigation, Young coped with the parents' fear and suffering on a daily basis, making time each night to update them on the investigation and answer their questions—a painful process because so often, despite his efforts, there was little to offer. Later, he would stay in daily contact with Dennis St. Laurent, while Amy's mother gravitated toward Lieutenant Loughlin.

Developing such a close relationship with the victim's family was unusual. In an ordinary case, police involvement would begin with the crime and the crime scene. Police might have a few contacts with the victim's family to gather information about the victim or solidify a case, but later contacts with the family to update them and guide them through the process would be handled by the department's victim witness advocate.

Here there was no crime scene, and no evidence or details of the crime to work with. The family needed answers. When the detectives couldn't provide those answers, they felt an obligation to offer the family whatever support and information they could as well as the comfort of knowing that the investigators who were working on Amy's case never flagged.

But there was something more going on in the Amy St. Laurent case that police officers normally didn't experience. Police are trained from the day they arrive at the academy to maintain an objective distance from their work. Then, the day-to-day experience of policing brutally conditions them not to get emotionally involved. They learn to insulate themselves against the constant barrage of horrific things they see. In an essay about the life of a patrol officer he wrote for the *Portland Press Herald* when he became patrol captain, Joe Loughlin described it vividly:

I'd forgotten so much—the broken glass, the smell of body odor mixed with feces and urine. I forgot about the sobbing, weeping, rocking, muttering and groaning. People screaming, flailing about, smashing their heads into cement, into walls, into anything. I forgot about the depressed, the drugged, deranged, suicidal, homicidal, the self-inflictors. The puking, biting, punching, kicking, charging, bleeding and crying. I forgot about being on the front line, facing violence, the danger, the hatred and disrespect and that stomach shot of adrenaline surge. Voices screaming out in different languages, pointing mutely in fear, the barriers, the confusion. The tense moments when you must act with no time for reflection or consultation. Those men and women in uniform on your streets have the toughest and dirtiest job. They see things you'll never see, hear sounds they'll want to forget. Police officers work and function in a world that goes far beyond the realm of normal experiences. They may be exposed to and bear witness to more horror in a single shift than most people will experience in a lifetime.[1]

Police officers learn to protect themselves from the job, to compartmentalize the work and not take it home. They know enough not to let it get personal, understanding they need that objective distance or they can't do the job. But there are always cases that get through the barriers, cases that stick in the mind, and this was one. They couldn't protect themselves from Amy.

Everyone who worked closely with the case became, in Sergeant Stewart's words, somewhat obsessed with it. This may have been, in part, because it differed so much from the usual case. Sergeant Stewart says he likes to be at the crime scene so he can view the victim and promise that victim to secure justice. Crime scene promises like that are made with a head that is actively engaged in assessing the clues and information. Here the investigators came to know and imagine Amy alive and lovely, without the intervening picture of a body or a crime scene.

Danny Young said that the strength of people's attachments to Amy didn't really hit him until he went with MSP detective Rick LeClair to speak with Amy's supervisors and coworkers at Pratt & Whitney. Going from office to office and from interview to interview, he realized that to those who knew her, Amy St. Laurent was a very special young woman, an unusually generous and optimistic person who contributed her positive spirit to the workplace.

She had been forthright and independent and genuine. Open about her pleasure in becoming good at her job. Open about her relationship struggles. Friends told Young that she was outspoken and would let her feelings be known if she felt uncomfortable or threatened. She was a competent young grown-up who might be spontaneous but wasn't impulsive and didn't take careless chances. Everything he heard told Young that Amy would never deliberately put her family through the agony they were experiencing. It was then that his suspicion that she had been the victim of a crime hardened into certainty.

On Thursday, Amy's family stood tearfully before the media as they offered a $35,000 reward for information leading to her discovery and safe return. Chief Chitwood told reporters that rewards were often quite successful. On Friday evening, concerned citizens joined Amy's family and friends for a candlelight vigil in Portland's Monument Square. These events helped put a human face on the situation, reminding the public, and witnesses who had not come forward, that this was a real tragedy happening to ordinary people.

During the first week, everyone working on the case had been hitting it hard. There were endless meetings to sort out what they knew, to prioritize interviews, and to decide where to search. One morning, driving to work, Young passed an old tote road going off into the woods not far from Gorman's mother's house and thought, "Maybe Amy's down there." Later in the day, he sent Sergeant Joyce and Sergeant Bruce Coffin out to walk the area.

During that same week and in the weeks to follow, Young would order numerous searches to be conducted in and around Portland. Community policing officers tromped through the cold and squalor of abandoned buildings, railroad police officers searched along tracks and rights-of-way, and Portland patrol officers conducted ground and woods searches. Marine Patrol was searching the harbor, around and under docks and piers and along beaches. National Guard helicopters searched forests and waterways.

Because they could pinpoint no particular site, investigators had to assume that Amy could be anywhere. Maine state police and Portland police conducted searches of the woods and areas around Amy's house. State police interviewed Amy's neighbors, searched around her house, and searched junkyards, state parks, and roadsides along the turnpike. Police in South Portland and other adjoining towns were searching. Detectives would spend their own time in the evenings and on the weekends, checking out locations that might have been overlooked.

Cemeteries and parks were searched. Industrial parks and dumpsters were searched. The Coast Guard and the Portland fireboat conducted numerous searches of the dock and waterfront areas and throughout the harbor. Lieutenant Loughlin began attending roll calls, reminding patrol officers about Amy St. Laurent. Patrol officers were instructed to get out of their cars and check hedges/patches of woods/underbrush/parks, any place they spotted that might hold a body. Soon you could see empty cruisers all over the city, as these patrol officers joined the search.

State and local police agencies weren't the only ones searching. On weekends, after work, whenever they could, Amy's family and friends, including Richard Sparrow and people from Pratt & Whitney, and her mother's coworkers from DeWolfe Realty, were searching, too. They searched beaches and marshes and wooded areas, peered into drains and pools and culverts, returning repeatedly to Danny Young for new ideas. However weary the detectives might get, they found it impossible to slacken their efforts knowing Amy's mother was out from dawn until dusk, searching for her lost daughter.

For everyone, the time of year, and the impending winter, increased the sense of urgency. It was the end of October. The days were getting shorter and colder. Even as the falling leaves left the woodlands easier to walk through and see into, those leaves piled up on the ground, masking clues and perhaps covering a body that might be lying there.

As the investigation focused in on Gorman, detectives tried to imagine different scenarios of Gorman and Amy in the car, leaving 230 Brighton Avenue. They retraced routes he might have taken heading back toward the Pavilion and arranged for detailed searches along those routes. Imagining themselves in his car, they considered other places Gorman might have gone—back toward his mother's house in Scarborough, for example, into an area that was familiar. Or heading toward Amy's mother's house in South Portland, a route that would have lulled Amy into a false sense of security. They also imagined Gorman offering Amy a ride back to her house in South Berwick. In each case, they drove the routes looking for places a man with sex on his mind might take a girl where he could control her and be alone and undisturbed long enough to attack her and then, when his plans went awry, kill her and dispose of her body.

The different detectives' speculations about what had happened would precipitate many arguments over the course of the investigation as they tried to narrow down their theories and mutually/collectively agree on some common stories. The primaries and their sergeants sat down two or three times a week to evaluate and reprioritize the case, constantly identifying new areas to be explored and new subjects to be interviewed. At the same time, they were imagining and reimagining the night Amy disappeared, trying to assemble a set of facts that would let them find her.

By Thursday, the fifth day of Amy's disappearance, Lieutenant Loughlin braced himself to tell Amy's mother she should expect that her daughter was probably dead.

She knew what I was about to tell her. I could see it in her eyes—sad, beautiful eyes that pleaded for me not to go on. But she knew. She started to talk before I could speak because she knew. "I have some items of Amy's that might interest you. Some letters and . . . but I know that Sergeant Stewart has her diary."

I got up and closed my office door to get the bustle of the detectives' bay out of our ears. Don and Diane Jenkins sat in my office like many parents and relatives before. I always try to box it up but can never predict. Every cop will tell you . . . one can rarely predict the reaction. I've had people smashing furniture in my office. I look at the eyes first. Is this a screamer? A pounder of furniture? Or a sobber, a vile curser, an attacker, a fainter, or a mute?

Diane Jenkins is a beautiful, graceful woman, but there's such sadness in her eyes and she's so weary and Amy's only missing five days.

"Did you know Amy loved cats?" she continues in an effort to stop me.

Don speaks a few words and I can tell there is tension here and not just because of Amy. I let them talk. Diane goes on about how she feels Amy is trying to communicate with her spiritually. A lot of cops might dismiss that but they always listen if they're good. I believe, and listen.

Diane continues, talking of Amy's consistent behavior in calling her, taking care of her cat, being responsible about her job, et cetera. Then our eyes meet and my stomach flips. "Do I know?" I ask myself. Yes, is the answer. Yes, Amy is dead and it is probable that Gorman did this. Okay. Get ready, Joe.

"*Diane . . . we believe that Amy is dead and no longer with us.*" *It hangs in the air. Through the door I hear the bustle and hum of detectives working. Diane looks at the carpet. My phone rings, breaking the silence.*

"*I know . . .*" *She pushes out.* "*I know.*" *I watch her lips move in slow motion, waiting for more. Don holds her hand. Diane's deep sadness moves toward me, forging a connection that will grow stronger as the case progresses. Diane creates in my mind, in all our minds and hearts, a connection with her missing daughter.*

But there is always hope. "*What if . . . How come . . . Maybe it's . . .*" *I allow her to theorize, but she knows. She knows.*

I know, based on everything we have learned and based on my experience, that time is no longer on our side. I keep picturing Amy in the water, removing images from my head as we speak, my mind going through a Rolodex of death scenes I've witnessed. Then I think, no, not water. Woods off the interstate. Yeah. Woods.

I can hear Diane's voice through the tunnel of crime scenes. An intercom page breaks through the commotion in my head and the quiet murmur of Diane's speech. It's Sergeant Joyce. I call 8526. "*Yeah?*"

"*Listen, we got a guy hanging in the basement up on the hill, looks like a suicide but I'll let you know. The kids found him so it's a pretty bad situation. Fagone is there, so the scene is all set. But get this . . .*"

I try to mask my feelings to spare Diane any more grief as I press the receiver into my ear. "*It's the same house where that poor Newcomb girl was murdered and the boyfriend shot himself after, out back. Remember? Weird, huh?*"

Kelly Newcomb was the daughter of a Portland firefighter, a great, jovial guy who died soon after in my local gym of a heart attack. I saw him a day before he died. Another sad story.

"*Oh, and Joe?*" *Tommy continues,* "*the chief wants to see you about that last press conference . . . he was pissed.*"

"*Oh, great. Thanks, Tom. Keep me posted.*"

Don and Diane hold hands and I see the strain between them. Diane talks more about Amy and the spiritual connections she feels. I explain that we are searching everywhere and are focusing on one or two individuals. Inside I really know who we're looking at. I know he's responsible. We're working so hard to get him—often right through the night.

I tell Diane I may call Vicki Monroe, the clairvoyant. We speak about our own spirituality and life, and death, and life after death. I know it's true. I've seen enough people die and enough death to become spiritually connected. Cops usually go one way or the other regarding mortality and death—either spiritual or cynical and fatalistic.

I see my brother's swollen head after his car accident. Is Amy's head swollen? I think—what might have happened? Diane's voice comes at me through the tunnel. "I feel her presence trying to guide me. We were so close. I truly feel her."

Again the phone rings. The building page blares. We rise and I shake Don's hand. I hug Diane and I tell them we are working very hard to find her daughter. "I know. I know," she says as she glides out of my office.

It's true we do notifications all the time, but if they were all like this, no one could do the job.

There's no time to process it, to feel it. The fact that we've got a big case doesn't stem the normal flow of work. As I walk them out, Sergeant Jones catches my eye. Then Sergeant Coffin. The bureau is buzzing with detectives on phones, people being escorted to interview rooms, the chatter of dozens of cases. Jones grabs me and asks to talk.

"Make it quick, Mike. The chief wants me."

"Yeah, yeah. Look, Lieutenant, we've got two burglars in jail waiting for arraignment and we can't find the report from the officers last night and the computer system is down. . . . I got a search warrant going over on Brighton Avenue and I'm down two guys because of this jerk's interview in the other room."

We move it into the office for privacy and Sergeant Coffin comes with us. We start with all the problems of the day and it's only 1015. On the video monitor behind me, I hear Coons and Teceno talking to a pedophile, his low voice explaining how he had anal intercourse with a nine-year-old girl and a seven-year-old boy like it was a normal conversation. God, I can't believe he's saying it like it's okay. But we've heard it many times before. I tune it out, getting back to Jones and Coffin with a bunch of instructions.

"Get patrol out to Brighton and make sure that thing is secure. When I get back from the chief, I'll get on the computer thing with Deputy Chief Burton. Bruce, make sure that shithead goes by the numbers with Coons."

Gotta see the chief. I move through the desks, the paper, the phones. "Hey, Lieutenant, you going to the gym tonight? Looks like you need it," hollers Detective John Dumas.

"Don't push me now, Clownie."

I'm in the corridor door to Chief Chitwood's office. It's like going before the Wizard of Oz and I'm the Cowardly Lion. I pause to collect myself, then open quickly. He's down the hall by the personnel office. A man with amazing energy. Always moving. Now he's coming toward me like a train.

"Joe! You're not the damned spokesperson for the department. Got it? Everything on the St. Laurent case goes through me from now on."

I try to interject. "Chief, I thought you were okay with it. I believed . . ."

"Joe!"

I know he's really mad when his ears are hot red and the spit starts coming out the corners of his mouth. No sense in arguing. "Okay, Chief. It will never happen again."

He moves back to his office and I sneak back into the Detective Bureau. My pager goes off again. It's Tom out at the death scene. The bureau's hopping. The city's hopping. It's only 1100.

Detectives went on with the detailed work of checking Gorman's story. On Thursday, Young and Detective Scott Dunham, one of the department's computer forensics experts, went to 230 Brighton Avenue and met with Jason Cook. In order to establish more exactly the time Gorman had returned to the apartment on Sunday morning, Cook agreed to allow them to search his computer for the e-mail message he had sent to his aunt at the time Gorman arrived.

Detective Dunham, Cook, and Gorman all attempted to find the message but there was no such message on the computer. Cook said he had a program that automatically erased e-mails a few days after they were sent. He was unable to explain how other e-mails, sent between October 1 and October 17, were still present on the computer.

Young obtained the name and address of Cook's aunt in Hollywood, Florida, and asked the Hollywood police homicide unit for assistance in locating the aunt. Hollywood police Detective Phil Reingard reported that he had contacted Cook's aunt, had explained the circumstances, and together they had examined her computer for e-mail between October 18 and October 21. There were no messages from Jason Cook. Cook's aunt said she'd received no messages from him for some time.

Young then spoke with Jamie Baillargeon, Gorman's ex-girlfriend, one of three persons Gorman said he might have phoned on Sunday morning. Baillargeon confirmed she had not received a call from Gorman between the hours of 1:00 a.m. and 7:00 a.m. on Sunday, October 21, although she had subsequently spoken with Gorman about Amy St. Laurent. Detectives already knew he hadn't called Matt Despins. When they finally tracked down Kermit Beaulieu, the third possibility Gorman had named, they established that Gorman hadn't called him between 2:00 a.m. and 7:00 a.m. but might have called earlier, asking for information about finding a cheap motel room.

Police talked to bouncers and bartenders at the Pavilion, using information gleaned from them to begin tracking down witnesses who had been present on Saturday night. Detectives sat outside the Pavilion at closing time on the nights it was open (Friday, Saturday, and Wednesday), speaking with patrons as they left to locate those who might have been in the street early that Sunday morning. Tracking witnesses this way led them to people as far away as Boston and Burlington, Vermont.

Amy's mother, unable to sit on her hands and wait for news while her daughter was missing, also visited the Pavilion the next several nights that it was open, hoping to locate people who had seen her daughter or who might have information about her disappearance.

Detectives collected reports from police on the late out shift in the Old Port, including a plainclothes liquor enforcement officer who had been in the area around the Pavilion at the time Amy St. Laurent was allegedly dropped off. The officer's presence was part of a joint effort with the Pavilion's owners to enforce a new security plan to quickly clear the sidewalk and street to prevent chronic Old Port problems such as fights and intoxicated people in the road. She reported that the streets and sidewalks had been nearly clear, that few people had been around the Pavilion, and that anyone walking down the street would have been clearly visible. The officer had not seen Gorman, Gorman's car, or Amy.

Since getting the first call about Amy on Monday night, Young and the other detectives had been working virtually nonstop. Working the phones, interviewing, writing reports, briefing the brass. Searching. Following up on phone tips—a strange-acting neighbor here, someone digging on the beach there, tips about a gang murder in another city, a body found on a beach in Massachusetts. Detectives had been meeting regularly to share their collected information. They would throw it up on the dryboard and see what avenues needed pursuing, what stories didn't mesh, decide which witnesses needed to be reinterviewed, what names witnesses had given that needed to be followed up, and in what order.

When they weren't doing all that, they were sorting through the piles of messages, or the jammed voice mail. So-and-so says he doesn't know anything, but his friend such-and-such knew Gorman and he might. They were working against the fundamental detective's clock that says the first few hours, the first few days, are vitally important because of how quickly memories fade, stories get concocted, evidence gets destroyed.

At the same time, they were working with a second fundamental rule, which told them to take as much time as they needed to get things right the first time. Interviews with important witnesses had to be recorded and took as long as necessary to get through the stories. It was also standard investigative protocol for these interviews to be observed by a second detective who would be able to concentrate on things the interviewing detective might miss or switch with the interviewer if the chemistry wasn't right. That meant important interviews often tied up two detectives.

In the center of the case, Danny Young, the primary detective, needed to have many different abilities. The ability to work in a calm and focused way in the chaos of the Detective Bureau, breaking down the investigation into pieces and parceling them out to other detectives. The ability to take in massive amounts of scattered information, process it, and connect seemingly disparate dots. The ability to organize the paperwork that was piling up at an incredible rate. The ability to constantly reprioritize and focus on a particular thread of the investigation. Most of all, the wisdom and experience to keep thinking through the stories and details and putting them all together.

The primary detective is the "funnel" that everything comes through. By SOP, every interview must be reduced to writing, including times, dates, names, addresses, and dates of birth. All the information collected by anyone goes to the primary, is cross-referenced, and goes into a notebook on the primary's desk. All internal reports and all supplemental reports from other cops, evidence technicians, the medical examiner, and so on, are collected by the primary and signed off on by the supervisor, who is ultimately responsible for their content and for ensuring that SOPs are followed. The primary is the person who will ultimately testify in court. To ensure continuity and security of the information, there will be many pieces only the primary and the supervisor will know.

An investigation is a kind of controlled chaos. The control that was needed in order to free Danny Young to concentrate on the St. Laurent case came from Sergeant Joyce. Joyce was very comfortable and adept at handling all the confusion of an intense investigation in the midst of the Detective Bureau's routine, ongoing chaos, where everything was always time sensitive and an emergency. Situations that made others cringe made him smile.

In the police hierarchy, Lieutenant Loughlin would say, "Tommy, you run it and tell me what you need," and then Joyce would farm out the jobs. As the eighteen-hour days went on, though, Loughlin worried that Danny Young was trying to do too much on his own. He and Sergeant Joyce argued about it.

"Tom, he's doing too much."

"He's fine, Joe. Fine."

"Dammit, Tom, he's not fine. You're working him like a mule. Even your other people can see it. His phone never stops. He's got a constant stream of interviews and people. He's been called in on other shit."

"I'm watching it, Joe. Alright! What am I supposed to do? Thorpe and Rybeck have two death scenes going. Dumas and Krier the Asian gang interviews. All the past cases and those two stabbings. A trial next week . . ." He goes on.

I hold up my hand for him to stop. "It's about control, alright. You have to control everything. I know that you're good. I believe in you, but you're pushing him too hard. You know what I want. Get it done. I've got too many other distractions and issues. I have to depend on you, Tom. Get it done."

Tom placates me and includes others in peripheral work, but it does help Dan.

It's 1100. Dan comes into my office and tells me he's fine. He can do it. He updates me. Fascinates me. We compare notes. He's fielded twenty-two messages over the morning. I've had seventeen and everyone wants answers now.

"Jeez, Dan, I wish I could join you on police work. This admin stuff is bullshit."

Danny adjusts his belt. "Hey, you're losing weight," I say. "This might be good for you after all."

The case is starting to boil over with information and legal concerns. Posturing. Egos. Media. Family. Anxious queries from the public. And we've got all these other cases.

Amy St. Laurent had been missing almost a week. Despite a full-court press, police still had no idea where she was or what had happened to her. No witnesses. No physical evidence. No crime scene. Just a void where a warm and vibrant woman had been and an increasingly disturbing picture emerging of their prime suspect.

7

Amy St. Laurent disappeared in late October, just as the glorious crescendo of a Maine fall was fading away. It was a fall most public safety personnel missed. Now Halloween loomed, and November. The days were getting colder, shorter, and darker, and no one had time to notice. The detectives working on the case felt the weight of those days. There was always more to do, and the urgency of the case didn't diminish.

By the end of that first week, their belief that Amy St. Laurent had been murdered was reinforced by what they were learning about Russ Gorman, the last person known to have been with Amy on the night she disappeared. Long before FBI specialists were writing books about criminal profiling, detectives were doing their own sort of profiling. Not the type made famous by FBI agents trying to identify the unknown subject, or UNSUB; police were building profiles of known suspects. In the case of Amy St. Laurent, they had studied the victim so that they could understand who she was and predict how she would have behaved; now they had to fill in the other side of the equation.

The picture they'd built of Amy St. Laurent told them that she was a thoughtful and responsible young woman who was that rare thing in the police officer's daily cavalcade of life's underbelly, a truly innocent victim. The picture they were building of Gorman told them he was exactly the sort of guy who would glibly try to charm a girl when it was sex and not a relationship he had in mind, then react with violence when she resisted.

Gorman's criminal record and interviews with his friends revealed a twenty-one-year-old man who lacked empathy, had an extremely negative attitude toward women, had demonstrated a propensity toward violence, and had shown a willingness to exploit anyone to satisfy his needs.

Gorman was born in Alabama to young parents who divorced when he was one and wrangled about his custody until he was six. Although provisions were made for each parent to have partial custody of the boy, disputes, lack of cooperation, and new relationships kept the arrangement from working. Eventually his father moved away and later started another family, ending most contact with his son. His mother had another child and began drifting in and out of Gorman's life, often leaving him behind in the custody of his grandparents.

Gorman was unsuccessful in school, eventually repeating first and fourth grades, ending up at age fifteen in seventh grade. He was diagnosed as hyperactive and Ritalin was prescribed, but he refused to take it. He frequently refused to go to school in Delray Beach, Florida, because of gang activity there, dropping out altogether after the seventh grade. During his teenage years, he was shuttled back and forth between his mother, Tammy Westbrook, and his paternal grandmother, Dot Gorman, living part of the time in Troy, Alabama, and part of the time in Florida.

Between thirteen and eighteen, he amassed a significant juvenile record in both states. From 1993 to 1998, Gorman's record showed twenty-four incidents in which the Troy police were involved, including auto theft, robbery (in one case befriending an eighty-one-year-old man and then stealing his few valuable possessions), breaking and entering, trespassing, punching a teacher in the head, and making phone calls of a sexual nature to a thirteen-year-old girl. In many instances, he served as apprentice to his uncle, Danny Gorman, already a convicted criminal. At one point, he served thirty-nine days in the city jail for theft. He began abusing drugs and alcohol early in his teens. Along with his criminal activity, Troy police reported that Gorman was known for his terrible temper when he'd been drinking.

Gorman's record in Florida was no better. In 1994, at fifteen, he attacked his mother after he had broken into a neighbor's house and stolen guns, frightening her and convincing her that she could no longer handle him. She told police that he refused to obey her, swore at her, punched holes in the walls, and wouldn't attend school. A CHINS (Child in Need of Supervision) petition was filed, and Gorman was taken into state mental health guardianship.

A psychiatric evaluation determined that Gorman was depressed and suffering from oppositional defiant disorder, the old-fashioned term for which is "stubborn child." Psychiatrists found that Gorman's judgment and impulse control were poor and that he lacked insight into the effects of his actions on others.

Gorman spent time in an institution and was prescribed psychoactive drugs for his depression. As with the Ritalin, when he was out of an institutional setting, he would not take his medication. Eventually, as a result of his behavior, he was placed on probation until his eighteenth birthday. His grandparents in Alabama petitioned for guardianship and then changed their minds, but Gorman did end up living with his grandmother in Troy. When he was eighteen and living with his mother, he again attacked and punched her.

Witnesses described Gorman's terrible relationship with his mother. Matt Despins said, of Gorman, "He's not a grounded guy with a family behind him." Despins told investigators that Gorman absolutely despised his mother, adding, "I've seen some of the stuff she says to him. She deserves every bit of hate that he gives to her." An ex-girlfriend told them that his mother was very hateful, often not wanting him. Gorman and his mother would have screaming arguments; often, she would throw him out of the house only to take him back a short time later.

During one of the periods when he was living in Florida, Gorman became involved with a woman named Kathleen Ferguson, with whom he had a daughter when Ferguson was seventeen. For a time, they lived together with their child, but the relationship failed, in part because of Gorman's negative attitude toward women and his treatment of Ms. Ferguson, which included hitting and punching her while she was pregnant. Child support was ordered but Gorman never complied, although he always managed to find money for drinking with his friends or for drugs.

Approximately eighteen months before Amy St. Laurent's disappearance, he had come to Maine to join his mother, Tammy Westbrook, and her boyfriend, Rick Deveau, who had moved to Scarborough with her teenaged daughter and Westbrook and Deveau's two young children to live in a house belonging to Deveau's mother. In Maine, Gorman held numerous menial jobs.

In September of 2000, he was working at Bill Dodge's auto dealership, cleaning and prepping used cars for resale, when he approached a fellow worker asking if the man wanted to buy some high-end car stereo equipment he'd stolen from a customer's car that had been left for service. His coworker reported Gorman's offer to the employer, the employer went to the police, and once again Gorman was convicted of theft.

At the time Amy St. Laurent disappeared, he was still on probation for that crime. He was later arrested for leaving the scene of an accident. Shortly before police interviewed him in connection with Amy St. Laurent's disappearance, he was arrested for operating after his license had been suspended and illegally attaching license plates and sentenced to twelve days in jail. The process was under way to suspend or revoke his driver's license.

Gorman's unstable temper quickly showed itself in Maine, where he was often involved in fights. A witness described Gorman at a party suddenly punching someone in the head and finding it amusing. In any group he was the loudmouth. The cocky, confident one. He was an adept manipulator and a first-class moocher, highly skilled at getting other people to provide him with housing, rides, and drinks.

Despite his criminal record and his unstable personality, Gorman was a kind of hero to many of his slacker friends and acquaintances in the Old Port because of his incredible facility for picking up and bedding women. "Quality women," in the words of one friend. At the time he crossed paths with Amy St. Laurent, Gorman, who prided himself on keeping score, bragged that he had slept with over ninety women even though, for much of the time, he had had one or another steady girlfriend.

Often he would go to the Old Port with his friend Ryan Campbell. The two would pick up girls, take them to Campbell's apartment in his parents' house, and have sex with them. On the night Gorman met Amy St. Laurent, however, Campbell was away on an overnight cruise on the *Scotia Prince*, the ferry from Portland to Nova Scotia, with his family. Although there was some suggestion that Campbell's friends came and went rather freely at his parents' house, Campbell's father, who had not gone on the trip, might have been home, making it difficult for Gorman to take a woman there for sex.

Gorman was so successful, sexually speaking, that some of his friends told detectives they believed he was using drugs as well as alcohol to ensure his luck with the ladies. Gorman was reported to be a big dealer in the popular club drug Ecstasy, which he sometimes exchanged for sexual favors. But there also appeared to be girls who had no memory of what had happened when they were with Gorman. Amy St. Laurent's behavior in leaving with Gorman was sufficiently uncharacteristic that detectives joined his friends in speculating that a date rape drug such as GHB (gamma hydroxybutyric acid), Rohypnol (flunitrazepam), or Ketamine (ketamine hydrochloride) might have been used.

As Gorman's story crumbled under police scrutiny and the details of his character began to be known, Danny Young determined that it was important for them to search Gorman's car. He reasoned that it was highly probable that some part of the crime against Amy St. Laurent had occurred in the car—a controlled environment where Gorman could be sure of having his victim confined. If something had happened in the car, evidence might still be recovered that would give them information about what had happened and possibly bring them a step closer to an arrest.

Even though they knew that Gorman had cleaned his car (behavior that only confirmed their suspicions something might be found there), they also knew that evidence could be tenacious and might still be discovered using forensic investigative techniques. A good evidence technician—and Chris Stearns and Kevin MacDonald were very good—might still find something.[1] There might also be dirt, debris, or vegetation stuck to the underside of the car that might lead them to her body. Since Gorman had refused to consent to a search of the car, such a search could be conducted only if a judge could be persuaded to grant them a warrant.

Here Young ran up against the hard reality of his case. In a normal suspicious-death case, you have a body. Police get a call. Go to the scene. Determine from the information at the scene whether the event looks like a homicide or is suspicious enough to warrant further scrutiny. If so, they proceed to investigate with a medical examiner. But the Portland police had no evidence that a crime had been committed other than their strong suspicions based on their knowledge of criminal behavior and the fact that there was no other reasonable explanation for Amy St. Laurent's disappearance.

In Maine, all homicides are prosecuted by the attorney general's office. Young had already been in contact with Deputy Attorney General William (Bill) Stokes with questions about the progress of the case. It was usual for prosecuting attorneys to be involved from the very earliest stages of a homicide; indeed, prosecuting attorneys often began their involvement in cases at the crime scene. Now Young asked Stokes about the possibility of getting a warrant to search Gorman's car.

The response Young got wasn't encouraging. Bill Stokes informed him that he knew of no prior case in the state of Maine where a judge had granted a search warrant when there was no body or other evidence of a crime. Stokes then told Young he had nothing to lose by trying.

So Danny Young tried. Young had written at least fifty affidavits in his career and was well schooled in how to write one that wouldn't get flipped and lose them their evidence at trial. Now he gathered together the facts he and other detectives had amassed from their interviews and drafted a twenty-page affidavit, which he submitted to Stokes for review. Following his summary of the facts then known, Young stated:

> as previously set forth in this affidavit I believe there are reasonable grounds that probable cause exists that Amy St. Laurent is deceased and the victim of a homicide. The last time Amy St. Laurent is accounted for, based on Jeffrey Gorman's own statements . . . is in the vehicle of Jeffrey Gorman. There is no evidence at this time that anyone sees Amy St. Laurent after she is in Gorman's vehicle[2] . . . [I]n my training and experience as a homicide detective with the Portland Police Department, I believe that any evidence in the crime of homicide can be readily destroyed or lost if a substantial amount of time elapses between the time of the event and the crime scene search . . . [I]n homicides such as this, often forcibly removed hairs, blood, fibers, bloody clothing or material, semen and other body fluids are found even after the scene has been cleaned.

A week after Amy St. Laurent disappeared, on Saturday, October 27, at 3:00 p.m., a state court judge persuaded by Young's compelling affidavit signed a search warrant authorizing the seizure of Gorman's 1991 red

Pontiac Grand Am for the purpose of conducting a search of the vehicle. Gorman's car, which was found parked in the Old Port, was towed to police headquarters at 109 Middle Street, where evidence technicians Chris Stearns and Kevin MacDonald would spend twenty-five hours processing the vehicle.

The garage door at 109, a mechanical monster, chugs and screeches, then buckles and moves up slowly. My eyes are burning as the light slashes slowly across the cement floor of the underground garage. Only two calls overnight on different scenes. Not bad compared to some nights.

Still, I'm light-headed and rubbing my eyes as the monster rolls up. A kind of friendly monster today, I think, moving inside, but I don't know why. Some days, this same machine would greet me in the morning and churn my stomach for what lay ahead. Others, it couldn't move fast enough.

The light shoots across the cement. To my right, I see the parked cars of the command staff. The chief is in already. My pager splits my symphony music, summoning me to morning staff meeting as I move my Taurus into my slot. But wait . . . something's different there in the back . . . a car.

Gorman's car.

Shit! They got the search warrant! I'm banging my steering wheel like a happy drummer. We got him. We got his fucking car! More happy drumming. My pager bleeps as the monster screeches to a halt. I pound the steering wheel with my fist, hard. We got you now, you bastard! I slide into my slot and pop out of the car in my excitement. My anger.

I see the "Stearnman," the evidence technician, move around the car, slowly, mechanically flashing his pictures, the light bouncing into my bloodshot eyes. "Stearny" moves around the car like a spider eyeing its trapped prey.

"We got the freaking car. That's great. That's great!"

Stearny looks tired as he photographs. Just the beginning of a long, long day. There will be so much forensic work for him.[3] Gorman's had it, I think. My pager bleeps. The loudspeaker calls my name to report. Lieutenant Loughlin, call 8533. Lieutenant Loughlin, 8533. It's Penny Diaz, my assistant, and this sounds urgent.

I can't believe we got the car. Danny believed, but it was an incredible long shot. The monster slams shut and the garage is silent. I talk to Stearns as he works. This guy Gorman is done! I think of his arrogance, his almost laugh-

able post-offense behavior. Right out of a criminal psychology textbook. Is he organized or disorganized? Impulsive or methodical?

I recall that organized are usually psychopathic, with disorganized usually being psychotic individuals. Organized offenders are more apt to plan, use vehicles, display power and control, commit sex acts on the victim, use restraint. Yeah, Gorman's smooth—we've been told that over and over—but you're not that smooth, are ya, Gorman? So yeah, Tommy and Dan and I will bat this around, but I think organized.

But where's the girl?

I go back to my behavioral science from my FBI studies at Quantico. To identify and incarcerate, use the three-prong approach:

—do not underestimate your adversary

—know how he thinks and feels about the world

—study his behavior

Study his behavior. Danny will do this over and over. Constantly reevaluating what he knows about Gorman as he interviews those who knew him. And Gorman's out there laying a nice foundation, isn't he?

Getting the warrant was both exciting and satisfying to the detectives working the case; however, they also knew that it could be weeks or even months before any results became available from the state crime lab. Meanwhile, Amy St. Laurent was still missing. While Stearns and Mac-Donald worked on the car, state and Portland police continued to gather information about Gorman.

A quality not always appreciated about police investigators is their extraordinary patience and persistence. Patience in the face of resistance and lies. Patience when faced with almost unremitting frustration and legal hurdles. A patient willingness to stick to the routines, to follow the stories through as many witnesses or interviews as it takes, listening carefully to the facts, then checking and rechecking those facts, proceeding legally and prudently however frustrated they feel or however exhausted they get.

Once the first week of the St. Laurent case had passed, the detectives' race-against-the-clock approach gave way to steady, unremitting endurance. There was no longer much likelihood that the missing woman might only be injured, or a hostage, and that speed was essential if there was a hope of rescue. Nor did it appear that Amy's body or the crime scene were going to be in some obvious or clearly visible place. Recognizing that the event had already occurred and there was nothing they could do to stop it, they settled in for the long haul, focusing on building a strong case, making sure they got the guy before he did it again.

Their knowledge of human nature would play an important role. A trained detective knows how to spot a liar. Liars don't simply lie with their words or with their faces. They lie with their mannerisms, the nature of their responses, displays of nervousness and anger, the contortions of their bodies—folded arms, jiggling feet, leaning toward or away from the interviewer, shrugs of their shoulders. They lie with obfuscation, excess detail, and belligerent denial. Sometimes with stone-cold expressions that fool even seasoned detectives.

When Detective Young and the other investigators began to reinterview key people, they were looking as much at behavior—at how the witnesses spoke and moved and behaved—as they were at what was said. Gorman began his second interview attempting to focus attention away from himself with his tale of a man in a yellow suit and a raincoat acting suspiciously in the Old Port that the police really ought to take a look at. He tried to be friendly and engaging. He expressed concern about leaving Amy alone in the Old Port so late at night. He had a detailed timeline of his evening, complete with the names of his alibi witnesses and how long it had taken him to drive from the Old Port to the Brighton Avenue apartment, but refused to take a polygraph, give a DNA sample, and allow a search of his car. The detectives located witnesses who confirmed that, following that Tuesday interview, he cleaned his car and researched polygraphs.

As if those weren't enough flags for experienced detectives, he also engaged in the kind of post-offense behavior[4] typical of a guilty person. He cleaned the rubbish-filled car he had only a week before declared wasn't worth cleaning.[5] He tried to deflect attention from himself and show concern for the victim by calling her family (after calling the police department for a contact number). He called Young with a supposed sighting of Amy St. Laurent. When his car was impounded, he made outraged calls, demanding to know when he was going to get it back. And when the car was returned with fabric samples removed where luminol had indicated presumptive bloodstains, he called Young and furiously demanded compensation for the damage.

Gorman also changed his appearance. He abandoned the spiky, streaked blond locks in favor of a shaved head. A good strategy, one of his friends noted, to prevent the police from getting hair samples. When friends commented on the change, he asserted that he routinely shaved his head every few years, although one witness noted that when she had offered to style his hair, he had told her no one touched his hair. He got more tattoos and body piercings, trying to distance himself from the Old Port pretty boy with his new, tough look. He grew a goatee.

According to criminal psychology textbooks, offenders engage in various post-offense behaviors for a variety of reasons. The obvious one is disguise—to make themselves as unlike the person witnesses might associate with the crime as possible. Offenders also change their physical appearance because they are disgusted with themselves for what they've done and don't want to associate the self that committed the crime with their new self. Still others change their appearance and behavior because, as a result of committing the crime, they've just crossed a big hurdle and are now a changed, and different, person.

Police began tailing Gorman and monitoring his behavior, hoping he might say or do something that would give them a break. On Halloween, a big scene in the Old Port with a party at the Mariners' Church and noisy crowds and costumes giving a Mardi Gras feel to the evening, Detective Mark Teceno, Sergeant Jeff Davis, and Officer Tommy O'Connor followed Gorman. The three, dressed in civilian clothes, took turns following Gorman, who was dressed as a pimp, as he made his way from bar to bar, sometimes sitting only a table away as he drank with his friends. They hoped the fact that it was Halloween might spook or lure Gorman into leading them to Amy.

Certain that at some point Gorman would be compelled to visit Amy's body, Danny Young would have put twenty-four-hour-a-day surveillance on Gorman if the department's budget would have allowed it. As it was, the police did as much surveillance as their energy and budget allowed, doing surveillance on Gorman's friends as well.

It was hard for everyone to watch their suspect going on with the normal routines of his life—drinking and clubbing, playing pool, and hanging out with his friends—knowing that Amy St. Laurent would never do any of those things again. Hard to watch him putting on his smooth, cool-guy act, trying to pick up girls, knowing that those girls were seriously at risk. Harder still to watch teenage girls and young women responding to his smooth and charming manner, knowing that his slick exterior hid a violent nature.

At the same time, the detectives were working with Gorman's friends and acquaintances, looking for breaks in their stories about Gorman's alibi. As they interviewed, they asked the same questions. What has he said about Amy St. Laurent? Whom did he hang around with? Who knew him better than you? Who's told you things they won't tell us? And always, whomever they spoke to, they asked about places young men might take girls, couples might go parking, places Gorman might have gone with Amy.

Detectives were also looking for Gorman to begin to talk. Typically, except for the coldest sociopths, it is difficult for suspects to avoid talking to someone about their crimes, especially serious, guilt-inducing crimes. Such talking is even more likely when the perpetrators are young. The detectives hoped that eventually Gorman would crack under the weight of his conscience and steady police scrutiny and say something incriminating. Even more, they hoped that he'd get drunk, cocky, or careless and tell someone where he'd hidden Amy.

Detectives therefore kept pressure not only on Gorman but on his friends. One thing that's surprising to a layperson about a case like this is how readily friends will support a suspect's alibi and how slowly and unwillingly they divulge what they know about his character. The police are less surprised. They are used to people's reluctance to provide information. Sergeant Joyce summed it up in one cynical sentence: "Don't expect much; then you won't be disappointed." Police also know it takes time for people to get over their belief in a friend and to accept the possibility that someone they know might be a murderer.

There is also, particularly among adolescent and young adult males, a kind of "pack mentality" at work. No one wants to be the one who breaks the bond and becomes the snitch. In addition, although everyone wants the police to come when there's trouble, most people are relatively unfamiliar with them—the police are those blue lights in your rearview mirror that ruin your day—and are reluctant to initiate contact. This kind of reluctance was especially true for some of the teenage girls and young adult women acquainted with Gorman, some of whom had valuable information. Months after Amy St. Laurent disappeared, police would still be finding new witnesses and collecting new information.

Gorman's friends began their talks with the police with the attitude that Gorman was a good guy, always up for barhopping or a game of pool. Gorman was the life of the party, the willing-to-try-anything crazy guy. For male friends, Gorman's success at picking up girls for sex meant that hanging around with him improved their own chances. Others probably valued Gorman because he provided access to desirable drugs.

Some were reluctant to talk because they were afraid of him. Even though he wasn't a big guy, he had a terrible temper, especially when he'd been drinking, and was always ready for a fight. Shyla Cameron, a waitress at the Iguana, described him as "a vicious little guy." And he had boasted about having access to guns.

Detectives knew you couldn't always get a witness's story in one interview. It might take several sessions to get the whole story, or the true story, out. Sometimes this was because witnesses lied deliberately—because they didn't believe in cooperating with the police, were determined to protect a friend, or had something of their own to hide. Sometimes they unconsciously slanted the facts since the suspect was their friend. Sometimes witnesses didn't give the whole story because they weren't even aware of what they knew, or that what they knew might be important.

A chilling example of this kind of progression emerged from the interviews with Kush Sharma, Gorman's roommate. In his initial interview, Sharma insisted that Gorman, after leaving the Brighton Avenue apartment with Amy, was gone only about twenty minutes, then returned to the apartment and stayed in for the rest of the night, corroborating Gorman's story. In a later interview, Sharma told police that he *thought* that was what had happened, he didn't know, he couldn't be sure, and voluntarily took a polygraph to record his uncertainty.

Still later, Sharma said that when he and Amy were outside walking Jason Cook's dog, she asked, referring to Gorman and showing that she sensed something wasn't quite right, "Is he okay?" Amy, who had good intuition, was trying to put herself in a safer situation.[6]

A similar pattern appeared in the interviews with Jason Cook. Initially, Cook insisted Gorman had returned to the apartment after being gone only twenty minutes, offering as support his tale about being on the computer sending an e-mail to his aunt when Gorman returned. When the police were unable to verify the e-mail after checking the computer and contacting Cook's aunt, Cook backtracked a little, yet when roommate David Grazier commented to Cook that he hadn't seen Gorman at the apartment when he returned at 3:15 a.m., Cook insisted, "Well, he was there."

It took several interviews to uncover a version of the story that had Gorman stopping at the Iguana bar (in his interviews, Gorman never mentioned stopping at the Iguana) to ask Cook if he could bring Amy back to the apartment for sex (perhaps Gorman was looking for a more private venue than the living room couch where he was sleeping) and Cook telling him he could not.

As they took Sharma and Cook through the many different iterations of their stories, the detectives had to wonder something else, as well. Were Cook and Sharma lying because they, too, had something to do with Amy St. Laurent's disappearance?

Gorman's plan to have sex with Amy was also confirmed by a waitress at the Iguana, Shyla Cameron, who reported in a follow-up interview that Gorman had asked her, concerning Amy St. Laurent, "Should I take her home and sleep with her?" Cameron had told him he should just leave her alone. It would take several interviews to learn Gorman had called a friend that night, trying to locate a cheap motel, and had confided in another friend that he thought of Amy as nothing more than a "quick blow job."

Probably the most disturbing example of a reluctant witness was Ryan Campbell, a young man who at the time served as a reserve[7] police officer in Old Orchard Beach, worked at his sister's day care, and longed to become a full-time police officer. Police initially contacted Campbell when they learned that he was missing a gun, a Glock 9 mm. Matt Despins had told police that Campbell had last seen his gun between October 7 and 10 after an evening with Russ Gorman and that Campbell believed Gorman might have taken it.

When they contacted the Westbrook police about Campbell's missing gun, Portland detectives learned that, on the Wednesday following Amy St. Laurent's disappearance, Campbell had filed a report stating that his weapon was missing from his lockbox and that Gorman had been the last person to see it.

Interviewed by Detective Young and Sergeant Joyce, Campbell insisted that he had had his gun on the Thursday before Amy disappeared and denied that he believed Gorman had taken it. Campbell told them that he had left the gun in a lockbox in his room when he went away with his family for the weekend cruise on the *Scotia Prince*. Campbell said that the key to his lockbox was with his car keys and that Matt Despins had had the car for the weekend but probably didn't know the key was there. The only other key was in another lockbox in his uncle's room.

Campbell stated: "I remember, point blank, up close and personal, that I took it [the gun] out of that car . . . and it's, every night I take that thing out of my car and put [it] in that box and it's not, it's just not there this time. I remember." Asked why he had said Gorman was the last person to see the gun, Campbell became befuddled and was unable to give a coherent answer. Detectives made a note to confirm that Campbell had actually been on the *Scotia Prince*.

Detectives then asked Campbell about Gorman's conduct with girls. Campbell told them Russ would have a girlfriend and also go out and pick up girls on the side. Asked by Detective Young: "So it wouldn't be unusual for him . . . just to go home thinking he might get a quick piece and that's the end of it?"

Campbell replied: "Right, you know, it's almost like his goal every night . . . I'm serious, this is what he looks forward to every night, he wants to go out and get a new girl every single night."

Asked about places Gorman might take a girl, Campbell said: "Oh, well, we meet girls on their terms. Whatever it takes to, you know, get that piece of ass."

In a subsequent interview, Young and Westbrook detective John Des-Jardins tried to pin Campbell down about the timeline of the missing gun. Campbell was unable to recall what he had done that Sunday when he returned from the cruise. First he told them he knew he looked for the gun when he got home because he usually went out shooting on Sunday afternoon. When pressed, he acknowledged that the boat hadn't gotten in until evening and, because of the increased post-9/11 security, he and his family hadn't cleared customs until 9:30 or 10:00.

Despite the fact that he had a steady girlfriend, Campbell said he was supposed to meet a high school girl named Megan at the Game Room, the pool hall in Westbrook where he and Gorman hung out. He was unable to tell the detectives whether he had gone home or directly to the Game Room after returning from the cruise. Then he said he went to the lockbox to get some money and that's when he discovered the gun was missing. Then he said he didn't. He said that it was Sunday night when he found the gun missing and he had looked for it immediately after returning from the cruise because his mother ran a day care in the house and he didn't want a loose gun around.

Then he said it wasn't Sunday and his mother, who had told the police he went crazy when he found it was missing and she helped him tear the house apart looking for it, must have been wrong. He said he didn't tell his father the gun was gone until Tuesday, and it was only after that that he told his mother. Asked by DesJardins why, if he had known the gun was missing on Sunday, he waited until Wednesday to report it missing and why, if Campbell had put the gun in a lockbox, he reported that Russ Gorman was the last person to see him with his gun, Campbell had no good answers.

It seemed improbable to both detectives that a police officer could be so careless about a missing firearm unless he was hiding something, so they pressed him. Detective Young: "Do you remember you said your gun's missing and it was in your car not in the lockbox in your frigging house, and that you think Russ might have it . . . Do you remember telling that to Matt Despins?"

Campbell: "I seriously don't."

DesJardins, interrupting: "You told me that you believe that Russ took your gun. What made you feel that? When did you form the opinion in your mind that Russ Gorman took your gun?"

At another point, exasperated with Campbell's stories and perhaps hoping to appeal to his conscience, Young told Campbell: "This has gone on for a long time . . . all I'm trying to do is find Amy. Right now, finding her is the first thing on my mind. I pray for it every Sunday when I go to church. I'm hoping to bring her back so she can have a good Christian burial with her family. That's what they're looking for. They know that somewhere, she's dead."

Despite Young's appeal, it took three interviews (all by Detective Young, with three different co-investigators) before Campbell, in an interview with Young and MSP detective Scott Harakles, finally admitted that, sometime a week or so before the cruise, he had been out for an evening with Gorman. That they had picked up some girls from Munjoy Hill and brought one of them back to Campbell's room. Campbell said he had worn his gun that evening although he was just out for a casual night on the town, eventually taking it off and putting it under the seat of the car. When they got out of the car back at his house, Campbell forgot the gun. Gorman reached under the seat and handed it to him.[8]

Campbell told them he had dropped off to sleep, leaving the gun lying around in his room. Later, Gorman came in, mumbled something, and went out again. When Campbell woke in the morning, the gun was gone. Gorman probably took the gun, Campbell surmised, because he had so many people after him.

There was more. The detectives had been told by Kristin Langmeier, Campbell's longtime girlfriend, that she was in his room on the Monday night after the cruise, the day after Amy St. Laurent disappeared, and Campbell's gun was there. It was lying on the floor, she said, and Campbell picked it up, said, "That's odd," and set it on the bookcase. Campbell claimed to have no memory of this but agreed that Kristin was a truthful girl. Eventually, Campbell admitted that he believed the gun disappeared—a second time?—when he was in his apartment on Tuesday night with Gorman, researching polygraphs. He said that Gorman was in the room alone for a while and that he hadn't seen the gun since.

It took nearly eighteen hours of various detectives' time trying to get Ryan Campbell, himself a part-time police officer, to tell the truth.[9] In the end, maybe he did. Maybe he didn't. Maybe he himself had something to do with the gun's ultimate disappearance.[10]

Sometimes it was loyalty. Sometimes it was fear. Through it all, the police persisted. Asking, checking, comparing stories, and asking again. As the weeks went by, Gorman and his pals roamed the Old Port, drinking, drugging, and looking for girls. And Amy was still missing.

8

Early in the second week, Sergeant Stewart came to a meeting with the Portland detectives and brought along Scott Harakles, a young state police detective who had been away at a training the previous week. Until that meeting, Harakles was unfamiliar with Portland, having patrolled over near the state's western border in Kezar Falls. Nor had he ever met Danny Young, but on the drive to Portland, Stewart told Harakles, "I know that we're going into enemy territory, but you're going to love this guy, Danny Young."

Detective Harakles came into the meeting not knowing much about the case. The first time he'd heard of a missing woman had been from his wife, Rachel, who'd seen one of the "Missing" posters, been concerned, and asked if he knew anything about it. Beyond that, he hadn't heard much more than the public had—a young South Berwick woman named Amy St. Laurent had disappeared after a night of dancing in the Old Port. She had left the dance club with a man other than the one she'd come with and never been seen again.

Hearing only that part of the story, it looked to Harakles like this was a case of an easygoing young woman out for a good time who'd ditched one date and picked up another. Not that that made her any less a victim if something bad had happened to her—the police care about all their homicide victims—but going into the meeting in Portland, Harakles had no idea how wrong he was, nor how deeply attached he would become to Amy St. Laurent.

By the end of the meeting, Sergeant Stewart could see that Danny Young and Scott Harakles would be a good match, and he assigned Harakles to be Young's counterpart, the primary case detective on the state police side.

It was an inspired decision. In pairing detectives, it is valuable to choose people who will get along and who have complementary skills or attributes. Danny Young was, in Stewart's words, an exceptional, old-fashioned investigator who had great people skills, tremendous insight, knew his city and its people, and wasn't burdened with ego or his own agenda. He was compulsive about keeping orderly case files. He had an uncanny ability to memorize and recall the facts of a case. Harakles had been a detective for three years and was the age of Young's sons, with extremely deft skills as an interviewer.

Physically, they were both wide-shouldered men with deceptively pleasant looks and styles. Young's comfortable manner made him easy to talk to. Harakles, with his youthful looks and boyish energy and enthusiasm, didn't seem like a thirty-two-year-old with eight years as a highway trooper and three as a detective. Both were adept at gathering information from a particularly difficult group—the community of young adults and teenagers scattered throughout the cities and towns surrounding Portland who frequented the pool halls, bars, and clubs of the Old Port.

What made Young and Harakles the perfect team to pursue the disappearance of Amy St. Laurent was that they shared some of the most essential traits of a successful detective: passionate commitment to securing justice for victims, stamina, intelligence, creativity, and incredible stubbornness. They were the type of investigators who, once they had their teeth into something, didn't care how long it took or how hard they had to work—eventually it was going to go down.

Almost from the start, the two detectives, in the words of a coworker, "married up." Despite the age gap, a strong bond arose from the value they placed on family. Danny Young had married his high school sweetheart and raised three children, two of whom were police officers and one of whom was married to an officer. He was enjoying being a grandfather. Scott Harakles was just starting out with two young children. His family, and the special time they spent together, were central to his life.

The strength of that bond would prove a critical factor in solving the case. While the intra- and interagency conflicts inevitable in such a complex case swirled around them, Young and Harakles ignored such distractions and kept their broad shoulders to the wheel. They were such a dedicated and effective team that their superiors were repeatedly motivated to set the usual conflicts aside in order to give the two detectives as much support as possible.

Harakles quickly learned that his earlier impression of Amy St. Laurent was all wrong. From her diary, from interviews, and from information supplied by her family, he began to see what an innocent person and nice girl Amy was. Far from being someone who would casually leave with a man she'd just met, Amy St. Laurent was the kind of girl who wouldn't kiss on a first date. He repeats a story from Eric Rubright in which Rubright, having taken Amy for a ride on his motorcycle, suggests a kiss to Amy. Her response was, "Don't even think about it, and take me home right now."

In their meetings, the detectives would share and argue over their theories about what had happened the night Amy disappeared.

"Ahh, shit, Danny! You've been married too long. Whaddaya think? He's on a leisurely drive to take her back? No way! He's got a plan after he leaves Brighton Avenue. He's probably hit her with a roofie. She's somewhat relaxed and as he drives down the industrial part of Douglas Street, he pulls into a lot. It's there where he puts the moves on her and guess what? Wrong girl."

They're waiting to jump in, so I push ahead with my theory, knowing we've each got our own, that everyone's driving those routes and checking those places.

"Yeah, so it goes bad in the car and he what? Beats her, strangles her, maybe even shoots her . . ."

"If he shot her, it wasn't in the car," someone interrupts.

"So maybe that's after he drags her out of the car. Then what? Then he's gotta get rid of the body. But where? Is she in the water by Merrill Transport? Hobo jungle? Dumped along the highway? We know something bad happened in the car, 'cuz he cleaned it. Then how about the thing you told me he says about some weirdo in a yellow raincoat might have got her?"

"Yellow suit, Joe. Suit."

"Suit. Okay, Dan, so maybe he was trying to get her over to Campbell's. I'd go for that. But where's the girl?"

As ghosts and witches were replaced by turkeys and Pilgrims, and then the red and green of Christmas, Harakles would make the daily drive to Portland to meet up with Young. Two or three times a week, Sergeant Stewart might go, too, and the two primaries and their sergeants would go into the conference room, alone or with other detectives who'd been working on the case. Sergeant Joyce would make notes on the dryboard as they shared newly collected information and strategized about the next steps to take.

After the meeting, or right away if there was no meeting, the two primary detectives would drive off together, usually taking Young's car because Danny had his bomb dog, Karla. Karla would ride along in the backseat. Some days they would meet Young's wife, Linda, at the end of the day and hand off the dog before they headed on into an evening of interviews.

The pain of Amy's family weighed heavily on the detectives. It was hard to keep repeating, "We're working on it, we're doing our best, we're *going* to find her," even though they meant it. They were doing everything they could do and constantly asking themselves, Where else can I look? What am I missing here? Everyone working closely with the investigation became obsessed with it, stopping their cars at likely woods roads or along the highway and getting out to search. Scott Harakles said he'd never had a case like it, where they would search and search and never come up with anything, and yet, each time he stopped somewhere and got out of his car, he was filled with a sense that yes, this time I'm going to find her!

There was pressure from the media, looking for fresh information in a story that had riveted public attention. Detectives had to be constantly alert to avoid revealing the details of their investigation or the identity of their suspect. Chief Chitwood and Lieutenant Loughlin gave frequent press conferences, responding to pressure from a community horrified at the disappearance of a lovely young girl and fearful for the safety of themselves and their daughters, fears that didn't diminish as weeks passed without a resolution.

Detectives were also under pressure within the Portland Police Department. The case consumed a great deal of CID's resources, leading to grumbling from detectives who felt they should be more involved or should have had the case. There was a fair amount of quarterbacking from detectives who thought the investigation should be conducted differently, details assigned different priorities, different avenues followed. There were arguments about how the case should be staffed, complaints from detectives who had to pick up more work. Wounded pride, short tempers, the weary impatience of exhaustion. Subtle pressure from higher up the food chain to produce some results that could be used to calm the public.

In our own house, things were tough. Vernon Geberth's advice on interagency cooperation is laudable. But I think, yeah, okay, Vern, sounds good but apply it to reality and the dynamics of human beings. Forget about other agencies. How about in our own unit? Our own backyard?

1900. Thorpe lumbers in from a job. Rybeck follows. Both slam their shit down on their desks as I happen to walk by. There's so much going on I don't even know what they're working on.

"Hey, Gary. Karl. What's up?"

"Ahh, these fuckin' people keep dying," Thorpe grunts. "And you might get a call about a complaint. Guy shot himself and I got into it with the landlord who, by the way, is a dink."

"Okay, what do I need to know about the call I'll get?"

I already know it's inbound, owing to Gary's gruffness. He tells me. "Yesterday, I call over to the next town for them to do a note [death notification] and they screwed it all up. So get this, I'm on the phone with the mom, telling her that her son is at Hay and Peabody funeral home and those idiots didn't even tell her that her son is dead. They just handed the phone to her. So the mother goes . . . my son is where? Where? So now I realize that she doesn't even know her son is dead yet. She screams and howls and drops the receiver and falls to the floor in their police station. Only me, Lieutenant. Only me. So . . . you're gonna get a call on that."

Rybeck's on the phone with a family member, trying to calm that poor person down. Tommy, Dan, and others are in a conference room discussing the St. Laurent case. The property crimes people are out on a job.

I start telling Gary about the case on Amy St. Laurent and he starts with, "Whatever, Lieutenant," as I hear a scream and a sob through Karl's receiver.

"Whaddya mean, Gary?"

"I mean, it's fucked up, that's what I mean. Danny is running around like a lunatic. Tommy is this and that. Bruce is . . ."

I listen, because Gary Thorpe, despite his thorny personality, is a great investigator. The six-foot Thorpe has a heavy, athletic build, thick graying hair, and bright eyes that can also look right through you. He's got a gruff, truculent affect that says you don't want to piss him off. He's adept at crime scenes and reconstructing the days of the dead. You'd never know he loves birds and paints watercolors.

Karl hangs up and hears us talking. "Don't get me involved in this. I have enough problems," he states. Rybeck, who we sometimes tell kids is one of Santa's elves, is a short, stocky Frenchman with gentle eyes and great people skills who is fascinated by the Civil War.

When I roll up at a bad crime scene and observe either one there, I'm relieved, although inevitably I'll get a complaint on the methodical Thorpe telling someone to "get the fuck out of my crime scene."

We go around about Gary's screwed-up notification and other things. Then I look dead at this seasoned pair. "What about the St. Laurent case?"

Both detectives stop what they're doing and start in on me. Did those guys do this? That? Check this? How come Danny . . . ? These guys are good so I listen to their insights, theories, and conjecture. They have good points and I end up getting Tommy into it with us.

At the center of the case, however, the greatest pressure came from two sources within the detectives themselves. First was their deep affection for Amy St. Laurent. Danny Young kept her picture on his desk. Every morning when he woke, it was with the feeling that something might have happened in the night, something Gorman had done, that might have helped them break the case if only he'd been awake and out there. It was the same if he took any time off.

Asked why the case mattered so much, detectives would say, "because she was such a nice girl. Because she was a real victim." Scott Harakles explained it this way: "Every homicide investigator doesn't like to lose. That's part of who they are, but every now and then, along comes a case that you let in. The Amy St. Laurent case was like that . . . because of who she was, your conscience tells you that you just can't let it go. Amy

St. Laurent," Harakles said, "was the kind of girl you'd want to raise, and the men sitting around the table evaluating her case were a bunch of dads." From the beginning of the case, Harakles said he was haunted. He had a pit in his stomach every single day. It never left him, but constantly reminded him: We *have* to get this done. If we can't get justice for this victim, we shouldn't be doing the job.

Then there was Gorman—his arrogance, his deception, his freedom. The more the detectives learned about him—about his early family life, prior criminal acts, his attitude toward women, and his goal of having sex with as many women as possible—the more certain they were that they were looking at a serial sexual predator whose need to "score" depersonalized his victims, reducing them to numbers on his scorecard. Now, he had moved on to sexual homicide. Having killed once, they believed, he would eventually do it again. Even to experienced police investigators, it was a chilling prospect.

So, they slogged through the bleak chill of November with two goals driving them—to find Amy and to build their case against Gorman.

The search for Amy took as many forms as detectives could conceive of. Sergeants Joyce and Coffin headed up a group of detectives who searched all the hiking trails on Mount Agamenticus, near Amy's home in South Berwick. They visited every hotel and motel on Route 1 from Falmouth to Saco. Young and Harakles checked motels in other towns. Detectives drove around, trying to think like their suspect, searching pond areas and sand pits. Peered under cars in junkyards.

State police conducted ground searches of the entire potential route of travel from exit 6 on the turnpike southbound along the pike to the Wells exit and then along Route 9 to South Berwick. Everyone walked roadsides and examined gravel pits, woods roads, fields, abandoned houses, and anything that caught their eyes as a potential disposal site. MSP used troopers and tracking dogs and detectives on foot. Detective Lance McCleish and Sergeant Stewart did aerial surveys with the state police pilot.

The Portland Department of Public Works searched all the storm drains—an event Gorman learned about because a friend's father worked for the city DPW, and which Gorman reported to another friend with a sneer.

Following the trail of potential witnesses was like working in a gigantic maze and consumed hundreds of hours. Detective Mark Teceno and evidence technician Chris Stearns conducted many of the follow-up interviews with young women who had known Gorman through the Old Port bar scene. Often one witness would lead them to another, and to another, and another. Each casually dropped name, or "Oh, you should talk with so-and-so, she used to hang out with Russ," or "I've heard that this girl knows something she isn't telling," or "Russ said something to so-and-so, but she's afraid to talk to the police," or "So-and-so knows more than she's telling but don't let her know that I told you" led to a name on the dryboard, a phone call, and often an interview.

Over and over, detectives would say: Tell me about Russ. How do you know him? Have you ever seen or experienced Gorman being violent toward women? Have you heard anything about Gorman supplying drugs or using drugs to obtain sex? If Gorman were going to take a girl somewhere for sex, where would he go? Where did he take you? Have you or anyone you know ever seen Gorman with a gun? Has he ever mentioned Amy St. Laurent or spoken about what happened that night?

As the days ticked by without a body or a break, Lieutenant Loughlin decided to consult a psychic.[1] He had heard Vicki Monroe on the radio and read a very convincing article about her in the newspaper.

I call Vicki Monroe, a popular local psychic who has turned many nonbelievers into believers. What the hell? It can't hurt. We're at the point where we'll check anything. Everything.

I explain who I am and she has heard of the case. I say, "Tell me where Amy is, Vicki."

Vicki tells me that something happened in a car with Amy. This is what we believe and at this point there is nothing in the press. She gives me the first name Jeff or Jay. Amy is telling her that she is underneath something but cannot say where. It is near water. There were other guys around and in the car but "J" is responsible. She tells me that the suspect has an enraged personality and a criminal record, which I suppose is pretty obvious.

She also thinks that Amy was given drugs and she would not normally go with a stranger. This we also believe was true, as does Amy's mother, Diane. Vicki tells me that Amy is definitely deceased and keeps saying it was violent and that she is under something. Vicki tells me that we're looking in the wrong direction and we should look north. Vicki wants to talk to Diane, as well.

We receive a lot of calls from psychics, and although we never discuss or reveal anything in an investigation, some of their thoughts may trigger events or thoughts in us. Dan told me he had had calls from another woman named Marie Roberts of Westbrook. Marie drew a map of where she believed Amy was but could not say exactly where the body was.[2] These individuals are passionate about what they do and sincerely believe in their abilities. I do not dismiss the possibilities of another developed sense or sixth sense.

I agreed to meet one psychic near my home on a sunny November Saturday. This woman had had a vivid dream of Amy calling to her from her burial spot. It frightened this woman, the hideous image that she saw of Amy buried in the sand around a river in Yarmouth. She was very convincing. We often worked through weekends anyhow, so we met and drove off to the woods of Yarmouth.

We walked through fields, woods, down to the river for several hours. One vivid memory I have is of this woman hugging a tree and telling me she feels Amy's presence and message but Amy cannot place exactly where she is. A few feet away, I'm wrapped around another tree, pleading with the spirit world and this woman, "Okay, okay. Just tell me where she is! Tell us where you are, Amy." Silently praying to God.

On the way back to Portland, empty handed, I heard Danny Young over the police radio calling for a patrol car to meet with an officer. Danny just couldn't stop.

9

Because criminals are devious, the police are constantly creating their own equally resourceful—and legal—strategies for tripping criminals up. Sergeant Joyce put it this way: a good investigator needs to know where the line is, legally, and then walk right up to that line.

The detectives working on the St. Laurent case would think of many ways to get Gorman to lead them to Amy's body. At one point, in mid-November, they sat down in their "war room" to put together a complicated joint surveillance operation. Their plan was to attach a tracking device, a "birddog," to Gorman's car, then let him know that a body had been discovered, hoping that he would be spooked into checking his hiding place and lead them to the body. Attaching such a device would be legal so long as the car was parked in a public place.

Like any well-planned operation, their plan had several alternatives, depending on Gorman's whereabouts. As part of the operation, they had recruited two attractive female state troopers, Detective Angela Blodgett and Trooper Cory Pike. Dressed in plain clothes, the two women were going to stop at Pizza Time while Gorman was at work, order a pizza, and, while they waited, discuss the news that a body had been found so they could observe Gorman's reaction.

Scott Harakles's job was to guard the rear door in case Gorman came out while Lance McCleish was putting the birddog on Gorman's car, which was usually parked behind the building. If Gorman got through the door, they joked, he might just have to get mugged. "I was really looking forward to that," Harakles said. After all their planning, on the day of the operation, with all the vehicles in place to follow him, Gorman didn't show up for work. He had quit his job.

By that time, the police had many cars rolling, including a unit by Gorman's mother's house and one by the Game Room. Eventually, word came in that Gorman's car was parked at the Game Room, and plan B began. Blodgett and Pike went into the Game Room and hung around, hoping to meet up with Gorman, while other detectives rolled into the lot to put the device on Gorman's car.

Sergeant Bruce Coffin described the event: "It was a crazy night. We were doing everything we could think of to find Amy. Our challenge was to find Gorman's car in a public place and then attach the device securely in a place that wouldn't interfere with the signal. We waited until his car was parked at a pool hall in Westbrook, the Game Room. I was in one car with Sergeant Matt Stewart and there were two other troopers, Scott Harakles and Lance McCleish, in a second car.

"We all pulled into the lot, putting our cars between Gorman's car and the group of guys standing outside the pool hall smoking so they couldn't see what we were doing. Then we all got out and stood around, making like a bunch of good ole boys who'd been drinking, lots of noise and handshaking, backslapping, while McCleish crept out of the car, crawled under Gorman's car, and installed the device."

It was a very tense scene. Once the device was in place, they all got back into their cars and drove away, waiting at designated places for word that Gorman had returned to his car and was rolling. Nothing seemed to go as planned. Although his car was in the lot, Gorman never did go to the Game Room that night, so they were unable to drop the rumor about the body. Eventually, he returned to his car and drove to his mother's house.

With as many as six cars parked at strategic places up and down his street, the detectives revised the plan to get word to him by having a friend call Gorman at home and tell him that a body had been found. Later that evening, as they did surveillance on Gorman's house, Matt Despins called Gorman to say he'd heard that a body had been found. Sergeant Coffin was outside in the cold, walking up and down the road, keeping an eye on the place, waiting for Gorman's car to leave. Everyone had expected movement, but Gorman didn't budge. Finally, late into the night, they called the operation off.

Police also worked closely with several of Gorman's friends, hoping that, in an unguarded or intoxicated moment, Gorman would confide something incriminating. On his side, Gorman, who was an experienced criminal, was engaging in "disinformation" to test his supposed friends. He would tell them stories that weren't true to see if those stories got back to the police. At one point, for example, he told a friend, "If I had killed that girl, I would have dropped her off the B & M trestle and let the crabs get her." Police had to assume that this might be the truth, and so they searched the area.

Early in the investigation, the Maine State Police had done some aerial searches. Now Lieutenant Loughlin and MSP detective Lance McCleish conducted another set of aerial searches arranged by Diane Jenkins's employer, DeWolfe Realty, with a helicopter and pilot donated by Sam Hamill of TCI Aircraft. They were hoping that with the leaves off the trees they might have a better chance of spotting something.

11/21/01. The rotors are still thwapping and the fast air washes across my face. Out pops this small man with dark hair and bright eyes. After introductions, he starts blurting out questions and orders. Did you guys do this? And that? How come you haven't arrested him?

"Whoa, Airwolf," I say to myself but entertain his questions because this man is willing to help. All the while I want to scream. What? Are you frigging kidding me? Do I tell you how to fly the chopper? We are all so exhausted and frustrated at this point.

I've just been introduced to Mr. Sam Hamill, aka "Airwolf." I'm so backed up at work I don't have time for this, plus we've already done aerial searches, but these people want to do something to help. I tell myself, okay, let's just try to enjoy the ride and who knows? It's another chance to find Amy.

We're in a beautiful sleek black Bell helicopter. It's Lance McCleish from the state police, David Gulick from DeWolfe Realty, who's a friend of Diane's, me, the pilot, whose name is John, and Sam. Over the intercom, Sam barks orders to John and we lift off. What a great view of Portland! Only we're not up here for the view.

We travel south over the interstate, chugging and chattering, about two hundred feet up, studying the woods/road border. I keep hoping we'll see something. Anything. All the way down to Berwick, nothing. We head back northbound over the pine trees. Amazing the amount of ground you can see. We stare 'til our eyes hurt, but there's nothing.

Over the noise of the flight, the headset clicks as Sam continues his line of questioning about what we did or didn't do. I'm exhausted. I've walked through the woods, over bridges, down tracks, along the water almost every weekend and some nights after work. When I jogged Riverside Industrial Parkway, near my home, I would check behind the buildings for Amy. If this is how I am, how does Danny function?

I ask Amy, show us, please show us! I have a list of areas we want to check and I relay that to Sam and the pilot. I still think—from things that Gorman's said—that she's in the water and we head toward the Fore River. The vibrations chugging with a downdraft every now and then help keep me alert.

We fly over a wooded area called the hobo jungle, across to the Merrill Transport. Looking. Searching. It's low tide and the water is clear. It's amazing how far down we can see. Every now and then something looks odd but turns out to be nothing or debris. Airwolf's chatter breaks my concentration.

"Yes, sir, we have investigated that point."

"Yeah, we have a suspect but no Amy."

"Why don't you bring this guy in and beat the shit out of him? Ya can't? Let me talk to him."

"Well, Sam," I respond, "we have a Constitution, you know, that protects people from that. It's not like on TV, you know."

"Well, can't you guys tell me who he is?"

I chuckle, but I'm exasperated and tired. There are so many goddamned quarterbacks I can't go five fucking feet without running into one. I know Sam cares and means well, but he hasn't been doing this every day for a month! I bring my mind back into the search. Amy, where are you? We bank left and the centrifugal force pulls on my belt. A Coast Guard boat below in Casco Bay is also searching for Amy.

"Go over to the B & M factory and fly over the tracks."

Of course, Airwolf's first question is an excited, "Why? What's going on over there?"

"Well, Sam, it's something in the investigation I can't discuss right now and I just want to see it by air."

"Whaddaya mean?"

"Look," I say, frustrated, "can we just look?" He talks to the pilot, a staccato "Whiskey Bravo Tom 179er, changing vector to . . ." and we change course.

The noise fades into the background. I'm thinking about what Gorman said to a friend about how, if he'd killed her, he would have dumped Amy off the B & M trestle, and my anger burns.

Imagine. Imagine. Now, I know this guy killed her and did something with Amy but where? And I imagine killing someone and then making a statement like that! I think of all of the victims I've seen over twenty-two years and the shitheads who do despicable things and walk away. The arrogance! The GP [general public] has absolutely no idea of the horrors that occur each day. That occur right here in Portland.

At one point we're near Gorman's mother's house and she comes out and stares up at us. She doesn't wave. As we move off, Sam shouts, "Guilty! Guilty! Guilty! People always wave. I've never seen that."

Chugging slow with a thwap over the terminal and factory. I can see down into the water. Last weekend I spent hours walking over the trestle and peering down into the cold azure water. Hoping to see something. Begging Amy to show me. She was on my mind all the time. But God . . . what was it like for Danny?

I know he's at another interview while I'm flying. Danny has his own daughter Amy, yet when we say "Amy" he thinks about Amy St. Laurent. My mind drifts as we thwap along. Danny walked by my office last night around 1900 and no doubt he was ill. Pasty, pale, sweaty, and heading toward the bathroom. "Danny. Go home. You're not going to be any good sick."

He looks at me directly and says, "I can't, Lieutenant. I can't." I know he's right but I say, "Try to get some rest, Dan. Try." We hear him in the bathroom, throwing up. Running a fever and sick as a dog. He looks like hell but he won't go home.

"Whiskey, Bravo, Tom 179er, changing course to . . ." I'm back to Airwolf and we're winding down. We fly Back Bay, which is crystal clear—it's almost tropical in the warmth of the chopper—and head back to the terminal. All the while, the Wolf chatters. What about this? How about that? How come? Lance and I catch a glance and we know.

Out of the wash on the helipad we shake hands with the Wolf. I am grateful for the man's generosity. He's a good man, if quirky. I get into my car, dreading what awaits me when I return to the office. My message bank will be maxed, my e-mails maxed. People will be waiting.

On the way in I'm stopped by Penny Diaz, my assistant, who must work diligently through all the chaos and personalities and who does a great job. But right now, Penny's not feeling patient. "Call this person now," she says, "and I am really sick of Tommy. You have to do something."

"Penny. Not now! Who called?" I am handed a stack of pink messages and I see Tommy is waiting for me about some news. "Give me a minute, Tommy. Just a minute!"

I see Detective Rick Swift, wide eyed, trying to catch my eye through the sea of detectives. The Swift One, as we call him, is not aggressive but I know he wants to talk to me now.

"Lieutenant, you wouldn't believe what happened on the Coast Guard boat today." I sweep him into my office and let him talk.

What happened was that they spotted a girl, fully dressed and in a heavy coat, a hundred yards out in the cold November ocean, trying to commit suicide in the forty-eight-degree water. As the boat approached, she turned and headed back toward shore, where officers and Medcu personnel they had called were waiting and took her to the Maine Medical Center. If they hadn't been out looking for Amy, they never would have seen her and she wouldn't have been saved. Many believed that Amy had led them to this girl.

To increase the pressure on Gorman, police decided to go public with a detail that had previously been kept under wraps—the fact that their investigation showed that Gorman never dropped Amy off at the Pavilion. Gorman had told police that there were people milling around in front of the Pavilion when he dropped her off around 1:45 a.m., yet it was well known that at that hour there were not many people around. The few people on the street would have noticed Amy St. Laurent. The investigation that disproved Gorman's lie had been vast. Everyone the detectives had spoken with, from every walk of life—bums, bouncers, bystanders, bartenders, customers returning to the Pavilion on other nights, and police professionals in the area—confirmed that neither Gorman nor Amy, nor Gorman's car, had been seen at the time he claimed to have dropped her off.

"Yeah, I agree, Tom. Dan. It's time to turn up the burners on this." I explain the plan to Chief Chitwood and he agrees with our strategy.

Tuesday, November 27, 2001, we decide to go public with the fact that Amy

was never dropped off at the Pavilion nightclub. We won't mention Gorman,
but he and his friends will know what we mean.

I contact David Hench of the Portland Press Herald. *Of all the media*
personnel I work with, I have established the most trust with him.

The next day it's front-page news, with Amy's lovely photo smiling at us
again. I'm quoted as saying, "We've substantiated Amy was last seen leaving a
Brighton Avenue address with a male. There is no evidence to suggest she was
dropped off. After extensive interviews and research we have not been able to
isolate that as a fact." The article reports that we have shifted our focus some-
what. I never identify Russ Gorman as the male . . . but it's out.

When the media ask about "the male," I respond, "He's one of many people
we're looking at."

So now it's out and we're hoping that Gorman will start a tailspin. We
shall see.

Suspicion about Gorman's involvement had been growing over the weeks
since Amy disappeared. Increasingly, when he went out in the Old Port,
he found himself not the center of an admiring and friendly crowd but
the object of questions and hostile behavior. When newspaper articles
suggested that this "male" was the primary focus of the investigation,
the revelation confirmed in the minds of many of Gorman's friends and
acquaintances what they had suspected.

At one point, he was assaulted in the Old Port by members of a gang
called FSU who demanded to know, "What did you do to that girl?" Getting beaten up really shook him. Friends reported that he was drinking
heavily and using more drugs. He was jittery, aggressive, and unstable,
his conversation frequently rambling and incoherent.

As life in the Portland area grew more uncomfortable for Gorman,
the detectives learned that he was planning to leave the state. Where he
was going was uncertain. He'd mentioned Alabama and Florida, where
he still had friends and relatives, but also California and Mexico. He'd
talked of making some quick money growing mushrooms and selling
club drugs. Gorman planned to travel south with a friend named Sean
Littlefield, using Littlefield's car.

The detectives believed that if he got away from Portland to a place
where he felt more comfortable, he was likely to let down his guard and

confide in someone about his crime. They expected that Gorman would stay in touch with his mother and that Littlefield would be in touch with friends and family in Maine so they probably wouldn't lose sight of Gorman. And, because he was on probation and required to report regularly to his probation officer, he needed Probation's permission to leave the state. Leaving without permission would be a probation violation and make him subject to arrest. Therefore, they could always arrest him and return him to Maine. Still, they were considering letting their prime suspect, a dangerous man and one they believed had committed a murder, out of their sight. It was not an idea they were comfortable with.

"Well . . . shit, Tom! You know the consequences as well as I do. What if this freak hurts someone? It will be me being asked in some federal lawsuit, Who was in charge of day-to-day ops? Can you hear it?"

"Yes, Lieutenant, I hear it, but it's worth the risk. He's nervous. Hot. And he knows it. He will talk. We both know that. We gotta let the line out."

"Tom, will ya just sit for a minute and stop pacing! You're making me dizzy."

"Joe, he's already saying stuff. You know he'll open to relatives down in Alabama and to this kid, Sean."

"Yeah, yeah. What about Matt [Stewart]?"

"He's worried. It's risky."

I look at the wall, at a painting of Back Bay, and think for a minute.

Tommy doesn't stop talking. "Do you want this guy?"

I look at Tom's piercing blue eyes, glaring under his unruly dark hair. We lock eyes. "Okay," I sigh. "Let the line out, Tom. Let him go. Keep it tight 'til I tell the chief the plan in the a.m."

Like a kid who's gotten his way, Tommy flies out of my room, the door vibrating off the wall.

The detectives knew that if they did let Gorman run, they could always bring him back on a probation violation. But arresting him for a probation violation would only put him in jail temporarily, and when he got out it might trigger him to run farther away. What they all wanted was for Gorman to be in jail on a murder charge. But they needed more than they had so far.

Before he left, Gorman had a conversation with a friend named Brent Plummer that Plummer recorded, using the message function on his cell phone and laying it casually on the table as they talked.

GORMAN: I don't want to leave on bad terms, and I do want you to know and I want everyone to know, no matter what the outcome is, I've got letters typed up at my house, at Mom's house, but I can't go back there right now. Uh . . .

PLUMMER: You've got letters typed to who? What kind of letters?

GORMAN: Explaining everything.

PLUMMER: Why everything?

GORMAN: Well, why I'm leaving, um, also saying that you, all you people know, Dude, all you fuckin' people that I know, my parents, everyone, know that I love my little girl and I couldn't possibly imagine my little girl twenty-five years old and disappearing or not knowing what happened to her. So that right there should just show something. Dude, I do, I do have fucked-up mental problems. I do, but I'm not that kind of person, Dude.

Shortly before Thanksgiving, Gorman and Sean Littlefield left Maine in Littlefield's small red Neon and drove to Troy, Alabama.

IO

In early December, a state police lieutenant received a call from a man who identified himself as Lieutenant Pat Dorian from the Maine Warden Service.[1] Lieutenant Dorian had been in the warden service for twenty-six years and had been head of search and rescue since 1986. Since the warden service dealt with over three hundred lost people each year, Dorian and his officers were very familiar with the challenges of conducting searches in wooded areas. Although Lieutenant Dorian lived far from Portland, like so many people in Maine he had been following the St. Laurent case from the beginning and had been increasingly perturbed by the failure to find Amy St. Laurent's body and the distress he knew this was causing to police agencies and to her family.

Dorian regretted that he hadn't called sooner, but he was stationed up in Greenville, nearly five hours northwest of Portland on the shores of Moosehead Lake. It had been foliage season and hunting season in Maine, and between hunting violations and hunters and hikers getting lost in the woods, the duties of his job had consumed all his time. Lieutenant Dorian said he might be able to help with the investigation and asked to be put in touch with the case detectives.

Dorian knew he was making a radical suggestion. It was a totally new idea for a conservation law enforcement agency to be working with criminal divisions on a criminal investigation. He risked running into the natural territorialism of both the MSP and the Portland Police Department as well as the skepticism of the police for outsiders, even outsiders in another branch of law enforcement. But Dorian was focused on the central issue in the case: finding Amy St. Laurent. He had been to seminars at national search and rescue (SAR) conferences on searching for abducted victims. He'd studied the statistics showing where bodies and evidence might be. He had a professional Incident Command Team that knew how to organize and manage major outdoor search and rescue operations. He believed that the warden service could help.

When he was connected with Sergeant Stewart, Dorian said he'd been thinking of ways that the warden service, utilizing experienced Maine Association of Search and Rescue (MASAR) teams, might be able to help them find Amy's body. He said that in 1999 he had been at an SAR conference and heard a talk by a Michael St. John, out of Oregon, reviewing a ten-year Department of Justice (DOJ) study on child abductions, which had established some parameters for searching for bodies.[2] In that talk, the presenter had raised the question: How do you use the expertise of search and rescue as a resource for law enforcement agencies?

Dorian knew that the wardens had an area of expertise detectives might lack, especially in the area of finding people who were lost in the woods, because wardens were attuned to subtle changes—broken twigs, disturbed dirt, leaves, or needles, things that don't fit in a natural environment—that a police officer might miss. He and some of his officers were also trained in managing large-scale search operations and outdoor crime scenes. He offered to bring some of his wardens down to sit with the case detectives, do an assessment of the case, and develop a methodology for conducting a search for Amy's body.

By the time they got Dorian's call, Danny Young and the other detectives had been working the case nonstop for six weeks. They had lost none of their fervor to find Amy and to give her family at least some closure and a chance for a decent burial, but they were exhausted. The pressure was particularly intense with the holidays coming. It was difficult to take pleasure in their own family holidays with visions of Amy and her family in their minds.

Danny Young was pacing the floors at 2:00 a.m., wondering if there was something he'd missed, racking his brain for things he might have forgotten to do, other avenues to pursue. Tommy Joyce was sleeping only because he knew Danny was up pacing. The were frustrated: it was hard for them to avoid feeling that while they were working their butts off trying to find Amy, Gorman was down in Troy, Alabama, laughing at them and thinking that he was home free. Also they were skeptical: they had tried everything, from searches by land, air, and sea to clairvoyance. And now here were a bunch of game wardens offering to help.

On the other hand, they were badly in need of a break in the case— some new way to crack it open. Winter was coming. If they didn't find Amy soon, they knew they might never find her.

And Dorian was making a very sensible offer. He had an expertise that they were willing to admit they lacked. They were city cops or, as Tommy Joyce put it, bricks and asphalt guys, while the wardens and the MASAR personnel were experienced outdoorsmen and women, trained in woodland searches. Dorian had a methodology for identifying and analyzing potential areas to be searched. His wardens had sophisticated mapping and GPS technology, which simplified identifying areas to be searched and produced an accurate and detailed record of the ground covered. Dorian knew how to take a profile of the lost person, a profile of the suspect, and test those against statistics and experience to identify sites with the greatest potential, and he could develop search parameters for those sites. He could also mobilize the many experienced personnel necessary to mount a massive outdoor search operation using the trained volunteers of MASAR,

On December 3, Dorian brought wardens from his Overhead (or Incident Command) Team, including Warden Kevin Adam, his mapping and GPS expert, Sergeant Roger Guay, and Sergeant Joel Wilkinson, and came to the Portland Police Station for a meeting. That meeting, held in the Detective Bureau's conference room, turned into an all-day session. Skeptical, bone-weary city cops sat on one side of the table, wondering whether these hillbillies from the north woods really had anything to offer. The wardens, with their computers, mapping programs, and GPS equipment, sat on the other. State police were in the middle. They had worked with the warden service before, though no one had ever done an operation like this. And always, despite the traditional separation of their agencies, Danny Young and Scott Harakles sat together, as partners should.

Right from the start, the wardens ran the meeting. Dorian and his team immediately started gathering information about the crime. This included first getting the lead detectives, Young and Harakles, to present the nucleus of the case. By questioning the detectives, the wardens gathered profiles of the victim and the suspect, along with the theories detectives had developed about what had happened the night Amy disappeared.

Once they had a basic picture of the case, they began to gather information to plug into what they knew about cases like this, employing their expertise in outdoor crime scenes. They asked for a detailed assessment of Gorman, including information about how familiar he was with the outdoors. Wardens asked whether Gorman was a hunter or a fisherman. Whether he was known to have spent time in the woods. How long he had lived in Maine and how familiar he was with the local area.

The detectives shared the picture of Gorman that they had developed. Gorman had lived in the state for about eighteen months. He was idle and lazy, working only when he had to in order to support his fondness for drink, drugs, playing pool, and other recreation. He had little respect for women, poor impulse control, and a violent temper. His principal drivers were pleasure and sex. He would go anywhere—her place, Campbell's place, on a beach, in a car, whatever it took to score—and, once he had made up his mind, do anything to persuade or coerce a woman to have sex with him.

Gorman wasn't a hunter, but he was a fisherman and had fished in the ponds behind his mother's house both during the daytime and at night. Gorman had also used the woods behind his mother's house as a hiding place, burying items there that he'd stolen from customers' cars at the car dealership where he had worked.

Next, the detectives reviewed the timeline of the crime. Gorman was known to have left the Brighton Avenue apartment between 1:45 a.m. and 2:00 a.m. The earliest time his presence back at the apartment could be confirmed was David Grazier's statement that he had found Gorman in the bathroom washing sometime around 4:30 a.m.

Using maps, detectives then identified possible routes Gorman might have taken when he left the apartment with Amy. During the course of the investigation, as routes were identified, detectives had driven them and timed the length of each drive. Along any route he might have reasonably taken, wooded areas, parking lots, and industrial sites had been noted. The wardens also asked for other details of the Portland area, such as what were the popular places for teenagers to go "parking." They asked where Amy lived and where her mother lived.

As the day wore on, a bond developed between the men. Going into the meeting, the wardens knew that 60 to 70 percent of their likelihood of success in the operation depended on the quality of the information they could get, which in turn depended on the thoroughness of the underlying investigation. They were very impressed by the information they were getting. The wardens listened to the detectives and asked questions, and together the different groups used their collective information to identify sites where Amy's body might be.

There were eight general areas they considered: areas near Gorman's mother's house, the roadsides on the turnpike going south, along Brighton Avenue, areas near Amy's mother's house, the Old Port area near the Pavilion, exit 2 off the Maine Turnpike near Wells, the area around Amy's residence in South Berwick, and a scattering of random sites Gorman had spoken about during conversations with his friends. They prioritized the sites using a technique called a Matteson Consensus, learned from the National Park Service, in which the detectives used a consistent, systematic method to rate the identified sites from highest to lowest in terms of the likelihood that Amy might be there.

The wardens would design their search criteria based on the timeline of the crime, their knowledge of Gorman's character, his experience, and his familiarity with the area, and their own information about killers' behavior when disposing of a body. Wardens knew, for example, that 72 percent of victims are less than 200 feet from a way or a parking lot. They knew, as the police did, that once a killer is sexually gratified and realizes what he's done, there's a sense of panic and a need to get out of there as quickly as possible. Also, that a killer is unlikely to go far into the woods at night. Police also knew that people believe they travel much farther than they actually do at night.

After the meeting, the wardens spent several hours driving around with the detectives, following the identified routes and studying the terrain. Kevin Adam, who would be developing the maps for the search teams, was trying to put himself inside Gorman's head as they drove around, trying to see what Gorman was seeing. "Okay," he imagined Gorman thinking. "I've got this girl in the car and I am going to have sex with her. Where can I take her? Pretty soon, she's going to notice that we're not going where I said I'd take her, and I've got to be able to control the situation. Where can I take her where there are no people around and I can have her all to myself?" It was the same scenario the detectives had run in their own heads for weeks.

Like Danny Young five weeks earlier, when the wardens and detectives drove along Route 22 past Gorman's mother's house, Kevin Adam saw the old access road leading back into the woods and thought, "She's there. Amy's there." Later he would say that, if they'd had Warden Sergeant Roger Guay's dog, Reba, a ten-year-old chocolate Lab, with them that day, they probably would have found her.[3]

At the end of the day, everyone was on board for conducting a massive search effort to take place on Saturday, December 8. The wardens headed back north with a lot of work before them, planning to return on Friday to go over the logistical details of assembling their teams, setting up a command post, doing the legwork for each of the designated sites, finalizing the maps for those sites, and designing the structure of each area's search. How a search team is deployed in a given area depends on the terrain. Where the terrain is heavily wooded, the searchers may walk practically shoulder to shoulder. Where it is more open and they can see the ground more clearly, they may walk five to ten feet apart.

The wardens left the detectives with some unanswered questions, including one that was very important. Had anyone, in the course of the investigation, been able to connect Gorman with access to a shovel? It would make a difference, in designing the search criteria, to know if it was likely they were looking for a buried body.

During the days that followed, Danny Young and Scott Harakles turned up two pieces of information that would be of major importance in designing and carrying out Saturday's upcoming search. First, in an interview with Gorman's mother's boyfriend, Richard Deveau, on Wednesday, December 5, Deveau told the officers that around the time Amy St. Laurent disappeared, Gorman had asked if he could borrow a shovel because he was going to help a friend put in a fence. Deveau had directed Gorman to a spade shovel behind the house, as well as to a posthole digger in the shed. Later, Deveau would observe that the posthole digger had never been touched. He didn't know about the shovel.

Detectives couldn't locate any friend who had asked Gorman for help in installing a fence. Based on their knowledge of Gorman's character—

lazy, unhelpful, and generally dedicated to avoiding physical work whenever possible (a characterization that Deveau affirmed, telling the detectives Gorman was too lazy to pick up a shovel)—they concluded it was likely the shovel might have been used to bury Amy's body.

A second significant piece of information was discovered the following day. As a routine part of his investigation, Danny Young had put in a request to the FBI asking for an off-line search of police records concerning Gorman through the National Crime Information Computer (NCIC). On Thursday, December 6, Young received the results of that search. The report revealed that at 3:14 a.m. on Sunday morning, October 21, the last day Amy St. Laurent was seen alive, and at a time when Gorman had claimed, and his roommates had initially confirmed, that he was back at the apartment, Tim Gardiner, a police officer in the neighboring city of Westbrook, had stopped Gorman for a high-beam violation at the corner of Main Street and Larrabee Road. Gorman was alone in the car.

For the exhausted detectives, it was a eureka moment. Although Gorman's alibi of being back at Brighton Avenue twenty minutes after he had left to drop off Amy St. Laurent at the Pavilion had been seriously undermined by subsequent statements from Cook and Sharma that they couldn't say when he'd returned, and statements from other residents of the apartment who had returned around 3:00 a.m. and not found him home, police now had an official source—another police officer and official police records[4]—confirming that Gorman had lied.

"My God, Danny . . . are you sure? My God!" Danny hangs in my doorway with his ever present notebook attached to his hand.

"Lieutenant, I feel bad I didn't check this earlier . . . we already ran plates and everything else but I . . ."

"Danny." I hold up my hand. "I don't know how much information a human being can handle, but you've taken on eight times the load."

I was stunned. Thrilled. I had the receiver in my right hand and I could hear a voice in the distance squeaking. I think I hung up on the person, I was so enthralled with this information. Danny's NCIC search showed Gorman was stopped in Westbrook at 3:14 on the morning of the murder.

This was huge. I slammed my fist into the desk. "My God, Danny. That blows him out of the water and confirms so much for us."

I was already framing up a map of Gorman's actions and the area he might have traveled according to this new timeline. Maybe he went around his mom's house. Or was he coming from Campbell's or the Game Room area? And Amy wasn't in the car, unless she was in the trunk, and that was unlikely, based on Stearny's search. He must have disposed of her in a quadrant of about four or five miles. But where?

Then I considered what Danny had just said, and the hairs on my arms bristled. That cop stopped a murderer! Gorman had just killed a girl and dumped her. Officers get shot, stabbed, beaten, and killed more frequently during traffic stops than any other type of police contact.[5] The "routine" becomes tragic within moments. You never know who, or what, is behind the wheel.

In our training, we observe dozens of videos of officers being killed during routine traffic stops, unaware of the monster lurking behind the wheel. Who knows what was going through Gorman's mind at the time. Was he armed? Did he have blood on his clothes? Evidence of Amy?

Gardiner had been incredibly lucky. I look at Danny's face and see he's thinking the same thing. He's elated, but it's just so goddamned chilling to think what a close call that was.

"Get to him, Dan, and find out what he remembers of the stop."

Danny leaves and I sit pensive for a few moments. It is such fantastic news. We were at the end of our rope and now we've got this. This and the wardens and the shovel. It's really coming together. And I wonder. Is Amy helping us?

The discovery of the traffic stop in Westbrook was vitally important because it confirmed a major lie. It also significantly narrowed the window of time during which the crime could have been committed, enabling the detectives and the wardens to focus on a much smaller search area in and near Portland.

Everyone settled in for the major effort of organizing a search involving more than a hundred people: search and rescue personnel, state and Portland police, game wardens, and dog handlers with trained cadaver dogs. Logistics included locating a command center where the wardens' Overhead Team could set up their mapping and communications center with space for the team commander, mapping and logistics, communications, operations, and a briefing/debriefing officer.

The command center also needed a space where search teams could be assembled and briefed, their vehicles could be parked, and searchers could be fed. Since the search teams would roll out early on Saturday morning, overnight accommodations needed to be arranged for those who had to travel. Arrangements had to be made to feed everyone. And all the arrangements had to be made with maximum attention to managing the media, which would be briefed at a press conference on the morning of the search. No one wanted to try to conduct the searches in the shadow of media vans. The press had to be informed, yet kept away from the actual search areas.

On Friday, the wardens returned to sit down with detectives and do the work of identifying final target sites, assigning teams to search those sites, defining the makeup of the teams, and doing the detailed writing of the search parameters for each site. This time the meeting was held at Crosby Farm, the highway maintenance depot and state police facility that would serve as the command post for the following day's operation.

The setup of the search had to be defined, with maps and written assignments, including waypoints and instructions to the search teams about ground to be covered, what they were looking for, and details such as the spacing of their grid searches. Because different conditions affect a dog's ability to detect odors, such as clay soil or bodies of water or extremely wet conditions, the wardens wanted to use multiple resources for each site. Therefore the plans called for each search site to be covered by both a dog and handler team and a search team.

As darkness fell on Friday afternoon and the lights came on, the wardens went back out onto the roads, checking and rechecking the loop from Brighton Avenue to Gorman's mother's house to the location of the traffic stop. They were on the road for five hours, checking out the lighting, visibility from the street, and the general appearance of the search sites at night, noting places that had appeared to be likely dumping spots during the day but were too brightly lit at night.

At nine that evening they finally checked in at their hotel. It was eleven before they had dinner. The National Weather Service was predicting snow for Saturday.

"Well, Tom, where are the hillbillies now?"

"They're all over, Joe. Some are in the gym, some are driving the route, and some are at the Sonesta."

Maine Warden Service overhead team. *From left,* Glenn Annis, Sergeant Joel Wilkinson, Kevin Adam and Lieutenant Patrick Dorian. (*Portland Press Herald*)

"The gym? Shit . . . just don't let them start any fires in there. Ya know, Tommy, I really like that Dorian guy. He's got clean, straight eyes and good humor, too. Guay, I like him, too. They are really sincere guys. This could work, ya know? How's Scott and Danny?"

"They're holding up. Running around like crazy getting ready."

"I still can't believe that freakin' car stop. Thank God!"

I see Sergeant Coffin in the bay. He looks whipped but, as usual, keeps his humor and tells us a joke. "Hey, mister . . ." His favorite phrase. ". . . there's these two guys in heaven . . ."

I go back to my office and call Diane one last time about the plans for tomorrow. I'm planning a press conference involving her in another public appeal for help on Saturday morning before we start this massive operation.

It's Friday night. 1915. Another long day. Tommy comes in and shows me the ops plan. It's huge.

Some of our detectives are pissed because we're dragging them in at 0700 on a Saturday. I've heard the mutterings. "Fuckin' Danny. This is crazy," one detective blurts out as he passes my office.

I'm not in the mood for it. "Just shut up and be there, crybaby!"

"It's like looking for a needle in a haystack," he continues.

"Just be there, Clownie. We've found needles in haystacks by the way . . . way before you were a frigging big detective."

Sergeant Coffin comes by the office. He's been pushing it hard and is red-eyed. "Hey, Bruce," I say, "I checked ops and you're not on it. What's up?"

"I'm beat. I need a day away from this. I made plans with my wife." I tell him it's no problem.

Tommy's excited and tells Bruce we're going to find her. Bruce says, "Yeah, like the needle in the haystack." Tommy and I go over the finals. I order a pizza for everyone and then head home, whipped. Danny and the others are still out there.

In bed at midnight, I stare at the ceiling. Please, God. Please, Amy, let us find you. Show us . . . I finally fall asleep with the light still on. At 0230 the phone rings. I jump up, my heart pounding, and mutter a garbled "Hello?"

"Ho, ho, ho, it's Bob O." Lieutenant Bob Ridge, the John Wayne incarnate of the Portland PD.

"What's going on?"

"Listen, you up with me?" Words I hear all the time in the dark. "Joe, we had another stabbing. Asian male victim up at the hospital, bad guy is another Asian. We got him upstairs and he's 46 [arrested]. The wounds are deep but not life threatening. He's gonna make it. Look, we got drunks and shitheads all over to interview and the crime scene locked up good although it's on Wharf Street outside. We need CID . . ."

I mutter the usual expletives. "We've got that search tomorrow, Bob. I'm down on people. Alright. I'll get some guys rolling." As if we had a choice and could say, "String up some crime scene tape and we'll come do it on Monday."

I call Tommy, like always. His wife, Alison moans, "Oh, no." I tell him we got a stabbing. "Christ," he says, "you gotta be shittin' me."

After the calls I'm awake, staring at the clock, watching the numbers tumble and click. Tumble and click. Eventually, I sleep awhile. At 0530, coffee going, I jump in the shower, pushing the sand from my eyes. Dressing for a press conference. Dressing for outdoors. It's another weekend with no weekend. This better work today. We've started catching breaks now and this is the big break everyone needs. Please, let us bring Amy home.

II

On Saturday, December 8, over a hundred people, including the wardens' Overhead Team, state and Portland police detectives, wardens, and about forty-five MASAR volunteers from units throughout the state, some of whom had slept Friday night in the gym at the Portland police station, assembled at a state Department of Transportation depot and state police headquarters off the Maine Turnpike just south of Portland known as Crosby Farm.

It's o630. Crosby Farm is swarming with police cars and other vehicles. It's a brisk morning. Nice sky but cloudy. Snow's predicted for later. A big smile from Lieutenant Dorian lifts my spirits. We've got a lot riding on this, but so does he. This is his baby. I go up to the command post and situation room on the second floor. These guys are organized and it's an elaborate operation. The computer search program is set up and one of the wardens is explaining how it will coordinate the areas and maps.

Through the window, I see people gathering. News teams are starting to show up. Tom, Matt, Scott, Danny, Dorian, Guay, and others cram into the room to go over the plan. Everyone is focused, hopeful, as Dorian goes over the procedures. Matt looks weary and, as always, serious.

"Hey, Sarge." I slap his back. "We're gonna do it today. Let's get ready for the news." Diane and her good friend Lucille are climbing out of cars. Lucille has been such a supportive friend. Diane looks tired and painfully sad. It's so hard for her to keep going through this, but she's incredible, the way she holds up. We bring them inside and offer coffee and bagels. And yeah, there are donuts, too.

Amy St. Laurent's mother, Diane Jenkins, and Lieutenant Joseph Loughlin speak with the press on the day of the search. (*Portland Press Herald*)

The news crews are waiting. Sergeant Stewart, Lieutenant Dorian, Diane, and I stand before the cameras in a final appeal to the public to help us find Amy. It's cold, and I start off nervous, so much to remember. Always a tightrope to walk with the media. Trying to ensure I include everyone and not compromise the operation.

"Today we are conducting a massive ground search with PPD, MSP, warden service, and MASAR in the hopes of finding Amy St. Laurent. There is an air wing up along with a helicopter thanks to Mr. Sam Hamill of TCI Aircraft." We've scripted this, I know it, but it sounds stilted. I continue, trying to stave off the incoming inquiry. "Based on our studies, we believe Amy could be in an area we have triangulated with the help of the warden service. We are not discussing any criteria concerning the selection of the sites and one should not conclude that these are the only sites."

Each time I pause, I see their mouths get ready to jump. "In addition, we have up to ten K9 dogs helping in this intensive effort to find Amy."

I turn it over to Diane. She pleads for any help or information. Her voice strong but cracking at times from emotion. She has such grace. Such dignity.

We all want, more than anything, to ease some of her pain by finding her daughter. Amy has been gone for seven weeks.

Sergeant Stewart's speech is clear and succinct. Finally, Lieutenant Dorian steps up to explain the wardens' perspective. I close with a final appeal for help and information about Amy. The questions flood us.

"Are you looking for a body?"

"Is this guy who said he dropped her off connected to the search?"

"Should the public be looking for a car or some item?"

We field the questions carefully. Finally, the reporters, cameras, and crew break away and pan the search groups as they move into a giant maintenance shed for briefing and assignments.

Thorpe and Dumas catch my eye and roll theirs like this is crazy. I close my eyes a moment and pray.

Cops, wardens, and SAR teams were packed into a big DOT garage as the wardens' Overhead Team told them what they should be looking for. Searchers were given the information about Gorman's borrowing a shovel and alerted to the possibility that Amy might be buried. They were given copies of the flyer with Amy's picture, her description, and a description of what she was wearing the night she disappeared.

Searchers were instructed to keep their eyes open, look for clues, and ask questions. The wardens reminded them that anything could be valuable information. Bent twigs. Scraped tree trunks. A thread. Scrap of paper. Disturbed dirt or vegetation. Dirt mounded up or dirt caved in. Shovel marks. Piled brush that didn't look natural.

As they went through the briefing, Sergeant Joyce remembered thinking, "Everyone else is home with their families today and we're going to be out in the cold tromping through the woods."

Getting things set up and ready to roll, the situation was best described as "controlled chaos," something all the players—detectives, wardens, and SAR teams—were familiar and comfortable with. It's amazing how emergency workers come together quickly when they need to. It was a massive operation, about which Sergeant Stewart noted, "Normally, you have to pull hairs to get resources, but not this time. It really came together."

Each team included state or Portland police and a warden, as well as the MASAR volunteers. Each team got a map, a detailed set of instructions for its search area, and a GPS device so that the teams could start and end the searches at established points and the Overhead Team could maintain a computer record of the areas searched. Things settled down as the teams rolled out the door to start their first round of searches.

Overhead, "Airwolf"—Sam Hamill—was up in his helicopter. With him were Portland detectives Mark Teceno and Don Krier, who would be conducting their own search from above.

Despite his optimism—and he had mentally assigned a 40 percent or better chance that they'd find Amy that day—Kevin Adam recognized that the information about Gorman's borrowing the shovel would make things harder. The grousing Portland detectives were right—it would not be like finding a needle in a haystack, but like finding a needle in a buried haystack. On his personal timeline, he thought that if they didn't find her by eleven, he'd start to worry.

To prevent information from leaking out to media monitoring the airwaves, the police and the wardens had chosen to use the phrase, "Code Blue" if a body was located.

Scott Harakles began every day with a prayer. He never asked God for help, because he believed God helps those who help themselves. But on this day, he got down on his knees and asked God for help in finding Amy. When he and Danny Young met up, Scott told Danny, "We're going to find her today."

Danny Young responded, "Yes, I know," and even gave Scott a time. He told Scott he felt really good about the prospects. Very optimistic. They had so much help with the search, and all the areas they were searching were associated with Gorman.

Young and Harakles didn't join a search team but traveled together in a car, staying mobile and on call in case a body or associated evidence was found. Since they had the time, they asked each other, Okay, so where have you always wanted to look? Unable to stay still, they were independently searching the woods between the Westbrook arterial highway and the Bill Dodge auto dealership, which Gorman was familiar with because of his employment at Bill Dodge.

Since getting the case, the two primaries had been working steadily, days, nights, and even weekends. But it was the holiday season. Young had made plans with his wife for the next day, Sunday, and was looking forward to finally having a day off.

Throughout the morning, as the search teams worked through the sites on their maps, the dogs repeatedly hit on things. Each time, the search would halt to determine if the discovery was significant. The airwaves sang with reports that turned out to be false alarms. Dead animals. Bad smells. A floating tarp. Bones. Deer parts. All had to be taken seriously. Like an erratic EKG, the mood was episodic excitement followed by depression or downright hopelessness.

In the midst of the morning searches, the wardens discovered there had been a glitch in the morning's dog search of the area surrounding some small ponds on a narrow tote road off Route 22 not far from Gorman's mother's house. The wardens determined to send both a search group and some dogs back into that area as soon as a team became available.

After the teams went out, Diane and Lucille visited the wardens in their command center. Diane was asking questions about the techniques of the search and the mapping technology the wardens were using to track the search results. Pinned up on the wall was a large map of the search area, with significant sites such as Gorman's mother's house and the site of the 3:14 a.m. traffic stop prominently marked.

Lucille studied the map and asked about the significance of the Westbrook traffic-stop site. Knowing that the police were keeping this information secret, the wardens invented an explanation. Unsatisfied and still suspicious, she asked Lieutenant Loughlin about the mark on the map as well. But no one was ready to reveal this valuable piece of information. It was a card the police wanted to hold close to their chests.

It was well past the 11:00 a.m. deadline Kevin Adam had mentally assigned. They had had a series of false alarms. It was cold, and it was hard to keep the teams' spirits up as they finished the lunch the Salvation Army food truck had provided and set out for their afternoon's assignments. It was also hard to balance the necessity of executing each search in a slow and methodical way with the sense of urgency imposed by the threat of approaching snow.

At approximately 1:00 p.m., a search team led by Warden Justin Fowlie and including Portland detective Gary Thorpe and members of the Mahoosic Mountain SAR team arrived to begin their search of an old, grown-up road extending approximately two hundred yards off Route 22. The road had been used to obtain the gravel needed to build I-295. Its surface was crumbling tar, and the road and surrounding woods were choked with trash, brush, and debris people had dumped there.

The road was bordered with scrub trees, thin birches, and small pines. At the end of the road, trails led off into the brush and circled around four small black ponds. It was an area popular with local hunters and fishermen. At its end, facing the road and peering through the trees like a lurking monster, was the carcass of a large abandoned truck. Scattered around it were the large white wooden forms contractors used for pouring foundations.

The Mahoosic team had come into the operation in a skeptical frame of mind, feeling that searching for a body wasn't part of their work. It wasn't what they were trained to do—the Mahoosic Mountain SAR always looked for live people. But inspired by Lieutenant Pat Dorian's enthusiasm and certainty that it would be a good thing to use their expertise to assist state and Portland police, they had joined the effort. They knew that everybody was looking for signs of a crime scene or a dumped, decomposing body, possibly hidden by brush or leaves. In the morning, they had also been instructed that there might be a grave.

Their team had already been out in the December cold for several hours. Now they gathered again to get their instructions for this site. Mindful of their instructions, their breath forming clouds in piercingly damp air that increasingly held the promise of snow, the searchers spread out in a line from the edge of Route 22 at approximately seven-foot intervals and began their slow, deliberate march along the left side of the old tote road through the tangle of underbrush and young trees. They were all aware that this afternoon's search would probably be the last chance to look for Amy St. Laurent until spring.

The team reached the end of the road, moved farther left, and made their way back out to Route 22. They then switched to the right side of the road. Slowly and deliberately, paying close attention to the woods around them and the ground beneath their feet, they paced their way from Route 22 back toward the ponds. At 1:30, just about twenty-five yards from the end of the road, they entered an area that alternated between open ground and pasture pines, pine trees with low branches that had spread widely at the bottom.

As he bent to go under a large branch, Landon Fake, an administrator with the Hurricane Island Outward Bound School, noticed that the soil just in front of him looked slightly depressed. Pine needles were scattered over ground that appeared to have been disturbed. He stopped, announced that he had found something, and knelt to examine the ground. When he looked more closely, he could see that one of the live branches of the pine tree was buried in the ground. It immediately made him stop and think, "Someone has been digging here recently."

Fake's announcement immediately stopped the line. Everyone came over, looked, and agreed that he had found something. Closer examination revealed shovel marks and an area of disturbed ground approximately six to seven feet in diameter. The disturbed ground was topped by sod that had been cut into pieces at one time. Brown pine needles had been sprinkled over the dirt to mask the signs of digging.

Portland detective Gary Thorpe, who was with the search team, acknowledged that he wasn't an expert on outdoor crime scenes. "Put me in any building, any room at a crime scene," he'd say, "and I know what's going on. Out here, I don't know a lot. But when I looked at what Fake was pointing out, even I knew that was wrong." Thorpe looked at live green pine needles buried in the earth and thought, "Oh, yeah, you're gonna hear a Code Blue on this one!"

Thorpe called on his radio for dogs to search the area. A call was also made to Detectives Young and Harakles, summoning them to the site. When he got the call, Young told himself, "This is it!"

The Mahoosic Mountain SAR team was immediately moved out and sent to another site. As Landon Fake said, "They couldn't get us out of there fast enough . . . in two minutes, we were gone." Out at the road, waiting to leave, they saw cars of senior police personnel arrive, along with the dog truck.

Warden Burnell and two volunteers brought in their dogs. The first dog didn't react well. The second dog reacted hard and began to dig. Warden Jacobs was called to bring in his dog. His dog also reacted and began to dig. At around 2:30, the wardens called warden Sergeant Roger Guay and his dog, Reba, to the site. Reba first focused on an area under some pine trees and then on the area of disturbed earth Fake had discovered.

A prickle of excitement went through the dozen men and women standing around in weeds and scrub on a cold, gray December afternoon. After a day of false alarms and seven weeks of high expectations but negative results, everyone was afraid to hope that this was finally it.

Young, who like Sergeant Joyce had begun his day thinking, "Hey, this sucks. It's colder than hell and here we are out in the woods," had been working toward this moment since the night he first got the phone call about Amy's disappearance. Afraid to believe this might finally be what they had searched for for so long, the detectives asked if this was likely to be a body or might just be buried clothes or another dead animal. Sergeant Guay assured them that Reba's reaction meant they'd likely found a body.

Not wanting to call a Code Blue too soon, and knowing that they'd found many dead animal parts already, Detective Young returned to his car and got some tools from the trunk. He returned to the scene and pulled on gloves. On his knees, using a trowel, digging very carefully to avoid disturbing any evidence if it was Amy, he dug a small test hole about four to six inches wide, at the opposite end of the site from where Reba had been digging. Approximately two feet down, he hit something that felt different from the soil. He cleared the dirt, exposing a small expanse of gray material. He reached into the hole and touched it, confirming that it was sweatshirt fabric. Amy St. Laurent had been wearing a sweatshirt the night she disappeared.

At 2:40, Young called a Code Blue, and the site became a crime scene. At 2:41, the search teams were recalled to Crosby Farm.

As the search teams set out, Lieutenant Dorian shouts one final message: "If you discover anything, call out Code Blue *over the radio so the news or scannerland doesn't pick up, and we'll get the dogs there. In a hospitable spirit, we also have food available."*

I plan to roam to various sites and check in at headquarters. Right now, I'm very glad to be inside where it's warm.

Within an hour, there's a hit in an area near where Gorman was stopped by Westbrook police. It makes sense, and I think, Oh, my God, what if it's her?

Detective Danny Young uses a trowel to dig a test hole at the site MASAR searchers and cadaver dogs identified as a possible gravesite.

But a short time later, they call in that it's a dead deer. A huge letdown. Time to get out there and poke around with the teams.

I watch one group probe the woods, moving in a line through the trees. There's another false alarm—a dead dog. A few more false alarms come in during the morning and into the afternoon. I go to 109 around 1300, have lunch, and update Deputy Chief Burton and the chief.

Tommy, Danny, and I have been on the phone, on and off, but I haven't heard from them for a while. Around 1430, I'm starting to lose faith. I head outbound on Congress toward Route 22, where I know they're starting to search near Gorman's mother's house. Suddenly, my pager starts beeping like crazy. It's Tommy. I think he must want food for the guys. It beeps again. Okay, Tommy, Okay!

I get on the cell and hear Tom's voice. "Joe? We found her."

"Really?" It floats in the air. "Really, Tom?"

"I'm telling you again, Joe. We found Amy."

"Where, Tom? Where?" I hear voices in the background. Dogs barking. "Are you sure?"

"We're off a short tote road off 22 near the mom's house. Danny's here. The dogs hit hard. Get out here, Joe. It looks like a grave."

I hardly believe what I just heard. I drive hastily to the site, still in disbelief. It's colder, the sky bruised and cloudy with a curious light. I'm shouting in my car for other cars to move out of my way. Still not believing. Maybe it's just her clothes.

Out of Portland, I drive past Smiling Hill Farm and spot numerous police and warden vehicles in the distance, their emergency flashers on. Dispatch is paging me. I tell the operator to tell the news media that we're still searching and conducting a meeting to make more plans, hence all the cars.

I pull off onto the dirt shoulder. It's all woods and unfamiliar territory. Officers and wardens out by the road say, "Lieutenant, they're up this road about two hundred yards. You'll see them."

I feel the weight of it as I move up the road through the skeletal wood. A gray landscape, bleak as a Goya painting. Will this be her, dammit? Will it? Will we finally have something to tell Diane?

I see a group and, yeah, there's Dorian, looking at me with a big hillbilly smile. My stomach flips. It's really true, I think, it's really true. Tommy walks jerkily up to me. I grab his arms and look at him.

"It's her, Joe."

Danny next. I hug Danny. His eyes are moist and I feel my own eyes getting cloudy and hot. Seven weeks he's worked toward this moment. "Danny. Oh, God, Dan. Great job!"

Dogs are probing the woods. There's a bustle of activity. I start noticing other people around me. Matt. Scott. Roger Guay with Reba. That friendly redheaded warden.

They lead me through the brush, ducking branches, into the woods about fifty feet. A branch snaps into my thigh, the sharp sting saying, "This is real. This is real." I smell dirt and see the outline of a grave. There's a small hole and Danny explains how he dug down until he felt something in his probe about two feet in. It was Amy! Her gray sweatshirt. I peer into the hole and see the sweatshirt.

I turn and look at Danny. Imagine him digging with his fingers and actually touching Amy. I rise, feeling thrilled, sad, troubled. "Roger," I ask Guay, "what if it's just her clothes?"

Guay and Dorian assure me. The way the dogs hit, it's a body. Buried. I

think, buried how? Buried alive? Strangled? Stabbed? Shot? What are we go-
ing to find? The Rolodex of crime scenes starts.

Finding what they hoped would be Amy St. Laurent's burial site was nothing short of a miracle. Murderers rarely take the time to bury a body. They
may shroud a body with brush or leaves, but usually they want to get away
from what they've done as quickly as possible. For more than a month,
everyone had been searching for a dumped body or a hidden body. Naturally, they had been alert to signs of recent digging, but mostly they had
been looking aboveground. Luckily, the wardens had asked their question
about connecting Gorman to a shovel. Even more luckily, the detectives
had gotten an honest answer to that question.

Amy St. Laurent's suspected grave was located less than four-tenths
of a mile behind Gorman's mother's house. And without Lieutenant Pat
Dorian and MASAR, it probably never would have been found.

12

Everyone was eager to get on with the work of getting Amy out of the ground. The small glimpse of gray sweatshirt Danny Young's digging had revealed had brought tears and a heartbreaking mixture of excitement and profound sorrow. But while Danny Young and Scott Harakles might have wanted to just grab some shovels and start digging, and all the officers would have liked to get inside out of the seeping cold, none of them, having come this far, wanted to take a chance on losing the evidence or information the burial site might give them by moving too quickly. They knew what they had to do.

It was only weeks away from the shortest day of the year. The weary detectives had no time, in the fading gray light of a December afternoon, to do much more than pat each other on the back and shake the grinning wardens' hands before turning their attention to the complexities of converting a major search operation into a crime scene requiring the meticulous exhumation of a buried body. Young said it was as though the minute they found her grave site, time slowed down.

Another time, another season, they might have discussed securing the scene and coming back in the morning. It is always best to work an outdoor crime scene in daylight.[1] But snow was coming, and a December snow in Maine might still be on the ground in April. The detectives couldn't risk losing days or weeks with their evidence buried.

Even if a tarp might have protected the grave site itself, and not collapsed under the weight of snow, the surrounding area as well as the access road needed to be carefully searched, and the investigators couldn't cover all that with tarps. They had already lost many weeks during which

Detectives walking down the rubble-choked road off Route 22 in Westbrook.

valuable evidence was being destroyed. They were also running on an adrenaline high fueled by their sheer amazement at having found Amy's grave. So no one wanted to stop. Everyone wanted to finish the job. They wanted to bring Amy home.

As civilian personnel were released, it was critical to make sure they understood that no information about what had been found and what police were working on could be released to anyone—not to family or friends and, most critically, not to the media. The Mahoosic Mountain searchers were pulled aside back at Crosby Farm and told, in cop-speak, that there had been a significant find. Their names were taken in case they would be needed later to appear at a trial, and they were released with profound thanks. As the story unfolded, the Mahoosic team could see that however reluctantly they had come into the search, their expertise had made a difference, and it had been worth doing for Amy's family.

Those in command also moved quickly through the business of thanking and dismissing the police personnel who had helped with the search, many of whom wanted to stick around and have a piece of the action. But everyone knew that crime scene processing worked better with a small, efficient crew.[2] There would be some bruised egos and hurt feelings; but there wasn't time to worry about it, there was way too much to be done. As Lieutenant Loughlin put it, "You feel bad, but you're already moving on and they've got to understand it's just part of the job."

As the scene was stabilized and decisions were made, the ranking officers on the scene, Lieutenant Brian McDonough, from the state police, and Lieutenant Loughlin, had to pass information up their respective food chains so that their superiors would be in the loop. Because the media were already focused on the search and aware that personnel and vehicles had converged on the area off Route 22, news vans had begun to arrive. It was necessary to agree quickly on a uniform story and to convey it to dispatch in Portland and to Stephen McCausland, the state police spokesperson.

Then came the complicated issue of staffing the scene. Although Portland and state police had worked side by side for weeks on the case, the grave site and surrounding crime scene were not in Portland but in Scarborough, resolving, finally, the question of jurisdiction. Amy St. Laurent was now officially an MSP case. The decision was quickly made, however, to proceed as a team, and the investigators moved on to the question of how the scene would be handled. Whose evidence technicians would do which tasks. Who would videotape the dig, sketch the scene, take the photographs, record and collect the evidence. Whether both the MSP and Portland crime scene vans would be used.

The chief medical examiner, Dr. Margaret Greenwald, and her deputy, Dr. Ed David, had to be located, notified, and summoned to the scene. The presence of a body meant that the exhumation could not proceed without Dr. Greenwald. A scene with a body "belongs" to the medical examiner. Because the body was buried, and the exhumation of a buried body is a detailed and complicated process, Dr. Marcella Sorg, a forensic anthropologist at the University of Maine in Orono experienced in such excavations, was also contacted.

Portland and state police evidence technicians had to be contacted. The parameters of the crime scene had to be identified and secured. Access to the scene was by the tote road, which was blocked by piles of accumulated debris. Somehow, Todd Coons, one of the Portland detectives, got a road grader that could be used to clear the tote road and allow the state's large crime scene van (a converted mobile home) and Portland's smaller one access to the site. Before any of that debris could be moved, however, it—and the road into the site—had to be searched so that no potential evidence would be lost.

Since it was obvious that the exhumation process would be going on long after dark, police borrowed a generator and large lights from Scarborough Rescue, which they set up to illuminate the scene deep in the woods, complementing the lights the state police had provided.

None of these steps took place without conferences among the ranking officers at the scene and often consultation with their respective command staffs. But all the investigators proceeded with the smoothness of professionals who were used to the complexity and chaos of crime scenes. Everyone clicked into gear and began to do their jobs.

All day long, the air had held the promise of snow. As darkness closed in, it brought a damp and biting chill. The detectives could feel the impending snow in the air and knew they were racing the clock. They also knew that one of the basic principles of crime scene investigation is that it cannot be rushed. Crime scene investigation is a detailed and time-consuming process designed to preserve the integrity of the scene and all the information and evidence collected there.

The suspicious site was first identified around 2:15 p.m. The Code Blue was called at 2:40. The medical examiner arrived at the scene at 6:15. During that time, there was a tremendous amount of work to be done before the exhumation itself could begin, following the site protocol. Identifying and cordoning off the parameters of the scene. Establishing designated paths into and out of the scene to avoid trampling on evidence. Documenting the scene in sufficient detail to allow an officer to later re-create it in a detailed written report.

Scene documentation involved the taking of detailed notes, not only about the scene itself, but also about the steps taken to capture those details. Mapping, for example, was a very complex and time-consuming process. First a rough sketch was made. Then, in order to reproduce the scene accurately later, measurements were taken to record distances, angles, fixed items, and movable items. The site was then photographed and videotaped.

The site was searched visually and with metal detectors. Every step of the process had to be photographed and videotaped. Evidence discovered was photographed in place with and without identifying numbers, a scale, and an arrow. Along with the usual crime scene requirements—never move, touch, or alter anything until it has been noted, sketched, and photographed—the detectives faced the additional complexities of conducting a forensic dig—the long, slow, careful process of exhuming the victim's body.[3]

The fact that it was night, and December, and that everyone had already been on the job for nearly twelve hours, was irrelevant. The detectives all had the picture of Amy's smiling face in their minds as they stood around what they now believed was her grave. Soon, perhaps, they would know how she had died. No one wanted to miss a shred of evidence that might help them understand the details of the crime or help them secure a successful conviction of the smooth-talking charmer who had offered Amy a ride home and instead killed her and dumped her into this hole in the ground.

Early in the process, Chief Chitwood came through the dark to the scene, congratulated Danny Young, and shook his hand. It felt good to Young to have his efforts recognized. What felt even better was when Detective John Dumas, who had started the day in a piss-poor mood, angry about giving up a Saturday and muttering darkly about finding needles in haystacks, came and shook his hand.

For Young, there would be some serious emotional rushes that night. It really hit him hard, he said, when he called his wife, Linda, from the scene. "You know how I told you I was going to have a day off tomorrow?" he said. "Well, it looks like I'm going to be working after all."

"You've found her, haven't you," she said. And only then did he realize that, yes, indeed, they had.

Chief Chitwood, bouncing with energy, snapping his gum, definitely Clint Eastwood–esque, moves up the tote road to me. When he gets close, I see he's got his jogging suit on. The chief is a workout fanatic. He knows crime scenes and starts off, "Great job, Joe. You guys did a great job."

"It was all Danny and Scott, Chief, believe me. And those warden guys are amazing. I still can't believe we found her. Still can't believe."

Chitwood moves to Danny, Tom, and others, shaking hands and congratu-

lating them, like they've won a sports event. It's pretty dark now. News teams
are choking up the road, I'm told over the radio.

Matt comes up to me, wide eyed. "Joe!" He grabs my arm. "Joe, you gotta
stop the chief from the news . . ."

This is MSP's biggest nightmare. They play it close to the vest, while Chief
Chitwood is a lot more open, more willing to speculate.

"Oh, yeah, Matt, real easy. Sure. Hang on a minute. I'll just go tell him."
Media Mike is a publicity hound. He loves the media so much it's almost like
an aphrodisiac. And he's good. The public loves him.

I walk up to the chief by the command post. "Chief, can you do me a favor
and talk to Matt before you go to the press so we can agree on issues?"

"Sure, Joe. No problem. Where is he?" The chief ambles over to Matt and
they converse.

Off to the side, I see white sneakers emerge from the gloom as if they are
walking on their own. Then I see it's Tim Burton. Thank God, I think. Bur-
ton has such good, logical sense, such a calming effect and a unique relation-
ship with the chief. He shakes my hand and congratulates me, then looks
around curiously. "Where did we get all this equipment and who's gonna pay
for it?"

"Jeez, Tim. Not now. We've got a potential conflict brewing, and fast. I need
you." I ask him to appeal to the chief before he goes out to the road. Everyone
huddles up and Tim does his thing with alacrity.

The last thing I see is Mike Chitwood walking down the dark tote road, jog-
ging suit reflecting the light, heading toward the news like a moth to a flame.

As I turn, Matt rolls his eyes because he knows what's coming, and strides
off into the darkness after the chief. Not my problem, I think, as I turn to the
scene.

The discovery of what they believed to be Amy St. Laurent's grave site in
Scarborough, which was under the investigative jurisdiction of the Maine
State Police, changed the dynamic of the case. Both police agencies were
still working side by side, and both felt it was crucial to the success of the
case to keep it that way; at the same time, the jurisdictional shift highlighted what had been an ongoing source of tension—the widely diver-
gent styles of the two agencies with respect to handling the media. It was
close to time for the 6:00 p.m. news. Media vans were lined up on Route

22, and Sergeant Stewart was very concerned about what Chief Chitwood would say to them.

Although the investigators all believed they'd found Amy's grave, what they had so far was a scrap of gray sweatshirt and the behavior of the dogs. The medical examiner hadn't arrived yet. The families had not been notified. MSP and Portland personnel, including Chief Chitwood, discussed the matter, and everyone agreed to say only that a significant discovery had been made, that detectives were now investigating it, and that in a short while, Portland police and the MSP would issue a joint press release.

Chief Chitwood then left the scene and went back out to the road. Sergeant Stewart, following, heard him speak with some reporters to the effect that a buried body had been found, a sweatshirt identified, and detectives believed it to be the body of Amy St. Laurent. Stewart subsequently spoke with the reporters, explained that the information was premature until the site had been examined and the families notified, and persuaded the reluctant reporters to hold the story. Stewart then returned to the scene, vigorously protesting the chief's actions, and tried to secure the Portland police department's cooperation in keeping a lid on public statements. While Stewart was back at the scene, trying to control what would be said to the media, the chief gave another interview that did make it onto the air, infuriating the state police and the stations that had cooperated in holding the story.

Route 22 was ablaze with the flashing lights of emergency vehicles. Scarborough police and state police were out there, preventing the media from having access to the site. Route 22 had been closed. Detectives and evidence technicians were in gear, searching the tote road and the area around the grave site. Now that the process was under way, it was time for Lieutenant Loughlin and Danny Young to make the painful phone calls to Amy's mother and father, informing them of the discovery.

"Yeah, yeah, okay, Dan, let me call Diane and you call Dennis."

I once again stomp my feet in the cold dirt. It's incredible, amazing, that we've found her, but I hate this part. I start my journey out to the road, trying to tell myself it's just another note, we do them all the time. But it's not.

How the hell do I say this one? Your daughter's buried? We found Amy?

How? Your daughter is in the woods? Hey, Diane, just wanted to let you know we're digging up your daughter. If I didn't know her so well, couldn't see her face so clearly, this would be easier. She's got the saddest eyes I've ever seen, and I've seen enough.

Out of the dark, a small cat appears and rubs up against me. I stop and scratch and am able to pick him up. "What are you doing out here, Bootleg?" I say Bootleg because of his black front paw, like he's wearing a little boot. I put him down and tell him to go home but he insists on following me. I think of Amy. Of how she loved cats. Perhaps she's sending an emissary to say it's going to be okay.

Ahead I can see the lights at the street. Cars, noise, the Salvation Army truck. There's that kitty again, rubbing hard against my legs. Amy? Is that you? Helping me? Comforting me?

I get to my car, parked on the shoulder away from the bustle of people. I want to get inside and start the heat but I pause and look at the gray Taurus. Hesitating. A voice in my head asks, "Do you find it hard to do your duty?" A movie quote that keeps coming back to me.

I'm inside, engine on, police radio spitting out info. Back in the city, it's busy. Gratefully, I suck in the heat. Delaying. Turn off the car radio, Bach mixed with police radio. I shut the police radio off, too, and stare at my cell phone on its mount. Hey, I can talk hands free. Delaying as I pull out my notebook to look up a number I know by heart.

I capture my own interest as I flip through my beat-up pocket notebook, flipping through a plethora of stories, destroyed lives, most of which I can no longer remember, escaping into other scenes.

I turn page after page. Some I remember, some I see. Some I smell. Some are just names and gross information. The pages are torn. White. Stained. Yellowed. Just people. Just life . . . to us.

Come on, you know the number. Just call, Joe. Call! The heat has finally seeped to my core. I see a hand reflected in my driver's side mirror. A knock jolts me. The electronic window hums down. "Hey, Lieutenant, there's a guy from Channel 13 news, wants to talk, etc. . . . ."

"Yeah, yeah. Hang on."

My leather jacket's creaking with noise. Why did I wear this? I turn down the heat, mentally creating a silence in which to speak, shutting out the world, the city, everything but the dark space in my car.

I press the numbers . . . beep, beep, beep . . . and the noise is almost deafening. I already see her eyes, asking why.

Third ring. "Hello?"

I know it's her. "Diane?"

"Yes?"

"It's Joe."

"Yes?"

"We found her . . . We found Amy, Diane. We found her."

Silence. Silence. A strange, muted sound of pain. Then she says, "Where?"

I tell where we are and how she must remain quiet for now.

"How?" she asks.

"Diane, she was buried in the woods." I'm grasping now, hoping to say the right thing, waiting for her reactions. "Diane, she was buried, but Diane, we found her. She's home." I repeat it. "She's home." Trying to avoid the barrage of feeling and questions she must have.

A muted, "Thank you." Then, "That bastard. That rotten bastard." I can see Diane's face through her voice. The pain. Anger. Her tired, beautiful eyes, hopeless but thankful.

"Diane, we will get him. We will. But you must remain vigilant. Prepare for the news. It's going to be all over the media. They will be calling so be careful in what you say." We talk about the next journey and all the work to do. I tell her about the kitty and how I felt Amy's spirit and comfort. I say I will call in the morning and update her.

Then, because I want to be sure she isn't alone, I ask, "Is Lucille with you? Julie? God bless you, Diane. Stay strong."

I hang up. Take a minute before I move on to the other calls I have to make. Stay strong. Diane is so strong. She's amazing. But I have just shattered those last faint hopes that Amy might be found alive.

As they removed the carefully cut sod that had been reassembled on top of the grave to mask the signs of digging, Danny Young couldn't help remembering how Gorman had told his friends that the police were never going to find the body. Gorman had tried hard to make sure that was true, but he hadn't counted on Lieutenant Dorian and the warden service.

To ensure that evidence from the body or clothing, including small hairs or fibers, wasn't lost, all the dirt was carefully removed with small trowels, whisk brooms, and soft brushes. It was carried in plastic buckets to detectives who sifted it through two screens. The work was physically hard because of the cold and the weight of the soil and the time and care it took to sift every inch.

All the excavation was done by Drs. Greenwald, David, and Sorg, on their hands and knees, peeling the soils away one slow layer at a time. Huge lights illuminated the scene with stark white light, creating a surreal patch of activity in the pitch black woods. There was noise but it was muted noise, everyone subdued by the circumstances.

Portland evidence technician Chris Stearns and MSP detective Angela Blodgett took photographs. Sergeant Joyce consulted with Portland and MSP evidence technicians. In the background, the generators hummed. Metal detectors beeped as they were run over the ground. The site began to be dotted with rulers and crime scene tape and little tented markers with numbers on them, marking places where evidence had been found. On the tote road, a single sock was found and then a hair scrunchie.

As the excavation progressed, the investigators discovered that much of Amy's body was covered by an old white foundation form, used for pouring cement, which measured approximately fourteen by forty-eight inches, one of many that were scattered throughout the woods at the end of the tote road. The form was carefully exposed, lifted off, and collected as evidence. Each hair or other object from the screening was carefully logged, bagged, and tagged. Dozens of pieces of potential evidence were collected from the soil, the body, and the area surrounding the grave.

Hours passed. The crime scene workers could feel that the snow was close. Everyone was bundled against the cold, breath steaming in the icy air, fingers and toes going numb as the chill worked its way to their bones. Except for brief trips to the heated vans to thaw their fingers, they worked steadily in the circle of light, toiling with warring senses of overwhelming triumph and profound sadness. We've found Amy.

For each of those who had been deeply involved in the investigation, there were two different "heads" reacting to the scene. The emotional head grasped the sadness of the moment and the tragedy of how two lives had intersected so briefly and things were changed forever. No one had ever abandoned the faint hope that their suspicions of foul play were wrong and one day Amy would turn up. Now they knew that wouldn't happen. At the same time, the professional investigator's head was excited. Now they could leap to the next plateau and get this guy.

Down in Troy, Alabama, Gorman was getting phone calls from his mother telling him police were digging in the woods behind her house and her road was blocked. Something big was going on, and it was taking a long time.

As the cement form was lifted off and the digging went deeper, maggots were spotted and the smells of dirt and pungent pine needles were joined by the unmistakable scent of decomposition. Gradually, Amy's head and the outline of her body began to emerge from the reddish brown soil. Despite the dirt, the Pratt & Whitney logo on her sweatshirt was still clear and bright, a disquieting image when the woman who wore it was so thickly crusted with earth she looked like a mummy. Dr. Sorg noted that the soils in which the body was found were dry and sandy. Top of body twenty-three inches below surface. Spade marks were found with an imprint nine by nine and curved.

Investigators eager for information about the cause of death observed seepage from what appeared to be a wound to the head. But little could be known for certain until Dr. Greenwald had conducted her autopsy.

A fairly wide excavated area was circumscribed around the body, with Amy's remains on a pedestal created by digging on all sides down to the lowest level of the body. As her hands and feet became visible, they were carefully covered with brown paper bags to protect against the loss of any evidence. Soil and hair from around her head and pubic area was collected and bagged. Samples of maggots and other insects were carefully collected and bagged for study by a forensic entomologist.

It's dark now and I'm in the command post with a few detectives and Lieutenant Brian McDonough, my counterpart on the Maine State Police. The news people are still out there and Brian is on the phone with Stephen McCausland, the spokesperson for the MSP. I can hear, from the receiver, "Brian, Brian! You tell Chitwood that I am the damned spokesperson for the state. You tell him that."

Brian looks at me and we both roll our eyes at our predicament. Eventually he hangs up and I ask, "Okay, Brian, would you rather deal with Chief Chitwood or McCausland?" Chitwood backs down from no one.

Matt pops into the trailer, glasses steamed, and notes that it's a lot easier when only our small group is involved. So true, Matt, I think. And things are about to get more complicated.

Outside in the cold, the exhumation is beginning in earnest. I hear the generators churning. Through the windows I catch slashes of bright lights. One of the detectives calls me on the radio and tells me the father is out on the road and wants to come up.

"No," I tell him, "no. Hold him there. Tell him I'm on the way."

I had met Dennis St. Laurent a few times but did not have a relationship with him like Danny did. I could have sent Danny out, but he was in the center of things, busy working on the dig.

I exited the command post van and noticed a leaning white birch lit up like a beacon, leading to the path where Amy was. The red plastic tape that led into the trail across the saplings and brown leaves was illuminated in the dark. That's not our tape. Must be the ME's [medical examiner's] or the state's. So strange to be doing a joint scene like this. We've got our own tape, equipment, SOPs, and techniques.

I could see a blue tarp through the trees and hear voices floating on the air, breath rising up in clouds on the fringe of the darkness. It was spooky, ghoulish. Got to get to Dennis. I walk through darkness toward the road, light from the site fading, and stop, snatching a moment's peace between the commotion of the scene and the chaos at the street, wondering how Dennis will be.

As I approach the road, I can see the red blinking flashers of several vehicles. When I'm closer, I see one is a Salvation Army truck with coffee and food. I'm thrilled at the prospect of eating something. But first, there's Dennis. He's standing there, shivering, his breath forming clouds. A small man, a quiet man. Brown hair starting to gray, thick eyebrows and a salt-and-pepper mustache. Absolutely destroyed by all this.

We shake hands and talk about Amy for a moment. I don't know what he'll do so I make some small talk while I assess him. He's calm and I start the process again and I tell him that I believe we've found her. That she's buried in a shallow grave up that road. I point. He wants to go up but I can't let him. "Let's get a cup of coffee, Dennis." I put a hand on his shoulder. I tell him we have a lot of work to do and it's going to take a while, but I believe in my heart that Amy's there.

We sip our coffee in silence. It tastes so warm and good and I'm reminded to be grateful for the simple things. Especially in this cold we're standing in. He's shaking with cold. We both are. He breaks his silence with "You, you guys did a good job."

I tell him it's important not to tell anyone about this except his partner, Kathy. The news doesn't know yet and we don't want to compromise things with the case. The next step will be arresting that Gorman bastard!

He looks at me with pleading eyes and asks again if he can go up. Again I tell him no. He's pretty good about things, compared to others I've seen, who are unable to listen through their pain and charge forward. The pain in his face is so clear it transfers to me. But I've given him as much time as I can. I've got to get back. "I'll call you," I tell him. "I'll call you later or Danny will. God bless and stay strong."

We shake hands and I move off into the dark. I wish he'd go home. There's nothing he can do here. But he won't. He's going to stay as close to Amy as he can. Later I learn that he remained there until they took her away and Danny went out to talk with him.

Up the trail, I feel angry and sad. Who knows what we'll find when . . . I think brutally . . . when we finish digging Amy up! I remember, again, "Do you find it hard to do your duty?" As a servant for those who can't possibly understand? My eyes are moist as I think of Diane, Dennis, and Julie and how grueling their wait has been. And how there's no way we can protect them from what is coming.

Up ahead there's a yellow plastic triangle in the dark, catching glints of light. Crime scene triangle number 4, then number 2, then number 1 along the road, marking evidence.

When I get close enough, the quiet is broken. Generators sputter and hum. Metal detectors zing. In the bright white light, green gloves, red ones, plastic gloves push and pull at the earth. Soil is loaded into green buckets and poured through the screens. The colors gleam unnaturally bright in the reddish dirt.

Around me, the crew are wearing dirty jeans, dirty sweatshirts, dirty uniforms. The air smells of dirt as it pours through the sifters. Flashes from the cameras document everything.

I can see the outline of a grave clearly now. Arrows, as in bows and arrows, stick up to mark points of contact and evidence. I've never seen that before.

Tommy stomps his feet. Scott stares at the earth, pensive, waiting, biting his

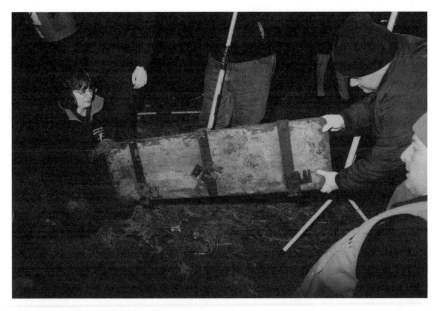

Chief Medical Examiner Dr. Margaret Greenwald and Detective Danny Young hold up the wooden form for poured concrete removed from Amy St. Laurent's grave.

left thumbnail. My pager goes off and when I return the call, someone wants to know if I'm coming to a Christmas party. Is it really almost Christmas? If so, then finding Amy is a good gift.

In the command post, symphony music drifts through the cozy interior as the backup camera shows the crime scene in all its eeriness. No sound, just ghoulish movements and slow digging as the music floats in the air and the warmth seems so welcoming. It's sad and strange and surreal. Is it Amy yet?

Tommy comes in. In the greenish glow of the backup screen we watch strange movements and a large item being removed from the grave. I pop out of the room, heading for the site. At the grave, Dr. Greenwald is kneeling, covered in dirt, her glasses steamed, holding one end of a large piece of board. Danny is on the other end. It's a two-by-four-foot board with metal straps. Danny is bent over, his watch cap smeared with dirt, as they hold the board for still pictures and video.

With the board removed, the dirt smells different. I know that smell. I see the outline of something. Are you there, Amy? The generators hum, producing a circle of light that looks like it ought to be warm, but it's bitterly cold. I stay and

watch. Tom, Matt, Scott, Danny, and I almost joined by the arms, like broth-
ers, our breath rising like smoke in the night. We're voices in the darkness.

Hey, there's that cat again. Maggots, I hear the ME say as I shove the kitty
and tell it to go home. It scuttles across the path and over the edge of the grave.
The searchers' voices are elevated now. We move toward the grave, where the
outline of a human head is now clear.

Brush, broom, and trowel move around the skull and upper body, exposing
the body outline. There she is. We are unearthing Amy and brushing back the
sadness. The how and the why are for other days. I blink back tears, letting
no one see. Maybe all of us who worked so closely on this are harboring secret
tears.

Amy, is that really you? The image that comes to mind is one of her posters.
Amy in a red dress, pearls, long, bouncy hair, earrings, and a subtle smile.

For a moment, I feel a flash of anger. I want to kill Gorman with my own
hands. I look around, see the seriousness in Matt's stare as he looks into the
earth, see Tommy's forensic mind working, Danny's sadness and exhaustion,
Scott's strength. Tommy and I speak for a moment about the next steps the
doctors are taking.

Let us whisper in the quiet horror of this.

Finally, the body is fully exposed, shrouded in brown dirt, her bagged hands
pointing stiffly up as though she's reaching toward us.

A large white plastic body bag is unzipped and spread out near the grave.
I think of Amy's bright and brave spirit. In a macabre silence, people posi-
tion themselves around the grave. Dr. Greenwald instructs on how she'll be
lifted out. Danny is in there, his eyes red from fatigue, with Scott right beside
him.

The "mummy" form is lifted slowly out and onto the bag, looking like some-
thing not even Stephen King could conjure up as it rests in the shiny white
plastic. The zipper closes with a whine, the body is carried out to the tote road
and loaded into a livery vehicle. Doors slam shut with a final, hard noise, and
the vehicle slowly moves away up the trail, bouncing red taillights gradually
fading away into the darkness.

I stare after it long after it's gone, then stamp my feet and turn to see the guys,
slumped as they stand. We still have to conduct a final search of the grave and
immediate area for evidence, then carefully brush down all the equipment.

People shuffle around recovering equipment. Finally everything is loaded up.

We shake hands, give a few halfhearted slaps, but there's no energy or feeling anymore. Stearns has the evidence tech van going. Dan, Tom, and I all hop inside. Blast the damned heat, Chris! We're all crammed into the vehicle, up front.

Matt, Scott, and the state police are in their command post, beeping as they back up, like leaving a camping trip. The autopsy will be tomorrow morning. We've been here at the grave since before three this afternoon, started our day at five a.m. Now it's after midnight.

Our van lurches forward, lights illuminating the dark road. We peer through the windshield like children.

Hey, is that snow? It's snowing! We look at each other for a moment. "God, are we lucky," Tom says. "Another day, we'd have a different story. Look at that. It's snowing." Big flakes quietly drifting down to cover this disturbed and eerie night.

Outside, in the "normal" world, it was a Saturday night in the Christmas season. People were crowding into the malls to do their holiday shopping. Going to parties, to dinners, to concerts and carol sings. People were baking. Decorating. Wrapping presents. Writing Christmas cards. While under the eerie, searing brightness of a bank of artificial lights, detectives toiled in a woodland clearing, unearthing the dirt-encrusted form of a lovely young woman who had had the misfortune to cross paths with a predator.

Finally, late in the evening, the excavation had fully exposed the body, and the surrounding earth had all been removed and screened. Around 11:00 p.m., the body presumed to be Amy St. Laurent was carefully removed from her grave and placed in a body bag for transport to the medical examiner's office. Before Amy was taken away, Detective Young asked the medical examiner to clean the dirt from her ankle. He was looking for the dolphin tattoo so he could give Dennis St. Laurent, still waiting out on the road, the real confirmation he'd been waiting for.

As the ME's van drove away and the evidence techs were snapping their last pictures, it began to snow.

It had been a long, grueling, miserable day and it had been as exciting as any the detectives had ever had in their careers. Danny Young said that, for him, finding the body was like getting to set down a hundred-pound weight. Tommy Joyce said, "the feeling you get when you succeed . . . it's why we do the job."

Tired, they stared at the snow, and looked at their watches, and found confirmation for their belief that for that whole day they had received the gift of divine intervention. Someone had sent the wardens, held off the snow, given them the faith and patience and willingness to come out this day and search. If they hadn't found Amy that day, they might not have had another chance to search until spring. And by then, snowpack, wind and rain, and freezing and thawing might have settled the disturbed earth, scattered the pine needles, and erased the shovel marks. Like many buried victims, Amy St. Laurent might never have been found.

13

On Sunday, the state of Maine awoke to snow on the ground and news headlines proclaiming that a body found in Scarborough was likely that of the missing South Berwick woman, Amy St. Laurent. A relieved public assumed that the job was done, now that Amy had been found, and looked for a quick arrest.

For the detectives, it was different. The case detectives awoke on Sunday feeling a hundred pounds lighter. They had worked hard to find the missing young woman they had come to think of as "Our Amy," but there was no time to relax and rest on their laurels. Now that they had a body and a grave site that should yield some information about the crime, and would soon have a cause of death, a new phase of their work had just begun.

Men who had barely slept were up and off at dawn to attend the autopsy. And the pace didn't let up. It wouldn't be until the following Sunday that Danny Young and Scott Harakles would get to spend some time with their families, after one of the most extraordinary weeks of their careers.

Sunday morning, December 9. I peek out my window and see the snow on the ground, everything clean and white. Not enough to clean the muddy image of Amy . . . not enough snow for that. Stumbling around to make coffee, I am thrilled that we found her. I know Dan and Stearns, Scott and Matt are already going to or are at the autopsy. They must be burnt toast, I think, as the smell of my own toast rises in the kitchen.

I still can't believe we found her. Days like that, you have to believe in divine intervention. And the way we found her . . . that bastard at least tried to rape her. *Maybe we'll know. Maybe we won't. The CSI-watching public has no idea how random forensic evidence can be. I'll bet he strangled her.*

"We will get you!" *I shout aloud, startling myself with the sound of my own raspy voice, as the image of Amy in the grave floats before me. I cannot clear my head. Joe! That's not her, Joe. The smell of dirt and decay mixed with cold and pine lingers in my nostrils.*

I shake my head. Why does this image bother me so? I've seen hundreds of dead.

That's not Amy, I think. Amy is the picture on the flyers. The pretty girl in pearls. I see her as an angel with a pink rose. Clean, floating smiling to heaven, not coated in dirt like a mummy.

I keep spitting and blowing my nose, trying to clear out the death smell.[1] *I think back to horrific scenes, the blood smell, the scent of physical matter destroyed. I would come home and throw my clothes off, discarded like a bad skin, and in the morning, putting them in the wash, I would hardly remember the scene, but Amy stays . . . so strong, so distinct right down to individual pieces of dirt. The tenacity of this image will not leave.*

Later, my pager goes off, and it starts again. It's Tom. I ask how he and Dan are holding up.

"Joe, they're done with the post and on their way back."

"Yes, Tom, yes. How?"

"Are you ready?" *He gives me a beat.* "Gunshot to the head."

Gunshot! Gunshot! It hangs a moment. God. That bastard. The downside of being taught to imagine it. I think of her fear. A lovely girl who thinks she can handle herself facing a guy with a gun. We've been imagining it all along. Now we'll have the details. Start all the arguments again. Was it Campbell's gun?

"Listen, Joe, we got a lot to do. I'm going back to 109 with Dan in a few. We gotta keep this tight when you tell the chief and command . . ."

I hang up and walk in circles in my living room. A gunshot. That explains the fluid we saw last night. God, poor Amy. Poor Amy. I gaze into the backyard, out to clean snow. A large crow looms in a pine, watching. I see you, deathbird. I see you.

Before they left the grave site, the medical examiner had scheduled an autopsy for 9:00 a.m. the next morning. Detectives and evidence technicians rose at dawn, gathered their equipment, and trooped up to Augusta, about an hour north, for the sad task of collecting evidence from the body and learning what the autopsy would reveal. For the last seven weeks, they'd been imagining the last day of Amy St. Laurent's life. Now they would get the information that would let them imagine her death.

The body on the stainless steel autopsy table, still thickly coated with dirt, looked more like a mummy than a person. After seven weeks in the ground, a visual identification wasn't possible. As the body was slowly cleaned, the investigators would get confirmation of what they'd observed the night before. Amy's sweatshirt, shirt, and bra were pushed up above her breasts. Her jeans, shoes, and one sock were missing. Her underpants were rolled down around her ankles.

With the same concern that had been used for preserving evidence at the exhumation, the clothing and remaining dirt were removed from the body with great care to ensure that any clinging hairs or fibers wouldn't be lost. Body hair, head hair, and fingernails were collected. Then the body was washed so that the skin could be examined.

Although formal identification would have to wait for DNA results or a comparison to Amy St. Laurent's dental records, there was sufficient information on the body or with it to make the detectives certain that this was Amy. Four details in particular matched information provided by Amy's mother. These were the surgical scars on Amy's hips, the tattoo of jumping dolphins around her ankle, her earrings, and her ring.

Once the autopsy was under way, detectives began to get more detailed information about the circumstances of Amy's death. They would learn that, prior to her death, Amy had been severely beaten about the head and face. Her skull would show evidence of several blows to the head. One of the bones in her face was broken. Her lip was cut and swollen and one of her teeth was freshly chipped.

Behind her left ear there was a large hole in her skull, which the medical examiner, Dr. Greenwald, pending the results of further examination, believed to be the result of a gunshot wound. A hole on the right side of the skull was probably the exit wound. Although the medical examiner had more work to do before she could officially state as a cause of death that Amy St. Laurent had been shot, detectives left the autopsy room knowing that their victim had been savagely beaten, quite possibly sexually assaulted, and shot in the head.[2]

Later in the day, detectives and evidence technicians would return to the burial site to finish digging out and sifting the soil that had been underneath the body and to take more photographs. Young and Harakles would return several more times to search the area, as well as conducting searches in other areas well known to Gorman, looking for Amy's clothes, Gorman's clothes, Amy's shoes, and the murder weapon. Since they hadn't found blood or a bullet, they surmised that the crime scene might still be somewhere else.

MSP detectives canvassed the homes in the area, searching for witnesses. Detectives also searched for hunters or fishermen who might have been in the area in October.

Danny Young returned from the autopsy to find an interesting telephone message. A woman named Mary Young (no relation to Danny) had called from Florida with information regarding the St. Laurent case. Told that he was the primary detective on the case, she had left a message asking him to call her back.

When Detective Young returned the call, he learned that Mary Young was a friend and former neighbor of Gorman's mother, Tammy Westbrook, when Westbrook lived in Delray Beach, Florida, and that Tammy's teenage daughter and hers were close friends.[3] Mary Young told him she had recently received a phone call from Tammy Westbrook, her first such call in many months. In that call, a distressed Westbrook described getting a phone call from her son, Russ, in which he'd said he had known all along that Amy St. Laurent was dead.

Gorman told his mother that it had not been he, but his roommates Kush and Jason, who had left with Amy, while he had never left the apartment except to go across the street for coffee. Sharma and Cook had been gone for several hours, and when they returned, they told Gorman they had killed her. They then asked him where was a good place to hide a body. After they threatened his ex-girlfriend, Jamie, and his family, Gorman directed them to the wooded area near a pond behind his mother's house, where they dumped the body and later went back to bury it.

It was ironic, after all their efforts to provide him with an alibi, that Gorman should try to explain the presence of Amy's body near his mother's house by blaming Cook and Sharma for the murder. The detectives, hearing Mary Young's information, understood exactly what Gorman was doing. Now that Amy's body had been found, he felt pressured to explain to his family and friends why it had been found where it was.

Since his departure for Alabama, Gorman's mother had been phoning him repeatedly, giving him details of the news reports and telling him how the police were coming around all the time asking questions about him.

The pressure on Gorman was cranked up on the Monday after Amy's body was found when David Hench, a reporter for the *Portland Press Herald*, reiterated even more strongly than in his previous article that police investigators believed they had been given inaccurate information by the last person known to be with St. Laurent, and that he did not drop her off in the Old Port as he'd claimed. On Tuesday, Gorman's name was publicly linked to the investigation when the same newspaper reported that a document filed in the Cumberland County Superior Court identified Jeffrey "Russ" Gorman as a suspect in the case.[4] Gorman's mother called his grandparents to warn them that his name was in the paper.

As the police had expected, down in Alabama, Gorman was starting to unravel. One of his first acts on arriving in Troy was to get himself a little .25 handgun. Shortly before Amy's body was found, he acquired a second one, telling people he needed them for protection or, alternatively, that he had them in case the police came after him.

He and Sean Littlefield had been staying with his paternal grandmother, Littlefield mostly moping around with little to do while Gorman wore Littlefield's clothes and drove around in Littlefield's car, looking for women to add to his list of conquests. At one point, Gorman might have taken off for Florida with plans to sell some drugs, leaving Littlefield behind in Troy.

When Russ Gorman's uncle, Danny Gorman, was due to be released from prison, his grandmother told Russ he had to leave because he had a record and she couldn't have someone with a criminal record staying at the house if her son Danny was going to stay there.[5] She said that Littlefield was welcome to stay. Russ Gorman and Littlefield went to stay with Erica Walker, a friend of the family.

Early in the investigation, Gorman had reported to friends that the police were interested in him but that they had no evidence against him. He had also stated that Amy St. Laurent's body would never be found.

Following a phone call from his mother, telling him that a body *had* been found, he went to the local college, Troy State University, and used the Internet to check the stories in Maine papers. Later that day, on December 9, at approximately 2:30 in the afternoon, he called his mother on her cell phone as she was on her way to the Maine Mall.

In response to her prompting that the stories he'd been telling her didn't add up, and that he should tell her the truth, Gorman said, "Mom, I did it. I killed that girl." He described walking with Amy by the lake, becoming enraged at something she'd said, and pulling out a gun and shooting her in the head.[6] He told his mother that when he was beating and killing Amy, he was seeing her (Tammy's) face, and that she should be glad she wasn't the one he'd killed.

Following the conversation on December 9, Gorman called his mother and asked her to send him money, which she promptly did.

Tammy Westbrook, having asked for the truth and gotten some version of it, did not report this conversation to the police. She did, however, call her friend Mary Young again and repeated the conversation to her. She also called an Episcopal priest in Florida, Father Fred Basil, and told him about her son's confession.

Although no official cause of death had been announced—the medical examiner would not release the information that Amy St. Laurent died from a gunshot wound to the head until March 22, 2002—information linking Gorman and guns continued to come in. Later on Monday, December 10, interviewing Jamie Baillargeon, Gorman's former girlfriend, Young and Harakles learned that Gorman had dropped what she believed was a plastic grip from a gun in her car three days before he left for Alabama. She gave the suspicious part to Young. It turned out not to be part of a gun; however, she also told Young that Gorman had told her he had a gun down in Alabama and that he'd had guns in the past.

In the same interview, the detectives learned that Gorman had told her the same story he'd told his mother—that he didn't take Amy back to the Pavilion, Kush and Jason did, and that they were gone three hours and returned with blood on their hands to say they'd killed her. She told them Gorman had said that Jason and Kush threatened harm to her (Jamie) and to his family if Gorman didn't tell them about a good place to hide the body, and he suggested they put it out by his "fishing hole."

She told them she was really troubled by the idea of a threat to her but also felt that it didn't quite ring true. Gorman was not the type of person to be intimidated by a threat. In that same conversation, Gorman had admitted to her that he had known all along that Amy was dead and where the body was.

In response to Jamie's shocked expression of how cruel this was to Amy's family—and didn't it bother him?—Gorman had responded that at first he felt bad but now he didn't really care anymore.

The following day, Detective Young heard from Jamie's mother, Dot, that Gorman had been seen at a party with a 9 mm Glock around the time Amy St. Laurent disappeared. And information from Jamie's current boyfriend was that he had heard that Gorman was looking for someone who wanted to buy a gun.

While Danny Young and Scott Harakles were interviewing Dot and Jamie Baillargeon, Tommy Joyce and Matt Stewart, along with five or six other Portland and MSP detectives and evidence techs, were executing a warrant Young had obtained to search Gorman's mother's house. Among the things police were looking for were the spade shovel he had borrowed from his stepfather; a firearm, firearm packaging, or ammunition; Amy's missing clothing or her driver's license; bloodstained clothing or clothing with soil or vegetation that might connect it to the grave site; a computer or other writing that might contain the letter Gorman told Brent Plummer he had left when he went to Alabama; and items that might contain Gorman's DNA.

It was an extremely dynamic scene as personnel arrived and began their search of a dwelling that, while not large, was cluttered and rambling, with small rooms and cubbyholes everywhere. When they first arrived, they found only Gorman's teenage sister, Britney, at home. Soon after that, the phone rang and it was Gorman. After speaking with him briefly, Britney handed Sergeant Stewart the phone, saying, "My brother wants to speak with you."

Stewart said hello and asked if the caller was Gorman. Gorman angrily stated that it was, and questioned their right to be there when his mother wasn't home. Stewart told him they had a warrant to search and that his sister was okay. Gorman ordered them to leave. Stewart responded that they would leave when they were finished and asked Gorman if he'd like to talk about things. Gorman snarled, "Fuck you, come get me, bitch," and slammed down the phone.

Soon after that, Tammy Westbrook arrived with her two younger children. From her behavior, Sergeant Joyce and Sergeant Stewart both had a gut-level reaction that she knew something. They also recognized that this might be their only chance to do an untainted interview with her, as she had refused to leave the house to be interviewed and they believed it likely that as the case against her son progressed, she might retain a lawyer and refuse to speak with them.

The two detectives sat down with her in the kitchen. Slowly, they eased into a superficially casual conversation about family, the challenges of raising children, and the holidays while the search proceeded around them, detectives coming and going in the room and her kids clambering in and out of her lap and clamoring for attention. She would alternate speaking to the detectives with little chats to her kids in a singsongy voice. Once Joyce and Stewart started talking to her, they became certain that what she knew was significant and that she was determined to protect her son.

As they attempted, through their questions, to bring her down the road to truth-telling and convince her to unload her heavy secret, her internal battle between telling what she knew about a horrible crime and her desire to shield her son was apparent. She seemed to teeter on the verge of control while her demeanor screamed anguish, conflict, and deception. As they talked, emphasizing her responsibility to do the right thing and not cover up for her son, she would visibly soften as the part of her that wanted to tell the truth would be dominant. Several times, they felt they had reached her and she was right on the verge of blurting out what she knew. Then her desperate desire to protect her son would surface. She would pull back. The sad, confused, and panicked looked in her eyes would harden into a flinty, determined stare, and her face and body would stiffen with resistance.

Eventually she terminated the interview, using her kids as an excuse, but she didn't shut the door on future conversations, telling the detectives maybe they could do this later. Although they abandoned their efforts to elicit the truth from Westbrook, the search of her house continued for most of the day and into the night.

Joyce and Stewart would stop by several more times—spontaneous visits rather than interviews by appointment, because people have a harder time telling the police they won't talk face to face than over the phone—hoping to catch her at a time when they could persuade her to tell the truth.

On Tuesday, December 11, detectives returned to the medical examiner's office to discuss her findings and get confirmation that dental records had positively identified the body as that of Amy St. Laurent. Dr. Greenwald confirmed from further examination of the skull by herself and Dr. Sorg that the cause of death was a gunshot wound to the head and that the death was, unquestionably, a homicide.[7] State and Portland police recognized that it was critically important that the cause of death, and the circumstances surrounding it, be kept secret.

Mary Young, during her conversation with Tammy Westbrook in which Westbrook revealed her son's confession, had urged Westbrook to report the conversation to the police. Westbrook had refused, saying, "I can't. He's my baby." So Mary Young made another phone call to Danny Young. She was Tammy's friend, and she sympathized with Tammy Westbrook's agony and her dilemma, but Mary Young was also the mother of a teenage daughter. What Gorman had done to someone else's daughter wasn't something she could just let ride.

Mary Young made her call at 9:30 in the morning on December 11. Detective Young got a page informing him of Mary Young's second call while he was in the meeting with the medical examiner. It was a big meeting, with Fern LaRochelle and Bill Stokes from the attorney general's office, Matt Stewart, Scott Harakles, Rick LeClair, Warren Ferland, MSP spokesman Steve McCausland, and Lieutenant Brian McDonough from the state police, Deputy Chief Tim Burton, Lieutenant Loughlin, Tommy Joyce, and evidence technician Chris Stearns from the Portland police department, and lab technicians from the state crime lab. When he could, Young left the meeting to return the call.

Young went back into the meeting clutching his notebook and shaking his head. "You won't believe the phone call I just had." He dropped into his chair, pushed his glasses back up his nose, and galvanized the meeting with the information he'd just gotten from Mary Young.

In this call, she told him several things:

1. Tammy Westbrook was afraid her phones were tapped and preferred to use pay phones.

2. Her son had called her on her cell phone while she was on her way to the mall the day after the body was discovered and admitted that he did kill Amy St. Laurent by shooting her in the head.

3. He was seeing her face (Tammy's) while he was doing it.

4. Tammy had called the grandparents to let them know Russ's name was in the newspaper.

5. When Russ was a baby, Tammy was doing drugs and so this is her fault. Her fault that her son turned out the way he is.

6. Tammy said Russ had told her she was lucky she wasn't the one he'd killed.

7. Tammy said that "he didn't mean it, it was an accident."

Mary Young also described Westbrook's anguish as a mother having such information.

Mary Young's call was like a shot of adrenalin to the tired detectives, putting the excitement and thrill of catching Amy's killer back into the air. It gave them the confirmation they'd been hoping for. It also gave them details they could use in their investigation, details only the killer would know. They had let Gorman run so he would talk, and now, finally, he was talking.

Suddenly, after seven weeks of drudgery, dead ends, and discouragement, they were on a crazy roller-coaster ride where information just came flying at them. Later that day, Mary Young called again to report that Gorman had called his ex-girlfriend Kathleen Ferguson, the mother of his young daughter, who lived across the street from Mary Young. Gorman had told Kathleen the following things: That the police wouldn't find DNA, because Amy wasn't raped. That there would be no gun residue and that his gun wasn't used. That after he killed her, he washed her body. Russ had made the call from a number belonging to friends of his relatives.

While the detectives in Maine were having another eureka day, having finally gotten a solid break in their investigation, down in Troy, Alabama, a stressed-out Gorman was becoming increasingly erratic. He made statements to various people that the reason he had two guns was that he was never going to be taken alive and he was never going to be taken back to Maine and put in jail.

An old friend from Florida who had known Gorman for years, Angela Pannell, was concerned about Gorman's state of mind after talking with his mother. She called him at his grandmother's home in Troy, trying to convince him to go back to Maine and deal with things. According to Pannell, Gorman told her that there was no way he would go back to Maine unless it was in a body bag. He'd kill himself first.

On that same Tuesday, while Danny Young was having his watershed conversation with Mary Young and describing it to his colleagues, Gorman had a dramatic encounter with a man in a Blimpie's parking lot. The man was coming out with a sandwich when he saw Gorman sitting in a car. As he passed the car, Gorman leaned out the window and ordered him not to stare. The man with the sandwich was Andy Bowen, the football conditioning coach at Troy State University. Not the type of man to be intimidated. He challenged Gorman, asking what Gorman was going to do about it.

In response, Gorman got out of the car and pointed a handgun at Bowen. A woman pulled Gorman back into the car, screaming at him not to shoot. After a few words were exchanged, Bowen walked back to his truck. Gorman drove away and Bowen contacted the police, describing Gorman and informing them that the man who had threatened him had driven off in a red Dodge Neon with Maine license plates.

Following the gun incident, Troy police searched for Gorman to arrest him on a criminal threatening charge. Gorman's dangerous behavior ended the Maine detectives' debate about putting the warrant to arrest him for violating his probation back into the system. They asked the Troy police to arrest him and hold him for return to Maine.

There's a bustle over by Danny Young's crowded desk. Voices are elevated and Matt's head is really red, his forehead furrowed in deep concern. He's pacing. I glide over and see Matt's face red in appeal and then he says, hastily, "This is not good, Lieutenant!"

Tommy and I lock eyes and he knows what I'm asking without uttering a word. Cavalierly, he says, "Yeah, hey, Gorman just stuck a gun in a guy's face down in Troy and the cops are looking for him." He chuckles.

Matt's got steam coming out of his ears and Tommy's acting very relaxed. Partly, Tommy's just jerking Matt's chain, but partly it's because he is cool with this. He's been making hard decisions in hot moments for a long time. Matt is extremely methodical, responsible, and not so flexible. Day to day, these two intense control freaks manage to put their personality differences aside in the interest of solving the case, but at moments like this, their truce can get a little frayed.

Many voices put their two cents in. I know this is serious—Gorman is crashing—but if he hurts someone, the blame will be on us. People will have the luxury of second-guessing our strategy and they'll disparage us with a vengeance. There will be legal and potential career implications. Meanwhile, there is chaos and Tom is thriving in the midst of it while Matt is truly in pain.

Casually, Tom rises from his desk and strolls over to Danny. "Dan, I think it's time we put that warrant back in the system." Dan, Matt, and the others look relieved. I'm relieved. As I head toward Chitwood's office to update him on the case, I call back, "Tom, keep me posted."

Following the incident in the Blimpie's parking lot, Troy police got a tip that the red Neon was parked at a Troy address. Surveillance was set up at the residence, but Gorman evaded police all night and into the next day. On the twelfth, the vehicle left the staked-out residence and went to a second residence a mile away. When the vehicle left the second residence, police stopped it, but Gorman was not in the car. The occupants told police that Gorman was in the attic of the residence they had just left, and that he was armed.

As investigators in Portland followed the incident from nearly fourteen hundred miles away via frequent updates from Sergeant Calista Everage—a Troy, Alabama, detective—Troy police arrived at the residence to arrest Gorman on a fugitive warrant. Gorman held guns to his head and threatened to shoot himself.

As Gorman held the guns to his head, the Portland detectives debated whether Gorman would pull the trigger. With typical sick cop humor, they started a betting pool.

"Tom, stop for a minute. First, where the hell did you get a tie like that? They don't even sell that shit in Kmart, and the sixties are over. Is that your

dad's stuff?" He's wearing a blue and white checked shirt and a brown striped tie. Tom's notorious for dressing like Sipowicz on NYPD Blue.

He's moving jerkily and I know he has good info for me, so I play to hold it all off, knowing I'm about to get a present. It's chaos out in the bay behind him.

"Ooookay, Tom, what is it?"

"Gorman's in a standoff in Troy and has two guns to his head," he says, smiling.

Bam! My fist goes onto the desk. "I hope that prick kills himself!"

"Hey, we're making bets in the bay if he's going to do it."

"Tom, send the Grim Reaper south. I don't want Diane, Dennis, and the family going through the pain and foolishness of a trial."

Tommy grins, liking the idea. "You think?"

As part of our constant black humor, the Grim Reaper had developed anthropomorphic attributes here in the office. It became the device to illustrate how we felt about certain crime scenes, to avoid lurid details. Sometimes we appealed to the Reaper to hold off his work while we caught up on other cases and crime scenes.

This time, I wanted to employ him. Send him down to see Gorman if it meant we could avoid a trial. A trial would be such a brutal extension of the family's pain and suffering. The system is slow, rigid, and confusing and a theatrical defense attorney can easily manipulate a jury into "reasonable doubt." I dislike trials, as they are not always about truth and the jury never gets to see the entire picture.

The standoff continues as Danny communicates with Troy. I tell Tommy I'm in for a ten on Gorman, just to keep it interesting. Tommy says Gorman won't do it, because he's a coward. I agree, but I'm still in for ten.

"By the way, Tom, did you get that Reaper sticker off the crime scene van?" At a recent death scene, I noticed the sticker, sickle and all and wearing a Sherlock Holmes hat, on the van.

"Yeah, Joe, we got it off."

From the tone of Tom's voice, I knew I had to check. This shit was fine for our survival but I didn't need some family member viewing that thing through tears. Guess who would be dealing with it? Lieutenant Loughlin, that's who. And Chief Chitwood.

"Lemme know about that freak Gorman, Tommy. Lemme know."

I went back to work. Four and a half hours later, the standoff ended. Gorman was in custody and alive. I was out ten bucks and it looked like we were going to have a trial.

Troy police safely evacuated the other residents of the house, friends of Gorman's family, two adults and a three-year-old child. The Troy police emergency response team and officers from the county sheriff's office closed State Highway 29. After a five-and-a-half-hour standoff during which, at one point, Gorman was holding two loaded guns pointed at his head and threatening to kill himself, negotiators from the Troy Police Department managed to end the incident peacefully. Gorman surrendered his first .25 caliber semiautomatic pistol for a soda and the second for a cigarette, and the Troy police took him into custody. Detective Young was notified and began extradition proceedings.

14

The standoff had ended and Gorman was in an Alabama jail, but the excitement wasn't over for the evening. The detectives and their supervisors had been engaged in an ongoing debate about whether Danny and Scott should go to Troy to interview witnesses or whether they should rely on the very able support they were getting from Chief Everage and Detective Sergeant Calista Everage (the chief's sister). "ALABAMA" had been up on the dryboard in the conference room along with the long list of potential witnesses to be interviewed, waiting to rise higher in the priority list or for the detectives to have time to deal with it.

Now, with Gorman in custody and Littlefield also in jail for shoplifting, and with many other friends and relatives in whom Gorman might have confided, Alabama had risen to the top of the list. Everyone agreed it was important to the case for the detectives to have face-to-face contact with the Alabama witnesses while the information was still fresh.

On that Wednesday evening, the decision was finally made that Young and Harakles should go to Alabama to interview Gorman before Probation and Parole arrived to bring him back to Maine, as well as to speak with other local witnesses. There was only one problem: with not much more than a twenty-four-hour window to conduct interviews before Gorman was returned to Maine, Scott Harakles stunned them all by declaring: "I don't fly."

It was incongruous. Harakles was a Maine state trooper. True, he appeared younger than his thirty-two years, but he looked like everyone's image of a big, tough cop, built like a football player with a firm jaw, broad shoulders, and a crew cut. He had all the command presence necessary to get the world to line up and obey. But he was a family man in a major way. He had two young kids. It was two months since 9/11. He had recently had a bad time in an MSP plane, and he didn't want to get on another.

On the surface, it wasn't a big deal. Harakles wasn't the only detective assigned to MSP Criminal Investigation Division 1. His supervisors suggested that the simplest solution was for another detective to fly to Alabama with Young. Young wasn't happy with that idea. He and Harakles had become extremely close over the weeks they'd worked together. Many of their days had been twelve to sixteen hours long. Despite the age and experience gaps, they had become partners, and a partner isn't fungible.

It wasn't just their personal relationship. Danny and Scott lived and breathed the case. They felt, and Lieutenant Loughlin agreed, that their joint view of the case and thorough knowledge of witness statements, the timeline, and autopsy results were important elements of the investigation and would be invaluable in speaking with witnesses in Alabama.

Lieutenant Loughlin also worried that splitting them up so far into the case might make them lose momentum—that not only would they lose Harakles's valuable body of knowledge, insight, and excellent interviewing skills but that, with a major personnel change so late in the game, Danny Young might also lose his intensity and focus. Sure, Young was a professional police officer, a highly regarded detective in a paramilitary organization. He was trained to take orders and obey the command staff. He was also human. He had been working relentlessly on the case from the first night of Estabrook's phone call, and that level of commitment and dedication arose in part from the fact that it was "his" case. Now Harakles had become "his partner," and it was "their" case. The same human qualities that fueled dedication and energy also fueled possessiveness. They had to be acknowledged and respected.

There was something else at play as well. Included in the qualities that made the pair such good detectives were stubbornness and tenacity. Harakles would be the first to admit that he was stubborn, especially when people were trying push their agenda on him. Now that Amy's body had been found, it seemed that everyone had an opinion or wanted a piece of the case; and now that it was a confirmed MSP case, people up the food chain were taking an interest. Chief Chitwood's habit of playing to the media, so different from the more cautious policy of the MSP and the attorney general's office of revealing little information, had led to discussions about pulling the case away from Young and the Portland police.

Those discussions made the partners feel threatened and distracted from all the real work that needed to be done. By early Wednesday no decision had been made, but the two detectives joined the debate that evening with the feeling that their backs were against the wall. Higher-ups were pushing them around generally and, in particular, pushing them to go to Alabama without giving them a chance to discuss it when they knew the case best. They didn't feel the same sense of urgency others did, but after ten minutes' discussion, they decided they should go.

"Matt, are you out of your friggin' mind? No. Absolutely no, we are not splitting these guys up. Not now!" The hair bristles on my neck. I can literally feel the problem.

The standoff is over, and Gorman is in custody. We've got work to do in Troy, and now Matt's telling me Detective Harakles will not get on a plane. He had a bad experience recently in an MSP fly and is adamant about not going. He and Danny want to go, but they want to drive.

Matt says, "My bosses are saying Harakles either gets on a plane or they are assigning someone else. Plus they are crazy to drive!"

I agree. "Well, shit, Matt, I think it's crazy to drive, too." It's 2022. We've all just been through this tense standoff. We're still at work and all we want to do is go home. But we've got this difficult situation.

"What time is the flight, Matt?"

"0830," he says. "They've gotta move if they're gonna beat the probation guys who will be down the next day."

"Matt, what is the freaking rush? Gorman's not going anywhere."

"Well, they have an obligation," Matt says, "and we need to interview down there before he's on uncomfortable ground. Probation is going to pick him up soon." He goes over reasoning and strategy, and I agree. Matt is a prudent man.

However, I'm sick of everyone poking their noses into our world after all the work our guys did on this. We've been at this almost eight weeks and I'm thinking, What? Command staff and outside forces are going to start influencing this now? There are so many players watching or wanting a piece of this. Our own and the MSP brass and administration, other cops, the public, the news.

Inside I'm shouting no! If it were up to me, I'd just send 'em by car if that's what they want.

But the situation has changed. Technically, it's now an MSP case and new people have access. It's no longer just our small working group. I'm doing a precarious and difficult balancing act, trying to keep everyone together. It means a lot of stroking egos. A lot of follow-up calls. A lot of diplomacy. Tonight my diplomacy's wearing kind of thin.

"Can't we talk Scott into getting on this fly?" *I ask.*

Matt is confused now, trying to calm me *down for once, his face returning to its normal color.* "No," *he says,* "he won't go."

I'm pacing now, nearly as jerky as Tommy. Nothing is easy with this thing. We've had a week of wild breaks and now this. "Ahh, shit, Matt. Go get those guys, please."

Matt leaves. I start on my messages to occupy me while I wait, knowing it will only aggravate me. "Yes, so, Lieutenant Loughlin, I have a problem. You people made an illegal entry into a dwelling . . . your detective had no probable cause to . . . Beeep. *A somber, low voice.* "Lieutenant Loughlin, my brother committed suicide last Wednesday and I need his personal effects, can you . . ." *I get through four messages before Scott and Dan are shadowing the doorway as the message voice continues,* "and I can't believe that the medical examiner never, never called my brother about . . ."

I push the "off" button, frustrated. There's so much to do and these are people's lives. I must attend to them.

"Scott, stop biting your nails!" *Scott's athletic figure leans in the doorway. It doesn't match his behavior. I've been biting my nails as well. Finding Amy has brought intense focus back on us. The press is full of the question, why no arrest? Of course everyone is tense. Right now, we have to put that out of our minds and deal with the business before us.*

Danny starts in. "Lieutenant, we can do this, I know it. If we leave at 0430, we can make it. If Scott doesn't go, I'm not going."

Oh, man! Now it's both of them digging their heels in. Dan is treading carefully, though. He is very respectful of the chain of command. Does Danny want to drive, too? Is that what I'm getting? One thing I'm sure I'm getting. These guys are crazy. It's over a thousand miles to Alabama.

Tension is high. I'm impatient. I want to argue but I stifle myself. Trying to be like Deputy Chief Tim Burton, to listen, absorb, and not judge. Yet.

"*Lieutenant,*" *Scott chimes in,* "*I am not being disrespectful, but I cannot get on that plane, and I'm with Danny. If you guys break us up this will go downhill . . . just the learning curve alone . . .*"

It continues and I listen to both of them go on. "*Lieutenant, I know we can do it. We want to do it. We can talk the case all the way down. It will be a good thing.*"

Finally, I'm out of patience. "*Scott, damn it, stop biting! Let me talk to Scott alone.*" *Everyone leaves.* "*Scott, you sure you can't fly? It doesn't make sense to me, based on what I know about you.*"

"*Lieutenant, I'm not flying. I have two kids, and ever since my last MSP fly and 9/11, I just can't, sir. I just can't.*"[1]

"*Okay, Scott.*" *Matt Stewart returns to my office and gives me this bewildered look.* "*They're staying together,*" *I tell him.* "*Give me Brian's number again.*" *Lieutenant Brian McDonough is my counterpart in the MSP food chain. A good man. A gentle, graying Irishman with a good sense of humor.*

I dial. "*Brian? Yeah? It's Joe Loughlin. What the fuck! We've got a situation.*"

Matt throws his arms up in disbelief at what I just said and starts turning red again. I'm talking to his boss. But I know Brian and believe we can work together on this.

McDonough and I start in. "*Look, Brian. I know it doesn't make sense, but we absolutely cannot separate these two.*" *I'm convinced that's the heart of the matter—the critical thing is keeping Danny and Scott together. I'm willing to fight for them to go.* "*Let 'em go,*" *I tell him. It gets a bit heated and I tread water for a few because now this is technically an MSP case.*

"*My bosses don't care at this point and will send someone else,*" *he says.*

"*Shit, Brian,*" *I tell him,* "*your bosses didn't know squat 'til now. They haven't been doing this since 21 October either, damn it.*" *I am frazzled and mad.* "*Gimme Chick's number [Captain Chick Love is next up the MSP food chain]. I'll call him next. Right now. The clock's running. If these guys are going, they've got prep to do.*"

I give it a beat, then go on, trying to convince him. "*Brian, if they stay together, they can and* will *do it. Pull 'em apart and Danny will shut down and then what? I won't even tell Tommy at this point. Brian, I appeal to your investigative sense. You know what I'm talking about.*"

"Joe, Joe, I agree," he says. "Hang on. Let me make some calls. Give me thirty and I'll call you back."

Matt's got that stare again. "What?" I ask him. "Go tell those guys to plan, but hang on, Matt."

Forty minutes later my pager goes off. I call Brian. "Joe," he says, "they go."

I breathe a heavy sigh of relief even as my headache sings. "Thank you, Brian. I'll keep you up on this. Tell you what. I'll keep Chitwood away from the news." We laugh and hang up.

Dan and Scott block my doorway, looking like hopeful kids, Matt's head behind them. "Get your shit and go, guys. I still think you're crazy, but go. And don't screw me up on this."

I'm about to punch my message button again when Danny says, "We won't let you down, Lieutenant. We won't let Amy down."

On Thursday morning, embarking on a crazy journey that typified Young's unstoppable, tanklike nature and Harakles's tireless enthusiasm, the two primary detectives climbed into Harakles's unmarked cruiser and left for Alabama. Everyone else might have thought it was crazy, but they really *preferred* to drive, welcoming the opportunity to thoroughly discuss the case and plan their approach to Gorman. As the miles flew past, however, Scott Harakles was feeling very lonely. It felt strange and wrong to be heading away from his family so close to Christmas.

He learned something interesting about his partner on the trip. Danny Young might be a fine detective, but he had a lousy sense of direction. Twice on the way down, while Harakles was dozing, Danny got lost.

As they got closer to Alabama, Harakles began to get excited. Unlike Young, he had never met Gorman. He'd only seen Gorman on video, observing Gorman's arrogance and disrespect. This would be Gorman's first custodial interrogation, as opposed to the voluntary interviews at the Portland Police Department. What they, and the attorney general's office, wanted was to lock Gorman into his initial story about dropping Amy off. Both detectives knew that a lot was hanging in the balance. They needed to manipulate Gorman into repeating the story and not let him see that it would be to his advantage to change it.

Like the day of the search for Amy's body with a snowstorm coming, this turned out to be another race against the clock. They wanted to get to

Troy in time to interview Gorman before the Probation and Parole officers returned him to Maine. When they left, they thought they'd have a day with Gorman. As it happened, they arrived at 11:00 a.m. on Friday to find that the probation officers were scheduled to leave Troy an hour later.

Their primary reason for going to Alabama right away was their interest in interviewing Gorman one more time while he was still on home ground, but shaken from his encounter with police. Once he was back in a Maine jail, even though the only crime he was accused of was probation violation, they knew he would lawyer up, and no one would be able to talk with him about Amy St. Laurent.

Part of their strategy as well was the element of surprise. If Gorman wasn't expecting to have to deal with them until he was back in Maine, he might be shocked by their sudden appearance. This, in turn, could throw him off balance, and he might inadvertently say things he normally wouldn't.

They were also eager to test Gorman's reactions to some of their newly discovered information, now that they knew many things that *only* he, or he and their witnesses, could know. In particular, now that the detectives knew about the Westbrook traffic stop, they wanted to see which version of the story he would give about the night Amy disappeared. Would Gorman stick to his earlier story that he dropped Amy off at the Pavilion, was back in twenty minutes, and stayed in for the rest of the night, or would he give them the same story he'd been giving his friends and relatives about Sharma and Cook having left with Amy while he stayed home?

Given Gorman's demonstrated familiarity with the criminal justice system and the police interrogation process, and based on his prior behavior, they also believed he would be interested in speaking with them to test *their* knowledge of things. It was a common practice with experienced criminals. With sociopaths. Gorman had engaged in various forms of testing and disinformation throughout the investigation. It would be, the detectives expected, a battle of wits in which their job was to be more clever.

Driving like teenagers on a road trip, they left Maine around 9:30 on Thursday morning, reaching South Carolina early Friday morning, at 2:00 a.m. They slept for four hours, leaving around 6:00 a.m. with about four more hours to drive.

They fought their way through the morning snarl of Atlanta traffic and reached Troy with only an hour to spare—an hour they got only because Troy is in another time zone. Troy is a quiet southern town of about fifteen thousand, located about fifty miles from Montgomery, which is home to Troy State University.

Although they had had a telephone relationship with the Troy Police Department (primarily with Detective Sergeant Calista Everage) since the initial request for Gorman's records, Young and Harakles had no idea what kind of a reception they would receive. Scott Harakles said that when you go into a situation where you have to lean on other agencies, you never know what you'll get—often there is a coldness or hesitation. But the reception and support they got in Troy were exceptional.

Because time was short, they were quickly provided with an interview room and taping capability. They immediately began taping an interview with Gorman, putting into play their plan to use Harakles as the interviewer. As expected, Gorman didn't want to deal with Danny Young. From the first, he'd known that Young didn't believe him. He tried to get rid of Young and speak with Scott Harakles alone, probably thinking he'd have a better shot at manipulating the younger detective. He couldn't split them up, and the interview proceeded with both detectives, Harakles sitting directly in front of Gorman with Young sitting behind Harakles.

Gorman began the interview as his usual cocky and arrogant self, projecting the attitude he'd exhibited all along—oh, yeah, you cops don't know anything. Harakles asked Gorman to tell them again about the night he dropped Amy off, and he responded, "I already told you all about that."

Harakles said, "Yeah, well, I haven't heard it, so just humor me and tell me what happened."

Gorman responded, "You know . . . I dropped her off and came straight home . . ." and went over the story again. As Gorman talked, Harakles felt the last uneasiness about leaving his family vanish, replaced by excitement.

Once they'd gotten him to repeat his story, and had seen that it was unchanged and that they had him on tape, locked into his lie, in Harakles's words, they took off their gloves and went at him with what they now knew—asking, Okay, so what about this, and what about that? Challenging his timeline, his lies, his accusations against Jason and Kush. The detectives wanted to see him dance, and they got what they wanted.

Suddenly Gorman the cocky loudmouth, the born manipulator, the slick liar, began to come apart. When Harakles asked what Gorman had to say about telling Jamie that his roommates had killed Amy, Gorman's eyes widened, and he abandoned his arrogant slouch. Looking like he'd seen a ghost, he told the investigators, "I think I need an attorney."

Since it was now legally a case with custody and interrogation, the investigators had to stop asking questions, but Harakles told Gorman, "No more questions, okay, but I'm going to talk and you're going to listen." Then he laid out what they had and told Gorman he was going down.

When they left that interview room, they could have gone straight home. They'd gotten what they came for. But they were there, so they went on working.

Their next interview was with Sean Littlefield, who had gone to Alabama with Gorman. The investigators had high hopes that Gorman would have told him something, since Littlefield was a good enough friend to have gone to Alabama with him and had been on the scene as Gorman was unraveling, but Littlefield didn't have much to offer. Littlefield told them that he and Gorman left for Alabama in Littlefield's car a week before Thanksgiving, driving pretty much straight through with Gorman doing most of the driving because Littlefield was sick. He said that Gorman's mother called frequently, reporting in one of her earliest calls that Gorman's driver's license was being suspended or revoked.

Littlefield described an occasion before they left Maine when Gorman stopped at the Pavilion nightclub, leaving Sean in the car, and went in to ask if they had cameras so he could prove that his car had been there the night he said he'd dropped Amy off. Gorman also checked out the presence of cameras at the Stein Gallery across the street. Littlefield told them that, in the beginning, Gorman maintained his story that he'd dropped Amy off and that all he'd done that night was kiss Amy.

Later, Littlefield said, after the Portland paper reported that police investigation showed Gorman hadn't dropped her at the Pavilion, Gorman's story changed. Littlefield overheard Gorman on the phone, telling a local friend that Kush and Jason had killed her, that he had told them about the spot behind his mother's house and they had put her there and gone back later to bury her. Littlefield said that Russ did tell him that Amy had been shot in the head, but that Jason and Kush had done it. At that point, no one outside the investigation except the killer knew that Amy had been shot in the head.

Littlefield also told them that his former girlfriend, Tiffany, had talked a lot about Gorman and his connection to the case. Tiffany had told people at her school that she knew what had happened and who did it, and that she could get a lot of money from him (Russ) but she wouldn't, because she thought he was cute.[2]

Littlefield also told them that the first week they were in Alabama, Gorman got a gun, a .25. That he got a second, similar gun just before the standoff and would sit around and play with the guns. Littlefield told them that when Gorman had to leave his grandmother's house because his uncle was getting out of prison, they were invited to stay with Erika Walker, a family friend.

When Young and Harakles finished taping their interview with Littlefield, they turned to the local police department for advice about who else it would be wise to speak with, including local people the two detectives had learned about in their interview with Littlefield. Having let Gorman run, hoping that he'd talk, they now wanted to find the people he might have talked with—friends, relatives, people he'd hung out with, and girls he'd slept with.

The cooperation of the Troy Police Department was amazing—another gift in the case. Detective Sergeant Calista Everage seemed to be on a first-name basis with everyone in town. As Scott Harakles put it, the Everages were a police family but they were also members of the community, and they knew their people. Calista Everage just asked the two visiting detectives who they wanted, took down a list of those people, secured their cooperation, brought them to the station, and marched them, one by one, into the interview room. For Young and Harakles, that generous assistance was another example of the unprecedented bond between police agencies that Amy's case had forged.

The next person they interviewed after Littlefield was a long-distance truck driver in her late thirties named Erika Walker, a longtime friend of the family known to Gorman and others as "Mamma E." Walker was a rough-edged, tough-talking woman who had her own history with the

Troy police, a history revolving around substances like mushrooms and crystal meth. She was an emotional woman, very volatile and unstable. In Harakles's words, "sketchy, bouncy, all over the place." She also had a good and valuable story to tell.

Walker was another of the witnesses in the case who were deeply pained by the conflict between their belief that they had to tell what they knew—Walker was the mother of a daughter herself—and their sense that in speaking with the police, they were betraying a close friend or relative, in Walker's case this kid that she'd known for most of his life. At first, she was reluctant to talk, expressing concern that either Gorman might come after her or someone who knew him might retaliate against her if she told the detectives what she knew.

After Young and Harakles reassured her that Gorman was going to stay in jail, and played on her evident desire to cooperate and clear her conscience of what was obviously troubling information, she quickly gave up her reluctance.[3] Danny Young just told her, very directly, "Come on . . . you *know* you want to tell us." And Young had a way about him that made people trust him.

After that, Walker relaxed and agreed to talk. About a week after he had arrived in Troy, Walker told them, Russ was visiting, and he said to her, "Mama E, I need to clear my conscience about something." She poured him a cup of coffee and said, "Well, go ahead and talk."

He took a deep breath and said, "I did kill that girl up there. We went for a walk and I was tripping and all of a sudden she said something to me that kinda slapped my face and I just went off on her and after I got done with her, I shot her in the head."

As Mrs. Walker was talking, Danny Young was thinking, "Boy, I sure hope the tape is working." With all his experience, he still listened with a sense of disbelief at what he was hearing. Even for seasoned detectives, getting information like this is exciting. Their training in interviewing and interrogation really comes into play when they're getting great stuff, and they have to control their emotions, their body language, and their facial expressions so their elation doesn't show. When a breakthrough moment happens, even as the information is coming in, detectives will check and recheck to be sure they're following protocol and that all the equipment is working, always fearful that this vital evidence will somehow be lost.

Luckily, everything was working fine for Young and Harakles, and they recorded a second, more detailed version of Gorman's confession than the one he had made to his mother.

Gorman told Mamma E that after he killed Amy in a fit of rage he then realized that he had done something wrong, so he cleaned himself up and he cleaned her up to make sure there was nothing of him left on her and then he dug a hole and put her in it, hoping that the ground would freeze before they were able to find her.

In response to the detectives' questions, Walker also told them the following: That Russ told her he had a big .45 gun at the house and asked if she wanted to see it. That he had walked Amy beside the pond to set the mood.[4] That Russ also told her he had slapped or punched Amy—at one point he even got down on the floor and demonstrated for Mrs. Walker how he had pinned Amy to the ground and beaten her. That after he had Amy on the ground, he pulled the gun out of the back of his pants and shot her.

At one point, in the middle of the interview, Mrs. Walker told the detectives she wanted to go outside and smoke. In response to her cooperation and in order to keep up the good relations, they had let her go, but they sweated bullets until she returned to the interview room, worrying that she might change her mind about talking and leave before she finished the story.

She did return to finish the interview. She told the detectives that with respect to women, Russ Gorman was a real whore dog. She'd known him to go with one girl, bring her home, and go right out and get another. Although he never came right out and told Mamma E that he'd had sex with Amy, those had been his intentions, and he also assured her that he'd kept himself protected. That later he had burned his clothes and burned Amy's so that there would be nothing of him left at the scene. That when he'd buried her, he had carefully put the grass back. And he hinted about getting rid of a gun by dropping it off a pier. Walker told the detectives that Russ also told all this to his mother, and told his mother why he had done it.

What Gorman had told Mrs. Walker meshed with the information Young and Harakles had learned from Amy St. Laurent's autopsy. It also gave them a better picture of their victim's last moments of life, and of the callous brutality of the man who had assaulted and murdered her. The gunshot, the assault, the carefully replaced clumps of grass, and the missing clothes were all pieces of information only the killer would know.

*

Back in Portland, an exhausted Sergeant Joyce had actually made it to the CID Christmas party, which is where he was when Danny Young called him to report on the Erika Walker interview. Sergeant Joyce grabbed Lieutenant Loughlin and they retreated into a corner while Joyce shared the news. The two of them stood there, stunned by this news of a second confession, as Christmas sounds echoed around them.

Everywhere you go, radios, elevators, store speakers are blaring holiday music. Who's got time for Christmas? It's incredible, the amount of work. The stresses and strains of a major case. The tensions between personnel. Do we search? Interview him now? Later? What about . . . what about . . . what about? A billion questions are thrown at me. On the phone with the press, the attorney general's office, the chief, state police, detectives, the mother, the mother's friends, the father, the VWA (victim witness advocate). Dozens of messages await me constantly. The guys are exhausted and we're worried about Dan and Scott out there on the road.

What about the Christmas party? Christmas party! We're working twelve-hour days, twenty-hour days. Running nonstop. But I'm the lieutenant. I should go.

At the bar after work, I feel surreal and spacey. People around me talk about normal life. Christmas parties. Going to eat. Going to shows. I shouldn't have come. I feel so out of sorts here. Everyone is in such an upbeat mood. The tinkles of glasses and silverware mix with laughter.

Tommy catches my eye. Something's going on and I know he needs to talk now. I bring my manhattan with me, as Tommy, parakeeting and jumpy, his tie swaying from the movement, backs me into a corner away from the noise.

He pauses, giving me that blue-eyed stare. I know he's got something good. Then he starts in, excited as he tells me Danny's just called. "The guys got a second confession from Gorman direct to a woman down there. She told them everything!"

Excitement grips me as I grab Tom's arm and shake him. "This is getting good, Tom." I clink my glass against his beer bottle.

Yes, I think, yes, we are gonna get this guy.

It's good news, but it doesn't put me in a party mood. I move through the crowd and out the side door into the street. It's cold and wet and I'm refreshed to be away from everyone. I'm heading home as soon as I stop at the station. I'm sick of the "station."

You can't explain the whole process to people. They're thinking, hey, you've found her, it's over, when it's just the beginning of a new chapter for us. A new chapter that is getting very interesting.

Walker's interview was followed by three more interviews at the Troy Police Station, including a woman Gorman had slept with who claimed to have had an out-of-body experience in which she saw the whole crime and knew that Gorman was innocent. Two others told the detectives that they had witnessed situations where Gorman had become uncontrollably angry when turned down by a woman. One said Gorman had been driving around with a gun in his lap. All the interviews were videotaped, and Young and Harakles brought those tapes back to Maine.

Later in the evening, around 8:00 p.m., the detectives, accompanied by Detective Sergeant Everage, went to the home of Gorman's paternal grandmother, Dot Gorman. Although Gorman had boasted to his ex-girlfriend Jamie that his "grammy" had plenty of money, it was clear this was a family that was just making do, as evidenced by the fact that although part of the living room floor had collapsed, the residents hadn't fixed it but were simply walking around the hole.

While Harakles took Dot's son, Daniel Gorman, out to the porch and spoke with him, Detective Young interviewed Dot Gorman. She told Young her grandson couldn't have done it and began to cry. Asked if she had ever seen Gorman with a gun, she stated that he'd gotten one when he arrived in Alabama, explaining that he needed it because he'd been "threatened." She then related Gorman's story about being threatened by Jason Cook and Kush Sharma. Gorman had told her he knew where Amy St. Laurent's body was only because of the threats and the fact that Jason had asked him where to put a body.

It was hard for the detectives, even though they knew she was "family" and had a difficult time facing the fact that her grandson had committed such a horrific act, to listen to the denials of a woman who had, herself, sometimes been the victim of Gorman's crimes.[5] To hear, as they so often did, about what a sweet little boy Russ Gorman had been, going to Sunday school and saying his nightly prayers.

When Young and Harakles arrived in Troy, they had gone straight to work. They interviewed steadily for about twelve hours. Around 11 p.m. Friday night, as the two weary detectives finished their last interview, they realized that they had been so focused they hadn't eaten all day. They also hadn't thought about a place to sleep.

Since there weren't many places to stay in Troy, they decided to drive as far as Montgomery, grab some of the fast food that Harakles loved, and find a motel.

In Montgomery, revived by food and coffee, Harakles decided he really wasn't all that tired and might as well drive awhile. Young agreed, and the two of them, running on only about four hours of sleep in the past thirty-six hours, hit the road again. From the start, these two men had been mission driven. Now, with their investigation finally going right, they were moving into another realm. A week of getting big breaks, which told them they were going to be able to get a killer off the street, had filled them with excitement and adrenaline. They just wanted to get home and start working with all they'd learned.

They never did stop for the night. Combined with their passion for the job was their passion for their families. Harakles was eager to get back to his wife and two small children. Danny Young had a grandchild appearing in a Christmas program on Sunday and he really wanted to be there. With all that on their minds, the two men figured, what the hell, why not, and kept on driving.

On Saturday afternoon at 6:00, Danny Young pulled into his driveway. His wife, Linda, came out of the house, ready to be mad at him for being so crazy. But it was just Danny Young, being, as always, unstoppable. A man who cut himself no more slack than he gave the bad guys and who believed in honoring his commitments. Young diffused his wife's anger with a tired grin. "Give me a hug," he said, "and welcome me home."

15

On Friday, December 14, while Danny Young and Scott Harakles were in Troy, Alabama, working on the case, and Probation and Parole was bringing Gorman back to Maine, Amy St. Laurent's family and friends gathered in the chapel at Conroy-Tully Funeral Home in South Portland to hold a memorial service for her. Although her principal champions were unable to be there, representatives from the Portland and Maine State Police were.

A large, framed photograph of Amy stood on a table at the front of the chapel, while twenty-five white candles set amid evergreens and pink roses marked the years of her short life. The same kind of roses Amy's father, Dennis, had given her every year on her birthday. Pink roses for Amy, yellow for Julie. A sad reminder that there would be no more birthdays.

Amy's mother, Diane Jenkins, told the listeners that her daughter "would rather we celebrate her life than dwell on how it ended," while her stepfather, Don Jenkins, reminded her friends to keep her memory alive by sharing their stories among themselves and with others who hadn't known her. Her mother recited the Prayer of Saint Francis:

> Lord, make me an instrument of Your peace.
> Where there is hatred, let me sow love;
> where there is injury, pardon;
> where there is doubt, faith;
> where there is despair, hope;
> where there is darkness, light;
> and where there is sadness, joy.

O, Divine Master,
grant that I may not so much seek
to be consoled as to console;
to be understood as to understand;
to be loved as to love;
for it is in giving that we receive;
it is in pardoning that we are pardoned;
and it is in dying that we are born to eternal life.

The prayer summed up Amy's character for those who had known her. Amy St. Laurent had been a loving and generous young woman, a giver, not a taker, and a consoler of those who needed consolation. Amy's mother chose it, as well, as a message from Amy to those she had left behind, about how their lives should be lived in remembrance of her.

The Reverend Eric Kelley urged his listeners to honor Amy St. Laurent's memory by making choices that would make the world a safer place for themselves and for others. "We are gathered today because of a profound tragedy that defies words. We also are gathered because of a young woman who packed a lot of living in twenty-five short years." Summing up the woman investigators had come to know, Kelley said, "Her living was marked by generosity, optimism, kindness, enthusiasm, humor, and love of life."

Amy Elizabeth St. Laurent. Her composed, smiling face staring at me again, only this time from the obituary page. 25, of South Berwick, who was missing since October 21, 2001, was found Saturday, December 8, 2001, in Scarborough.

0703. My TV LED blinks as the smell of coffee mixed with newspaper moves through my nose. Newsprint smears on my fingers, making them feel thick. Today is the day of the memorial service. The worst will be watching and absorbing everyone's pain and sadness.

"She attended Portland schools . . . was employed for the past five years as a secretary/technician at Pratt & Whitney. She was fond of her cat, Alex."

Oh, yeah. The cat. I recall the small cat at the grave site. So strange. So poignant. "She is survived by . . ." The list is long, ". . . and many friends that will miss her dearly."

My pager bleeps, jarring me from quiet thought. For a moment I think, Jeez, can't we ever have a little peace and quiet? But the truth is, with this job, we can't. It's Tom, explaining that there's a lot going on. Danny and Scott are in Alabama and soon they'll be sitting down with Gorman. There is an early morning staff meeting and a detectives' meeting in the case.

We still have a tremendous amount of work, documentation, and follow-up to do and, at this stage, we're proceeding with meticulous caution. We do not want to lose this guy to some loophole.

It's Friday, December 14, 2001. Another weekend approaching with no weekend for the guys. "Tom," I say, "I don't care. I am going to the service today. Did Matt call in yet? Hold off that meeting 'til 1300, and get Bruce to take over the evidence technicians."

The Conroy-Tully chapel is in South Portland. A funeral home, not a church like I'd anticipated, given my Catholic upbringing. It looks stark and cold from the outside. Matt and I park our cars across the street. Many times, police officers attend such services to survey the crowd and look for suspects and information, but our suspect is in jail. Our presence here is personal. Matt is once again perfectly dressed in a gray suit, freshly pressed shirt. Immaculate. The GQ detective. I adjust my suit and tie, polishing my shoes on the back of my pant legs. Matt looks at me funny.

"Listen," I say, "it works. I do it all the time."

Matt is polishing his glasses and we look at each other. This is going to be tough, but there is strength in numbers. I dread seeing Diane and Julie, recalling my own parents' pain when my brother Anthony was laid out in his coffin. That's the worst part of this job, the worst—observing people in such pain. We see so much pain. Sometimes you can just see it build up until the anguish is so great people are visibly searching for a way to escape, longing to leave their own bodies or just completely throw themselves into grief like screaming infants. It's primal and horribly disturbing.

The crowd is shuffling and snaking around to get in line, all those bodies giving off aftershave and perfume. Suits and nice dresses, ties and polished shoes mingle with dirty shoes and outfits hastily pulled together. The long line slowly moves into the funeral home and then into the chapel. People bumping into each other, distracted and numb. Inside, the funeral home is warm and inviting, but the air is heavy with sorrow.

I see Lucille first. She gives me a sad smile and we embrace. I ask where

Diane is, preparing myself for my first sight of her since the morning of the day we found Amy. I throw my arm around the ever stoic Matt as we move into the chapel. I see the familiar framed picture of Amy on the table, surrounded by white candles, greens, and lovely pink roses.

My neck is tight and my palms are sweaty. I spot Diane ahead, moving through the shuffling, halting line until I reach her. She is so composed and graceful, so elegantly put together, but her long, immaculate hair frames a face in which the eyes are tragically sad. She gives me a gracious smile, so glad and pleased to see that Matt and I have come.

I wrap my arms around her, embracing her with a heartfelt hug. We've been through seven awful weeks together. This is not merely a professional courtesy. This is for Amy. This is for her family. In my arms, Diane gives a slight heave, her body shaking, her head bent to hide her face.

We're supposed to box it up. Lock it out and get on with the job. I've stored up twenty-plus years of stifling my emotions while witnessing the howl of human agony. Now I worry it will come spilling out. I'm so close to this one.

"Thank you so much for bringing Amy home," she says.

"It was Danny, Diane. Danny and Scott and a lot of other people."

We move on to Amy's sister, Julie. The little sister. So close to Amy. Still struggling to comprehend all this. I know about losing a sibling, about the space it leaves in a family, in your mind. Poor Julie, eyes downcast, her blonde hair falling forward, eyelashes brushing the tops of her cheekbones. Her sorrow is weighty and tangible. She wipes a tear away with poise and precision. She has her mother's grace.

"Julie," I say. We hug and I feel her body shaking with tears. "Your sister is okay, Julie, she's okay and safe with God. I believe that. You believe that." It's true.

Then on to Amy's father, Dennis, and Kathy Emery, and to her stepfather, Don. All of them so terribly sad. We embrace. Shake hands. Dennis thanks me again in a sad, gravelly voice. "You guys did a good job." I know Dennis's life has not been easy and that his lovely daughter was a source of great pride and joy. Now, his suffering is mute and terrible.

As we take our seats and the ceremony begins, a whiff of pine flashes me back to the night of the dig. To the needles sprinkled on her grave, the pine needles buried with her. We are here to celebrate a life, but my head is full of death.

Diane is composed and eloquent as she speaks, telling us Amy would want us to celebrate her life rather than dwell on her death. She recites the Prayer of Saint Francis, which is something I try to repeat every day. Another strange connection in this case. Is it Amy speaking to me? Speaking to us?

Reverend Kelley tells us, "We are free beings in a world that is both wonderful and dangerous at the same time . . . We've had to recognize the reality of evil that can and does destroy so much of what we love, and it is something that must be confronted."

I know evil exists. All cops do.

I think of confrontation and of how I'd like to confront Gorman. I imagine . . . That's as far as it gets. As a caring human being, I'd like to confront Gorman. As a trained and experienced police officer, I've learned to handle those feelings and suppress the emotions. Always that split between the personal and the professional. It takes a toll, though. I'm sure Matt feels the same.

I quickly turn to prayer to stop the intrusion. I listen to the talk about Amy, imagining her as an angel now. Rest in peace, Amy, I think, and help us all in this crazy world. Move among us in grace.

Outside in the cold, Matt and I are approached by the news and each of us make statements.

Matt says, "All the investigators involved from both agencies have made a tremendous personal and professional commitment to the case . . . As a group we are extremely optimistic and resolved to see it to its successful conclusion."

Well done, Matt, I think. I am proud of him. And us.

I say a few words about how difficult the investigation has been . . . both with the situation and working with multiple agencies. That Amy kept us together . . . another positive influence of Amy in the midst of this horrible tragedy.

I reflect to myself that "tremendous" is a good word. In my entire career, I have never observed such an effective working relationship between agencies to get a job completed. Rarely have we had a case go on so long with such intensity. It was a monumental challenge—putting egos, rank, agency protocol aside and keeping everyone together.

In my leadership challenges, I felt it was a personal triumph, keeping everyone locked in. Thank you, Amy, I think. Dan and Scott the final glue that brought you home.

I leave feeling sad, but at least they can finally have a funeral. I think of all the cases where that doesn't happen. Where families wait years or decades or forever, and never get an answer, the missing person's room maintained, untouched. I've seen the toll it takes.

One young couple who had been recipients of Amy's generosity left a letter at the service. Their story was that, several years before, they had been financially strapped, their rent was due, and they were facing a bleak Christmas for their child. Amy, aware of their situation, had taken money out of her savings account, filled an envelope, and given it to them. Their letter read:

Dear Amy,

You're the truest most sincere friend we have ever had. You're a constant ray of light in our life, never judged or spoke unkindly towards anyone. You were there for us at our lowest points and we always swore if you ever needed us, we would be there for you. We were wrong and will be eternally sorry and heart struck that we couldn't help you when you needed someone the most.

We know you're in heaven. We think of heaven as a place reserved for the best of human kind, which does not even begin to describe you. The person or persons who did this to you must not have known you because anyone who knew you would have laid down their life for you. We can take comfort from knowing that you're looking down on us all and we pray we will see you again some day.

All our love, Amy.

Amy St. Laurent was the girl who used her own money to fly her best friend, Kate, home from Alaska as a surprise for Kate's grandparents' fiftieth wedding anniversary. She was the girl who took a leave of absence from work to sit in the hospital by the bedside of a friend who was in a coma, talking for hours about things they'd done together. She was the merry girl who played Mrs. Claus at the Pratt & Whitney Christmas party and hid Easter eggs for children.

Amy St. Laurent was celebrated as a person who was generous and loving, who was always thinking of others and giving them whatever she had, whether it was her time, her attention, or the contents of her savings account. And in the midst of their tears, as they recounted their special stories about Amy, those who loved her could not avoid the bitterness of knowing that a person who had done so much to enhance life had been taken from them in a brutal and horrific way by a young man who had never done anything with his life except indulge himself and prey on other people.

16

Danny Young and Scott Harakles might have taken a Sunday off to spend time with their families after their marathon trip to Alabama, but on Monday they were right back at work. There was a lot to process from their interviews in Troy. There would be more meetings with the medical examiner. More follow-up from the discovery of Amy's body. They continued to look for witnesses who might help them connect Gorman with a gun. They searched for Gorman's clothes and St. Laurent's clothes, or a place where they might have been burned, and the murder weapon.

On December 10, Portland police arranged to have divers search the small ponds near the spot where the body had been buried.[1] On December 21, responding in part to Erika Walker's statement that Gorman had told her he'd dropped the gun off a pier, state police, Marine Patrol, and Portland police divers searched Portland Harbor near Union Wharf and some of the adjacent piers.

Because of Gorman's familiarity with the Game Room and the Westbrook area, and the possibility that Gorman might have retrieved the gun from Ryan Campbell's room on the Monday or Tuesday after the crime, police divers also searched the Presumpscot River in Westbrook behind the Game Room.

They continued to question witnesses among the pool of young adults who hung around the Old Port or the pool hall, collecting information to fill out their picture of Gorman. Sergeant Stewart described these young people, with their marginal jobs and their pleasure-seeking lifestyles, as "like college kids without the brains and the classes. Every night is a party

Portland police Detective Sergeant Bruce Coffin with state police divers as they prepare to search Portland Harbor for the murder weapon.

and every day is the time to sleep it off." They were people just living day to day. Scott Harakles added: "Every time we went to the apartment on Brighton Avenue, they were all asleep."

As the detectives filled in their picture of Gorman's behavior toward women, they revised their original impression of him. At first, Young said, his view of Gorman had been that the word "predator" was too harsh but that here was a guy who used women for his own sexual benefit. Now that they knew more and had seen what he'd done to Amy, they concluded that Gorman was indeed a sexual predator.[2]

In the course of their investigation, Young and Harakles had located at least three young women who had had what they described as nonconsensual sex with Gorman. All their stories were depressingly similar. The women had been with Gorman, he had made them a drink or given them a drink, and they later found that they had had sex with him without a memory of the encounter, or recalled having a sexual encounter in which they were too dazed or helpless to protest or to stop it.

These stories were consistent with Ryan Campbell's speculation that

Gorman used drugs to ensure his success. When one young woman, after a forced sexual encounter with Gorman, told her girlfriends what had happened, they shook their heads and said, "Join the club." In each case, the woman did not report the assault or try to press charges, because she felt so guilty, believing that it was her fault for letting it happen. Like any successful predator, Gorman was adept at selecting victims whose guilt, low self-esteem, or passive personalities would ensure his success and protect him from repercussions.[3]

Along with the stories of women Gorman had assaulted, the detectives heard how he behaved when women were not compliant. Two of Gorman's friends in Alabama described him reacting badly or becoming explosive when a woman turned him down. One young woman described Gorman trapping her and demanding to know whether "it was going to happen" (i.e., was she going to have sex with him?) and slamming her roughly up against a building when she told him it wasn't. "He was really drunk," she said, "and basically, his character, when he's really drunk, he gets pretty violent."

Shyla Cameron, who worked in the Iguana, told them that after Amy St. Laurent disappeared, Gorman accosted her, Cameron, at work, complaining that she wasn't very friendly to him anymore. When she told him she was not his friend and she felt that people weren't safe around him, he suddenly grabbed her by the throat. Another of Gorman's acquaintances told Young that Gorman was very persistent about sex. She stated that she knew how many women Gorman claimed to have had sex with and that he would get angry if he was rejected by someone.

Gorman had a history of violence even toward those women with whom he was involved in long-term relationships. Gorman had beaten and kicked Kathleen Ferguson, the mother of his daughter, when she was a pregnant and vulnerable seventeen-year-old. Gorman had left threats in telephone messages to his ex-girlfriend Jamie, which her anxious mother had saved. Bob Milton, manager of the Game Room, who sometimes went out to eat or drink with Gorman, told how Gorman had expressed anger and hatred toward women, saying that he would like to shoot them in the face or cut their throat or put his foot up their ass.[4]

*

At some point in the early days after Amy St. Laurent was found, tension between state police and Portland police over Chief Chitwood's habit of speaking freely to the media boiled over. Since the night that Amy's body had been found, jurisdiction had officially transferred to the state police. In the interest of a good resolution of the case, the decision had been made to continue the cooperative relationship between the two agencies and to maintain two primary detectives. Concern over the chief's actions, however, eventually led to discussions about pulling the case away from Portland, leaving it exclusively with the state police.

Because of their long-standing relationship, Deputy AG Bill Stokes called Danny Young to give him a heads-up about the situation. The call came when Young and Harakles were doing an interview at Paradigm Windows. When Young got off the phone, he told his partner, "Scotty, they're going to take my box," meaning his box of notebooks containing all the case information.

Harakles, unfazed, said, "Well, don't worry. The box stays with you. If they took it from you, they'd only give it to me, and I'm not taking it."

Back at Portland police headquarters, Sergeant Stewart took Harakles out into the lobby on the detectives' floor and told him that steps were under way where they might be going to take the case. Just as he'd told his partner, Harakles told his sergeant that if they did pull the case from Portland, they'd better get someone else to work it, because he wasn't taking it. Later, Young grabbed a box of the case files and marched into Lieutenant Loughlin's office while Loughlin was talking with Sergeant Stewart. Holding it out, he told his surprised lieutenant, "If you want the damned box, you can have the box."

The matter was eventually resolved in a meeting between the two agencies.

On the phone in my office, I look up to see a bemused Bill Stokes leaning in my doorway. Just waiting, waiting on me, his shoulder pressed against the door frame. Typical Stokes, animated and slightly disheveled, suit opened, tie swinging.

I hang up and before I even speak, he starts, "Where's the iceberg, Joe? Are you gonna let me know before it hits? Where's the iceberg?" He removes his glasses as he steps into my office.

"What iceberg? What are you talking about, Bill?"

"I'm talking about Chitwood, Joe, Chitwood."

"Well, what about him?"

"He's going to hurt this case with his open mic to the press. You know, Joe, technically this is an MSP case. I don't want to take this away from you guys. But your department is going to hurt this."

Bill and I have a great relationship but now I'm getting mad. "Bill, Bill, why the fuck are you telling me this? Go to the chief. I can't tell the chief! I already went through this same shit with Fern on another case. This issue is with him, not me. You know our media views are diametrically opposed to your office and MSP. You know how he is with the press. But look, damn it! He's an honorable guy. Just talk to him. You're the prosecutor!"

We go on. Suddenly he says, "Heeey! Is that a granola bar?"

I look at my left hand, which has just automatically removed one from my top drawer. "Yeah. You want one?"

Bill has an amazing energy about him; it's like he's moving all the time. I see his lips smack and I toss a chocolate chip bar at him, which he snaps in midair like a frog catching a fly.

"You know, Joe, this is serious . . ."

"Yeah, no shit, Bill. No shit . . . and I don't need this now, when we've come so far. Come on, let's go to the meeting."

I get Tim Burton and tell him that I need his help at this meeting. We all squeeze into the conference room. Matt, Tom, Scott, Dan, Tim, Bill, and I. There are books, folders, case files all over the place.

It's his ball now as prosecutor, and Bill knows it as he starts out. We go over strategy and then he quickly gets to Chief Chitwood and the media, its impact on the case.

Tim knows it's going to be his job to talk to the chief, a precarious situation, as Chief Chitwood backs down from no one. He would unleash a tirade on Stokes, LaRochelle, and anyone else who confronted him. So it's a matter of presentation. Tim looks weary. He has so much going on managing this bureau. As the meeting continues, Tim slowly rises and leaves on his mission. In the end it all worked out.

The detectives continued to theorize and argue about what had happened the night Amy disappeared. Scott Harakles's theory was that, after a few

A strategy meeting in the conference room at 109. *Clockwise from front left:* Evidence technician Chris Stearns, Detective Sergeant Bruce Coffin, AAG Fern LaRochelle, Detective Sergeant Tom Joyce, Deputy AG Bill Stokes, Detective Danny Young, Detective Scott Harakles, Sergeant Matt Stewart.

days of dealing with Rubright, by Saturday night Amy was really anxious to separate from him. She was an attractive young woman who was fresh off a breakup. During the course of the evening, she met Gorman. He was charming, and he flirted with her. She wanted to send Rubright a message—look, guys are interested in me and I'm not interested in you. She exchanged phone numbers with Gorman in front of Rubright. Later, she danced with him.

Harakles thought that Rubright's story about not being able to find Amy after returning from the men's room was bullshit, that he got the message that she wasn't interested in him and got mad. That he thought, Screw her, and took off with her coat, purse, keys, and cell phone, leaving her stranded forty miles from home in the middle of the night. She needed a phone, and Sharma and Gorman seemed nice. They probably said to her, We've got a phone, come back to our place. We're having a party. If you don't want to stay, we can drive you somewhere.

Danny Young thought Rubright's claim that he couldn't find Amy was credible. That probably he was out of sight longer than he thought and that Amy had looked around for him and then left the club with Gorman and Sharma, waiting outside while Rubright waited inside. In any event, whatever had happened to keep Amy and Rubright from reconnecting, it meant that Amy was vulnerable without her coat, her purse, her phone, or a ride.

Detectives thought she might have been lulled into a false sense of security about Gorman because he knew a lot of the doormen, bouncers, and bartenders—the people in positions of perceived authority in the club world. Amy was not a party girl and wouldn't normally go off with a stranger—this was something her friends were adamant about—but she was stuck. She might have said, Well, I don't usually do this, but okay. And they might have reassured her, saying, Hey, we're okay.

Except that Gorman, the charming predator, wasn't okay. He was used to everything going smoothly for him as long as he picked the right victim—either an easygoing party girl who was out for a good time herself or, if he needed to coerce someone, a vulnerable young woman or teenage girl who would feel intimidated and guilty about what had happened. The problem arose when he picked Amy, a nice girl who wasn't easy. It explained why she was so badly beaten. Amy wouldn't have been passive. She would have fought back. And Gorman, who couldn't stand it when a woman said no, and who was known for his terrible temper when he'd been drinking, would have reacted with violent anger.

Everyone's got a theory. Mine is that after it goes bad in the car—we all figure he made his first moves in the car—after he's punched Amy in the face a few times, he takes the gun out and threatens to kill her. She's dazed and terrorized. And Gorman must think quickly. He knows he can't let her go now.

Where to take her? Campbell's house or familiar ground? Ultimately, he settles on the road near his mom's house. There he drags Amy from the car and marches or pushes her at gunpoint down that road. The scrunchie comes off. There aren't drag marks on her feet, so she walked, was carried, or went down there with shoes.

Maybe he dropped that sock on the way out. Carrying her clothes?

Somewhere near where we found her the assault continues, punching and kill threats as he tries to force her to have sex. She tries to talk to him, to resist, until ultimately he shoots her. Then he drags her to the pine trees and leaves her there, returning to bury her sometime later.

One thing we all agree on. The moonlight walk stuff is bullshit.[5]

Knowing who Gorman was and what he had done to Amy St. Laurent, it was a relief to have him locked up and off the streets, where he no longer posed a threat to the next young woman who had the audacity to say no. After all, the best predictor of future dangerousness is past behavior. Gorman had now moved from serial rapist[6] to murderer. A criminal profiler would agree that once a person has committed a sexual homicide, it is easier to commit the second. Detectives were very concerned that if Gorman ever got out, he would kill again.

Just days after Amy's memorial service, Danny and Scott are both back and the bay is busy. When the phone rings for the zillionth time, I snatch it up with irritation, expecting more work. It's Lucille Holt and she says that she and Diane want to bring us lunch to show their appreciation for all that we've done.

"Baked ziti?" I exclaim.

At noon, the food rolls in with Lucille barking out instructions. Together with their friend "Sonny," they deliver a huge Italian lunch. We all move into the conference room as they lay out our feast. As we gather around the food, it seems like it's the first time in months that we've stopped working.

Tommy's his usual fashion-plate self with a checked shirt and some kinda green tie. Matt's there, all smiles, with a crisp new haircut, the only one of us who doesn't take off his suit coat. Scott and Danny sit together, as always, smiling with pleasure as the foil is lifted off the spaghetti and meatballs and the air fills with the smells of spicy sauce.

Bruce Coffin's there, and Teceno and LeClair. Almost everyone who's worked on the case is crowded into the room.

"Tom," I call, "turn that damned TV off!" The closed-circuit TV behind us is monitoring another interrogation. He snaps it off and for a little while, there's no police work. It's just us, doing what ordinary people do in December, getting together with good people and eating great food.

It was so nice I got my camera and snapped some pictures. Comfort food, I thought. So appropriate and just what we needed.

As Diane and Lucille left us to the noise and chaos of the detectives' bay, bel-

lies full and comforted, I thought about how unusual the experience we'd just had was, and how typical of the Diane Jenkins we had come to know. In the midst of her own grief, she had taken the time to think of us.

In early January, detectives, prosecutors, and evidence techs met at the medical examiner's office for more discussion of the information about the gunshot wound gleaned from the reconstruction and testing of Amy's skull. Lab tests had confirmed chemical traces indicating that it was, indeed, a gunshot wound and identifying the entrance and exit wounds. The medical examiner explained the direction of the bullet suggested by the positioning and angles of the wounds, as well as other broken bones and a chipped tooth, which suggested that Amy had been struck with some object. The rest of the information available that day was grimly disappointing. There was none of Gorman's DNA on any of the dozens of items tested.[7]

Gathered around the table in the medical examiner's conference room, we await more news from the lab and medical examiner. Words I'll never forget. No DNA! I can hear the air hiss out of Danny's lungs. Scott drops his head. Tommy shifts in his seat. I know Tommy expects more and is very good at hiding his emotions. Matt's head is red again, so stoic that if it weren't for that color, you'd never know he felt a thing. But we're all reeling.

How can there be no fuckin' DNA? We've worked so hard. We've been so careful. I think of the Stearnman logging twenty-five hours on Gorman's car. All the work Kevin McDonald did. All those exhibits carefully collected and sent to the lab. Those miserable hours in the cold at the grave site, sifting, sifting, sifting. Plucking out the tiny hairs. Goddammit!

Peggy Greenwald's voice goes on, explaining the toxicity results. Amy's blood alcohol levels high. The presence of GHB (gamma hydroxybuteric acid). What we'd been wondering about. Did she maybe drink too much under all that stress? Rubright getting harder to handle. Making passes? Did Gorman put something in a drink? We believe maybe he did. It would explain her uncharacteristic behavior. And then another kiss of death—my God that term fits here, doesn't it? That none of the results are meaningful because of decomp. Because alcohol and GHB can be products of decomp.

Scottie looks at his clenched hands and I know what he's thinking. What we thought every day Amy was missing—that vital evidence was being lost. If only we could have found her sooner.

It's not like we didn't try. But there is still hope in the testing and review of evidence collected. DNA is only one part. Unfortunately, because of TV, CSI, the news, movies, and misinformation, it tends to be the part that the public focuses on.

With Gorman in the Cumberland County jail, held on probation violations, attention turned to the question of how and when he would be charged with the murder of Amy Elizabeth St. Laurent. On January 2, 2002, Gorman admitted to technical violations of his probation and was sentenced to ninety days in jail. Before those ninety days were up, the detectives wanted to be sure Gorman was under indictment for murder.

In Maine, all homicides are prosecuted by the attorney general's office. As the focus shifted from investigation to prosecution, Deputy Attorney General William Stokes and Assistant Attorney General Fernand LaRochelle, who had been advising the detectives on the legal aspects of the investigation all along, began to play a central role. Young and Harakles had already been consulting on questions concerning the legality of proposed searches and the necessity for, and language of, the various warrants they had obtained. Now the investigators and the prosecutors began preparing for an indictment.

In 2002, Stokes had been with the attorney general's office since 1977 and had tried about seventy-five murder cases. The dark-haired, engaging Stokes is lively and dynamic. He talks with his hands and his whole body in staccato bursts, leaning into conversation with the eagerness of a born storyteller. He delivers his words in a Massachusetts accent tempered by his many years in Maine. Detectives describe him as a passionate litigator, extremely effective in argument, forceful and persuasive with judges, and appealing to juries. He thrives on a good fight and isn't afraid to take risks.

Fernand LaRochelle, by contrast, is a much quieter man. He got out of the University of Maine Law School wanting to practice public interest law, interned at the attorney general's office, and found a career. He has prosecuted at least 150 murder trials in his thirty-year career. Middle age finds him graying and lean, with a face both distinguished and intelligent. He is low key, soft spoken yet authoritative. He is careful and precise, generous with praise for other lawyers' and police officers' hard work, and has a deep understanding of the pain and conflicts of the families involved in any murder case, both the victim's and the perpetrator's. After more than a quarter century on the job, he has a profound respect and appreciation for having had the opportunity to do valuable legal work that serves the people's interest.

Detectives who have worked with LaRochelle say that while Stokes is the more outwardly passionate, there is nothing lacking in Fern's passion. As one detective put it, "When Fern comes out and the gloves come off and he addresses the jury . . . you really see his talent. Once he's decided to fight . . . he will fight, and it's a beautiful thing."

Although they have both been trying homicide cases for many years, neither Stokes nor LaRochelle has ever lost sight of the particular responsibility their job carries. As the ones responsible for securing homicide convictions, they go into each trial feeling the heavy weight that comes with the necessity of procuring justice for the victim and closure for the families, as well as representing the interests of the people of Maine. So much, they say, rests on them. They also have a deep appreciation for the detectives' investment and interest in their cases. They understand the essential value of good detective work to a successful prosecution and how difficult it is for detectives to relinquish control of their cases to the legal process.

Now they began the preparations to take the case against Jeffrey Russell Gorman to a grand jury for a murder indictment. At the grand jury stage, the prosecutors generally haven't interviewed witnesses themselves but rely on information from the police and police reports. In many cases, only the investigating officer or officers will go before the grand jury, outlining the basics of their investigation. Other times, prosecutors put much more of their case before the grand jury because they want to see how a jury of citizens at the actual trial might hear and judge the story. In the case of Amy St. Laurent, the decision was made to make a fairly complete presentation of the evidence to the grand jury.

The grand jury process is a secret process; other than the citizen members of the grand jury itself, no one is present except the presenting witness, the prosecuting attorney, and, in Maine, if authorized by the judge, a court reporter. No members of the public are present, nor is the suspect or his attorney. The grand jury, which is a very old legal institution, is called the "conscience of the community," and it is this community that listens to the state's evidence and decides whether or not a person should be brought to trial. By law, for an indictment, a grand jury must consist of twelve to twenty-three persons. What the grand jury returns is known as a bill of indictment, what we call an indictment and what the lawyers call a "true bill."

There were several reasons why the prosecutors wanted to present a more detailed case to the grand jury. For example, because the matter of timing on the night Amy St. Laurent disappeared was critical, they called all the other residents of the apartment where Gorman was staying to testify in order to give the grand jury a clear picture of who was where, at what time, and what they saw and didn't see.

The primary reason they wanted to take the case to the grand jury rather than getting an arrest warrant, however, was that they wanted to get Tammy Westbrook's testimony on the record. At that point, they had no direct information from the mother herself regarding Gorman's admission that he had killed Amy. They had heard the details of Gorman's confession from Westbrook's friend Mary Young. Tammy Westbrook had also shared the story with an Episcopal priest in Delray Beach, Father Fred Basil. Mary Young and Father Basil were both honorable and credible witnesses; however, legally, their testimony was hearsay.

Gorman's confession was useful as factual testimony—as an actual, firsthand admission that could be used to convict him—only if it came directly from the source to whom he had told it, his mother. Therefore, they needed to get the mother on record with what her son had said.

They knew, from prior attempts to appeal to Westbrook's conscience, that she wouldn't talk about her son's confession. Twice, Tommy Joyce and Matt Stewart had talked with her at her home. On December 27, when they returned her computer, they had felt they were close to a breakthrough. Joyce spoke about how laying it out was one of the things people use to get themselves through tough times, like prayer.

WESTBROOK: I can't imagine him doing something like that.

STEWART: He did and you know he did.

WESTBROOK: No.

JOYCE: Because he's told you.

STEWART: Tammy, you know the truth.

WESTBROOK: You have to leave now.

JOYCE: You can get this out and you'll feel better.

WESTBROOK: No. I want you to go.

STEWART: Amy's mom no longer has her daughter because of what Russ chose to do.

WESTBROOK: Savannah's right there. Please respect that.

STEWART: Do the right thing, Tammy.

WESTBROOK: No. She can hear.

STEWART: The truth needs to come from you. It does. And you know that. I know you know it in your heart 'cause you're a good person. I see it in your eyes.

JOYCE: You're a mother, and you care very much for your son, but you do know what is right, the ultimate right thing to do.

In the end, Westbrook hid behind her two little girls, telling the detectives to leave as they were upsetting "her babies," so they left.

Scott Harakles had also had a conversation with Westbrook in which he almost connected. He was talking to her about doing the right thing, and she was pleading with him, "but this is my son." By the time detectives sat down with Fern LaRochelle to discuss strategy before the grand jury, they knew what Tammy Westbrook's position was going to be: Make your case any way you can, but leave me out of this.

Mary Young had told them that bearing the knowledge of her son's confession was a terrible burden for Westbrook. She wasn't eating or sleeping. She was deeply tormented by the conflict between shielding her son from prosecution when he should be punished for committing a terrible crime and not wanting to be involved in the process that would result in his arrest.

It is not unusual, in the legal process, for a year or more to elapse between an indictment and the time the case comes to trial. The detectives and the prosecutors knew that time has a way of allowing people to deal with guilty and troubled minds. Given enough distance from the event, a person with guilty knowledge can rationalize it or find a way to cope so that the knowledge is no longer so troubling and intrusive. They also knew that memory can fade. The attorneys reasoned that it was critically important to get Tammy Westbrook to tell the story of her son's telephone call and confession while it was fresh and immediate and she was still feeling the full impact of its horror, in a forum where it could be recorded and preserved and she would be under oath.

It was possible that Westbrook might come into the trial and tell the truth, but the grand jury process was the moment when they felt they had their best shot at getting her to do so. Also, if she was ever going to say anything officially, it would probably be before the grand jury, a closed and secret proceeding, rather than a public trial, and she was far more likely to talk before her son was formally charged with Amy St. Laurent's murder.

Gorman's confession, with its details about hitting Amy and shooting her in the head and sometime later going back and burying the body, was by far the best evidence they had. Although the prosecutors could place Gorman with a gun, they did not have the gun. Despite months of searching, the police hadn't found the missing clothes or shoes. Despite the more than twenty-five hours that Portland evidence technicians had spent on Gorman's car, and the meticulous work at the crime scene, the state crime lab hadn't come up with any DNA or other forensic evidence tying Gorman to the crime. Therefore, it was essential to get the details of the confession recorded as soon as possible so that the attorneys could use that information for further investigation and preserve it for trial.

Despite Tammy Westbrook's troubled conscience, they did not expect that getting her cooperation would be easy. It was possible that she would appear in response to her grand jury subpoena and either refuse to testify or tell an entirely different story from the one police had heard from Mary Young. Strategically, they had to decide how best to create a situation where she could be induced to tell the truth.

Part of that strategy was to send investigators to Delray Beach, Florida, to conduct personal interviews with Mary Young and Father Basil. This was another time-sensitive trip. With the grand jury session scheduled for early February, there was no time to drive. Scott Harakles didn't want to fly, and since the investigators already knew what they were going to get, this was a piece of the investigation that could be done by any competent detective. In mid-January, Danny Young and MSP detective Rick LeClair went to Delray Beach, Florida, where, with the assistance of Delray Beach detective Mike Miller, they recorded interviews with Mary Young and Father Basil.

When they visited Father Basil at his church, he questioned whether or not, as a priest, he could speak with them about what Tammy Westbrook had said. Assured by the detectives that since they had been conversations, not a priest-penitent situation, and that since he had mentioned the conversations to Mary Young, he had "published" the information and could claim no religious privilege, he agreed to come to the police station and give a statement.

In his statement, Father Basil told them that he was pastor of the Anglican church in Delray Beach. He told the detectives that he had had two conversations with Tammy Westbrook. Both times, she had called him at home. In the first call, she had sounded very upset and had told him her son's story about Jason and Kush killing Amy and threatening to harm Gorman's family unless he helped them dispose of the body and told them of a good place to put it.

Sometime shortly after, maybe a week or week and a half later, Westbrook called him again one evening between 8:00 and 9:00 p.m. and talked for about forty-five minutes. She asked, "Can I tell you something?" and then related her son's phone call in which he said he was walking with Amy and there was an altercation and he shot her.

Young and LeClair subsequently interviewed Mary Young, recording the information she had already provided by phone. By that point, Young said, he felt as though he already knew Mary Young well and that she was a friend. In a case where so many witnesses seemed indifferent or unconcerned, he appreciated dealing with a good-hearted woman who had a conscience. He understood that she was deeply sympathetic to Tammy Westbrook's dilemma but felt that the demands of justice, given what Gorman had done, far outweighed the demands of friendship. She was also concerned that if Gorman were released, another woman's child could be at risk.

Mary Young didn't just give the detectives her statement; she also allowed them to put a recording device on her telephone in case Tammy Westbrook called with further information. She offered to wear a wire in conversing with Tammy Westbrook's daughter, Britney, in case Britney had any useful information. She was very helpful in locating other witnesses for them, in explaining the situation to Gorman's ex-girlfriend Kathleen Ferguson, and in helping the detectives to get Ferguson's information.

Kathleen Ferguson confirmed what she had already told Danny Young. Gorman had told her, in a phone call, that Jason Cook and Kush Sharma had killed Amy St. Laurent. That they had hidden her body in the basement of the Brighton Avenue apartment for three days and had then taken it away and buried it. That it had been buried where it was found because Cook and Sharma had forced Gorman to suggest a good hiding place by threatening his mother and girlfriend. Ferguson also told the detectives that, in addition to Gorman's violent behavior, her relationship with him had foundered because he had such negative views of women and that these might have been fueled, in part, by his terrible relationship with his mother.

Young and LeClair returned to Portland with videotapes of their interviews. Acting with a cautious eye toward things that could trip them up at trial, they searched the basement of the Brighton Avenue apartment for signs that Amy's body had been stored there as Gorman had claimed, as well as searching Cook's truck for evidence that it had been used to transport her body.

On February 4, 2002, Scott Harakles served a grand jury subpoena on Tammy Westbrook. He told her that Mary Young and Father Basil would also be called to the grand jury, and that she knew why they were being called. In response to her protests, he told her that while she might hope otherwise, her conversation with Father Basil was not privileged. He reminded her that a grand jury proceeding was a very serious matter and that when she came to testify, she could not tell anything other than the truth.

As Westbrook protested, Harakles told her bluntly that lying to a grand jury would be perjury and she could be subject to criminal charges. After they had discussed the consequences of perjury, which included the possibility of arrest and incarceration, Westbrook told him that she did not believe her son had committed the crime.

"He did it," Harakles told her flatly. "He *told* you he did it."

As they had anticipated, she answered that she would not appear in response to the subpoena. If she failed to appear, Harakles told her, they would have to arrest her.

Along with preparation for their own case, the attorneys were preparing for the defense's right to cross-examine Westbrook at trial. At all stages of a case, the investigation stage, the grand jury stage, and the trial prep stage—police and prosecutors are always thinking ahead toward what will happen at trial, and how to do an investigation and present a case that will stand up to defense scrutiny. In the case against Russ Gorman, that meant getting the mother's testimony now so that the prosecutors could fit it into a factual matrix that would be hard to discredit at trial, even if the defense could show she was a volatile and vindictive mother who had a toxic relationship with her son.

As the prosecutors had anticipated, when Tammy Westbrook appeared at the grand jury in response to the subpoena, she refused to testify. To ensure that she understood that she was under subpoena and legally compelled to give honest testimony, and also to ensure that she understood she couldn't come before the grand jury and tell lies or claim that she didn't have any pertinent information, the attorneys took her through a two-step process.

On the first day, when she declined to testify, the prosecutors took her before a superior court justice, who told her she had an obligation to testify truthfully. He gave her the opportunity to consult an attorney about her rights and obligations and return the following day.

When she returned the second day, they sat her down with her attorney and played her the videotapes of their interviews with Mary Young and Father Basil. As a strategy, this was much more effective than saying to her, look, we know what you've told your friends. Here they were able to present actual visual evidence of what the police already knew, including the friends telling the police how heart-wrenching this knowledge was for Westbrook.

Ordered by the justice to cooperate, and told by her attorney she had no grounds to refuse, she went before the grand jury again on the second day. She was reminded that she had taken a sworn oath to tell the truth the day before and was still under oath. She was also reminded that if she failed to tell the truth, she would be subject to prosecution for committing perjury, making it clear to this mother with two small children at home that she risked being jailed if she didn't cooperate.

The decision to bring the suspect's mother before the grand jury was a difficult one. When calling members of the defendant's family before a jury, there is always a delicate balance to strike between the importance of any evidence the family member may have and the potential for creating animosity toward the prosecution or sympathy for the defense as a result of the family member's ordeal. Often prosecutors choose not to put family members on the stand even if their testimony has probative value, because of the problem of the jury seeing a family member in such conflict and pain. This was a consideration in the Gorman case, but the information Tammy Westbrook possessed was too central to the case. The state couldn't risk letting a murderer walk because calling his mother would cause her pain.

As her testimony began, Fern LaRochelle did the questioning, but once the testimony was under way, no prodding was necessary. Just as they had hoped, Westbrook decided to tell the truth. The story of the phone call from her son and their subsequent conversation came pouring out in a dramatic soliloquy. Fern stepped back and let her go without interruption. The grand jury sat mesmerized as Tammy Westbrook told the story of her son's confession. Don Mitchell, the court reporter, later told the prosecutors that it was the most dramatic thing he'd seen in more than twenty years of such proceedings.

On Friday, February 8, 2002, the Cumberland County Grand Jury returned an indictment. It stated that "On or about the 21st day of October, 2001, in the County of Cumberland, State of Maine, Jeffrey Gorman did intentionally or knowingly cause the death of Amy St. Laurent."

17

In the eleven months between the time he entered his "not guilty" plea and the time that Chief Justice Nancy Mills began to empanel a jury at the Cumberland County Superior Court, Gorman was twice involved in significant violations of jail and prison rules. Not long after he was incarcerated, he was found to have acquired razor blades by substituting foil in a disposable razor. Because of that violation, he was transferred from the Cumberland County jail to the new Maine State Prison in Warren. A few months later, he was again in trouble for trafficking in controlled substances.

But detectives and prosecutors weren't worrying about Gorman's behavior. They were busy putting together an effective case to present at trial. As the principal prosecutor in the case, Fern LaRochelle would receive from Danny Young five notebooks of interview transcripts and activities summaries, each more than 4 inches thick.[1] Along with the notebooks came boxes of audio- and videotapes of the many interviews in the case, as well as crime scene photographs, crime scene video, and reports from the state crime lab, the medical examiner, the forensic anthropologist, and a consulting entomologist.

Trial preparation would begin by reading all that material to get the story. The prosecutors' challenge was to sift through those hundreds of hours of detectives' interviews and thousands of pages of documents to identify the central story to be told and the best witnesses to tell it. It would involve extensive interviews with the primary detectives, followed by personal interviews with many of the prospective witnesses. All the documents and tapes had to be copied and given to the defense.

Gorman in Cumberland County Superior Court after being arraigned on probation violations. (*Portland Press Herald*)

It was very important, LaRochelle noted, for the prosecutors to both read the witnesses' statements thoroughly and also speak with potential witnesses. Often, a police officer will summarize the case and give you the good stuff but won't give you the potential bad stuff, the things about the witness that will trip you up at trial. Sometimes an officer's good relationship with a witness secures a level of cooperation that will fall apart under attack by the defense. The detectives are concerned with producing witnesses with probative information. The prosecutors' challenge is shaping that information in a way that presents an effective story for the jury.

During the two months leading up to the trial, Fern would spend long hours reviewing testimony and then coming to Portland to interview witnesses at the police station or at their homes. An extremely careful and detail-oriented litigator, his policy was to conduct a face-to-face interview with any witness he was considering calling at trial. It is only by personally interviewing witnesses and running them through their stories that a prosecutor can decide who will be the most effective witnesses at trial. Who will hold up under cross-examination. Who seems like a credible person to bring before a jury.

Sometimes a witness who looked great on paper and had useful probative evidence to offer would prove to be someone who couldn't be shown to a jury, or someone who could easily be taken apart by a defense attorney, or someone who turned out to be so flaky, shaky, shifty, unreliable, or easily discredited because of his or her own history that the witness couldn't be used. Sometimes important witnesses would have become sketchy about important details. Gorman's roommates, for example, appeared infuriatingly fuzzy about timelines on the night Amy disappeared.[2]

During the trial prep period, Danny Young would come to work on a Monday morning and find a whole series of messages left by Fern over the weekend. Posing questions. Asking for clarification. Asking for Young to arrange for certain witnesses to be interviewed. Meanwhile, Young had been promoted to sergeant and had a new job in the Community Affairs Unit and a new caseload.

A couple months before the trial, the attorneys got a trial date from the court: January 10, 2003. They would need that lead time to read through the reams of documents, interview witnesses, make travel arrangements for witnesses coming from out of state, prepare exhibits, and develop a trial strategy. All the out-of-state witnesses had to be contacted, schedules had to be arranged, and they would have to be flown to Maine and put up in hotels.

Just as it had been difficult initially to get witnesses to come forward and give their statements, now it was difficult to get witnesses to respond in a cooperative manner to the state's need to bring them back to Maine for a trial. Eric Rubright, for example, had left Florida and returned to the Midwest and was being very uncooperative about returning to Maine for the trial. David Grazier and his now-wife, Dawn Schimrich, had moved from Maine to Texas and had job commitments that made returning difficult. To free Fern for other things, Bill Stokes took over that chore.

As the weeks wore on, it became clear that the prosecutors *were* going to have a problem with Tammy Westbrook. At about the time her son was transferred from the Portland jail to the new prison in Warren, she also moved to Warren. She had been served with a subpoena, compelling her to appear at the trial, but whenever the prosecutors contacted her about coming in for a pretrial interview, she would be vague and noncommittal and tell them she'd get back to them. Then she never would.[3]

This pattern of phone call, explanation, and no response went on for weeks. Finally Stokes called Westbrook and told her that while he recognized her dilemma, she was under subpoena. He told her that they would do all they could to minimize the inconvenience, but they had to speak with her before trial.

Two days later, Bill Stokes got a phone message from Portland attorney Dan Lilley, saying that he now represented Tammy Westbrook. Stokes returned the call on the speakerphone, so that Fern LaRochelle could hear the conversation. Lilley told them that Westbrook didn't want to testify at the trial. Initially, Lilley took the position that the prosecutors couldn't seriously be planning to call his client in Gorman's murder trial as she was the boy's mother. He also asked for a copy of the grand jury transcript.

Lilley was asking for something he didn't have a right to see. The grand jury proceedings were confidential, and he wasn't representing a party to the case. However, after discussion, Stokes and LaRochelle arranged a conference call with Justice Mills and Clifford Strike, Gorman's attorney, and got permission to give Lilley a copy.

After Lilley got the transcript, and after his argument that they couldn't call Westbrook because she was the boy's mother had failed, Lilley contacted the prosecutors again, this time with the news they had long feared. Lilley told them that it wouldn't be productive to call Tammy Westbrook as a witness at her son's murder trial because she didn't remember anything about the phone call in which her son had made his confession. Nor, he told them, did she have any memory of the grand jury process. It was a frustrating, infuriating, and not unexpected piece of news.

Westbrook's testimony about her son's confession was the centerpiece of the story of what happened on the October night that Amy St. Laurent disappeared. The rest of the testimony the prosecutors planned to present would create the factual setting into which her story nested. Stokes and LaRochelle then had to decide what they would do when Westbrook came into court and said she didn't remember anything.

Faced with the possibility that Westbrook's testimony might be a problem, they looked hard at the second witness Gorman had confessed to, Erika Walker. Walker had come up from Alabama to testify before the grand jury, although her testimony was ultimately not used; now she readily agreed to travel to Maine again and make herself available. She was informative and cooperative, and it seemed clear, from what she'd told Danny Young and Scott Harakles during their interviews in Troy including her detailed knowledge about the way that Amy St. Laurent had been beaten and killed, that Gorman *had* confessed to her.

After she was interviewed by Stokes and LaRochelle, along with Sergeant Young, however, they felt that Mamma E, a tough-talking, profane, hard-edged southern truck driver, wouldn't play well to a Maine jury and that her tendencies to embroider on the story would make her vulnerable on cross-examination.

Here we are, over a year later, heading for a trial. By the time the trial actually arrives, everyone is exhausted from the process, especially the family. I mean really exhausted. In all that time, there can be no closure. No putting it out of your mind. No getting away from the fact that your daughter, your sister has been murdered, and moving forward with the good memories.

I am now a captain in the Patrol Division, far removed from criminal investigation. I face a whole new world of problems, organizational change, and management of a large number of personnel. I feel awkward in my uniform at first. I've forgotten how heavy the equipment is, but in a few weeks, it all feels like old jeans.

I have been away from the case and the developments for a long time, but Amy and her family never leave my mind. I see Danny, Tom, and the others periodically in the building, but we're like ships passing in the night. Danny is having similar experiences in the Community Affairs Unit.

He is taken off that duty to prepare for and attend the trial. He spends hour upon hour of his own time after work getting ready. He understands what a trial means and moves along with hope and trepidation. I can see the worry in his face when he and Tom stop by my office to update me on strategies for the upcoming trial.

"Whaddya mean they're not using Mamma E?" I shout. "That's crazy. She's heard it all. What's Fern doing, Dan?" I blurt out a dozen other questions to them, frustrated because I'm so removed from it all.

"Joe, she's so unstable and unpredictable they're not willing to put her up there," Tom explains. "Who knows what she'll do?"

"Well, so what! That's when the prosecutor controls her. Let the jury hear what she heard from that freak."

I am pacing now, all my uniform and equipment bouncing noisily. I'm worried about Fern's quiet demeanor. Fern is brilliant but he's gotta get in there and fight. If there is a theatrical defense by Strike and God knows who else, I want it countered with passion!

Tommy shakes his head as he and Dan explain it will be a joint prosecution by Fern and Bill Stokes. I consider that and think, Yes! A perfect blend of intelligent men. Great team. Fern is soft spoken, methodical, erudite, and experienced. A gentleman. His careful, low-key style is comforting to a jury. They see him as someone they can trust. Stokes is the perfect counterpart—upbeat, animated, quick thinking, energetic, and ready to argue passionately for a point.

As detectives, we're cynical about trials. Pessimistic about the possibilities of justice, of a process that rarely approaches the truth. And we're competitive. We want to win. We've worked our butts off building a case against Gorman and now it's out of our control.

Then Tommy drops a bomb on me. Tammy Westbrook has retained Dan Lilley as her attorney and wants to be excused from testifying, claiming that she doesn't remember anything about her grand jury testimony or her son's confession.

I am angry and frustrated by this news but not surprised. It's par for the course. With Lilley. With trials. With people like Tammy Westbrook.

"Well, Tom, isn't that just magic, huh? What is this, a magic show? And the ringmaster will be that character Dan Lilley. What a bunch of bullshit."

Dan Lilley is the nemesis of our police department. He loves the "show" and I know that's what it will be—a show. I expect he will challenge the constitutionality of information presented by the prosecution and manipulate the whole process until everyone's head spins. A trial is never the entire picture. The jury doesn't hear most of our information. With Lilley involved, it will be even more theatrics and less truth.

With Mamma E deemed unreliable, the prosecuting attorneys were back to Tammy Westbrook, and now they had to consider the challenges they would face trying to get her dramatic grand jury testimony before the trial jury if she persisted in her claim of lost memory. They wanted to get her statements into the trial as substantive evidence of a past recollection recorded, rather than simply using them as prior inconsistent statements to impeach her current "I don't remember" testimony.

The summer before, Fern had done an evidence seminar for attorneys in the attorney general's office, and among his research he'd found the Disher case, which dealt with how to proceed if a witness doesn't remember and you've got it recorded. As part of his pretrial prep, he wrote up a memo on the subject, covering both state rules and the constitutional issues including the Confrontation Clause, to have ready if needed during the trial.

There was also discussion among the prosecutors about whether to call Tammy Westbrook to the witness stand despite her claimed loss of memory. They might simply have taken her claim at face value and introduced her testimony via the grand jury transcript as past recollection recorded. They decided they wanted her on the stand. That decision—to call her as a witness despite her claimed lack of memory—was made in part because the Maine rules of evidence appeared to require her presence. They also felt it was very important to give the jury a chance to observe Tammy Westbrook, understand her dilemma, and assess her credibility, judging for themselves whether she'd had a genuine memory loss or whether it was just a mother's attempt to avoid testifying against her son.

Thus all the detectives went through another holiday season deeply immersed in the Amy St. Laurent case, joined now by Fern LaRochelle and Bill Stokes. The call went out for jurors, and on Friday, January 10, 2003, fifteen months after Amy St. Laurent disappeared, approximately seventy-five citizens of Cumberland County assembled in the county courthouse to begin jury selection in the matter of *State of Maine v. Jeffrey Russell Gorman*.

Jury selection was scheduled for Friday, January 10. I was on the phone most of the week with Diane, Lucille, and others between my new duties. I promised that I would make arrangements to attend part of the trial. I reassured them about the case, telling them I was very confident with LaRochelle and Stokes trying it.

As the trial is set to begin, Gorman is quoted in the paper, "I did not kill anyone . . . the jury is going to see I am innocent."

My stomach clenches as I read it, thinking about what lies ahead for the family. A jury trial is a peculiar, tedious process, a choreographed progression of information unlike anything that average citizens are ever exposed to. Unless you are exposed to society's true violence and horror, as we are, it's extremely hard to understand that human beings are capable of such hideous behavior as rape and murder, especially with the clinical and structured way they're presented in court.

It's not like in the movies or on TV. You never know what you'll get or what will happen. It's easy to plant "reasonable doubt" into the minds of a jury member, especially if there is a theatrical defense. I've seen the show many times over the years, all the things a jury never gets to hear. There's tremendous pressure placed on these ordinary people.

As a young officer twenty years earlier I was perplexed and bewildered when a judge glowered down at me and shouted that I would be held in contempt.

"Your honor, I am just trying to tell the story . . . the truth . . ."

"Just answer the question. Yes or no."

"Yeah, but I cannot explain it in that manner . . ."

"Answer," he orders. "Did you see him in the building?"

"No." The defense attorney smirks.

And so I saw my first burglary suspect walk away with a smile. Over the years I learned to adapt to this game. I always told the truth, trying to finish my sentences to make things clear for the jury. The objection might come, but they had heard it. In my cynical, jaded, seen-too-much mind, the thing that works best in our overburdened, underfunded, understaffed, and exhausted criminal justice system is the plea bargain. Inadequate and a corruption of the system, but at least there's a sentence and some certainty, and an expression of guilt by the defendant.

We do our best. We train and retrain and we've got good cops. But we all dread the confusion of the courtroom.

Diane is worried about how Amy's younger sister, Julie, will handle the trial, so a week before it starts, Lucille and I take Julie to dinner at Margaritas to prepare her for the realities of a trial and the difficulties she and her family will face. Julie brings her boyfriend, Tim, along for moral support. Two such innocent-looking kids. Seeing them reminds me of something the TV and media portrayals of crime so often miss—the wide ripples a crime like this creates, the pain of the innocent victims. Amy St. Laurent isn't Gorman's only victim.

On the crowded second floor of the restaurant, the four of us are snuggled in at our table. My rocks and salt Margarita gradually readies me for the difficult *conversation we've come here to have. Lucille is first to speak over the din of the restaurant, trying to lay the groundwork for what I've got to say.*

Julie tosses her long blonde hair back, apprehensive but brave and curious, staring ahead as she fidgets nervously. Tim gives her what I think is a protective hug. I realize this is the first time I've really looked into Julie's eyes—bright, smart blue eyes. They're usually downcast and sad.

"We wanted to talk about the trial and the realities of what you'll experience," Lucille says.

I grab my cue, leaning in, trying to be heard over the din without sharing this with the whole restaurant. "Julie, it's not like TV, or in the movies or on the news. A real trial isn't like that. It's going to be hard and frustrating." But broad strokes like this won't help her. She needs the gritty details in plain talk. "First of all, you will see Gorman up close and have to sit near him in the courtroom every day. I'm sure he will be cleaned up for presentation."

How many times have I seen it: a brutal thug comes into court groomed and shaved and wearing a suit and tie and the jury just can't believe such a nice person could do a terrible crime?

"You are going to hear things that are not true about your sister. They may try to twist things around . . . defense attorneys do that . . . there's very often an attempt to blame the victim. It can get pretty one-sided sometimes. The jury will not hear the whole story. Certain evidence and witnesses may be excluded. The prosecution won't be able to talk about Gorman's past or criminal history, yet the defense can say anything they want about Amy."

Julie interrupts, wanting to know why Gorman's history gets excluded. I explain as best as I can, and go on with what I think she needs to know, trying to give her a realistic picture of a jury trial without letting my own black cynicism bleed through.

"They will manipulate the truth and you must remain calm and controlled when people lie or turn things around on the stand. You're going to hear about the crime scene and the condition of your sister's body. It will be ugly and upsetting and hard to listen to. It's also a very slow process. Trials take time and you have to be prepared for that. You must be strong for your sister."

She straightens at that, wanting, as we all do, to get it right for Amy. We go on and take turns and field questions. After a while, we let the subject drop, talking about other things, trying to enjoy ourselves and our Mexican meal.

Lucille's staccato laugh interrupts the table near us when I act silly with my watch cap.

Back out on the winter street, I watch Julie walk away with her boyfriend—the bereft little sister who has had to grow up too fast. Young as she is, she has such strong echoes of her mother's dignity.

I go my own way, hoping I've done a good enough job. I'm overwhelmed with guilt telling Diane and Julie that the system will work and the jury will see through the muck and mire. Inside, I don't know what to expect.

Later, Fern LaRochelle would say it was the most amazing thing he had seen in thirty years of trying cases. Often, some members of a jury pool will have heard something about a case. Sometimes, several prospective jurors will have. This time, sixty-seven out of seventy indicated in response to the judge's questioning that they had heard something about the case. During the many weeks Amy had been missing, ordinary citizens all over the state had followed the news, hoping for the best and fearing the worst.

After a very long day of jury selection, which involved individual interviews by the judge and the attorneys with nearly every juror to ascertain what they had heard about the case and whether it had affected their ability to render an impartial decision, a panel of twelve jurors and three alternates was finally seated and instructed to be back at the courthouse on Monday morning by 8:30 a.m. to begin their service as the jury in the matter of *State v. Gorman*. The jurors left with instructions not to read about the case, not to watch or listen to any news programs about it, and not to discuss it with anyone, not even spouses or members of their family. LaRochelle, Stokes, and the detectives left with anxious stomachs and the certainty of a busy weekend ahead.

A criminal jury trial is a highly artificial process, circumscribed by a great number of rules that have evolved to avoid any prejudice to the defendant, who is, under our system of justice, presumed innocent until proven guilty. One of the hardest and saddest results of that, from the viewpoint of the investigators in a case and the victim's family, is how little of the story ever actually gets told. By the time the case to be presented in *State vs. Gorman* was delineated by pretrial discussion and agreement and by the amount of information about Gorman that was excluded because of its "prejudicial" value, the jury would get only a very diminished picture of his character or the extent of his personal corruption and his propensity for violence, and none of his long history of predatory behavior.

They would not hear about his extensive criminal history. They would not hear, for example, that he had befriended a man in his eighties solely for the purpose of stealing the man's few valuable belongings. They would not hear that he had assaulted his mother during a screaming fight after he had broken into a neighbor's house and stolen guns, nor would they hear he had punched and kicked his pregnant girlfriend and assaulted a teacher at school. They would not hear he had broken into customers' cars at the dealership where he worked and stolen stereo equipment to resell. No one would come to the stand to tell the jury that Gorman was a drug dealer, drug user, and heavy drinker. They would not hear the evidence that had led detectives to conclude he was a sexual predator. None of the women he had drugged and violated would take the stand.

The jury—which was to evaluate whether they could decide, beyond a reasonable doubt, that Russ Gorman had murdered Amy St. Laurent by shooting her in the head—might hear that Gorman didn't like guns. They would *not* hear that Gorman had gone to Alabama, because that might make it look as though he had fled the state. They would therefore not hear that Gorman had immediately acquired a gun in Alabama and had probably had another gun stored in his grandmother's ceiling. They would not hear about Gorman's using one of those guns to threaten a stranger in a Blimpie's parking lot. They would not hear how Gorman had hidden himself and his guns in a house with a small child, nor about the armed standoff that had followed.

Even sadder, they would hear little about Gorman's victim. Although the trial was for the murder of Amy Elizabeth St. Laurent, the citizens called to determine her accused killer's fate would learn little of what the investigators who had worked so hard on her behalf had learned. They would never get to imagine what the world had lost when a self-involved young man with sex on his mind, poor impulse control, and a total lack of empathy had snuffed out a bright light because that principled young woman had resisted a sexual assault.

They would never have a chance to picture the forthright, compassionate, and intelligent young woman Danny Young and Scott Harakles called "Our Amy." Nor would they have the chance to understand how two hard-boiled detectives who dealt with horrendous crimes and with crime victims every day of their working lives could become so attached to this victim that one kept her picture on his desk while another told people, "She was the kind of girl you would be proud to have raised."

A jury trial is also a highly scripted event. Because both sides have submitted their lists of witnesses and subpoenaed them to appear, the cast of characters is usually well known. The proposed exhibits have been identified, discussed, and largely agreed on before trial. Areas of potential conflict have also been identified. Experienced attorneys have anticipated legal issues that will be in dispute, often having researched the case law and prepared memoranda for the court in support of their positions.

Even with all this preparation, trial lawyers have to be quick on their feet and intimately familiar with all the details of the investigation and the reams of paper that a complex investigation produces. A case as complex as the Amy St. Laurent murder really needed two prosecutors—one on his feet and another listening, taking notes, ready to quickly produce documents or find a place in a document. For despite careful preparation, witnesses will lie, forget, change their stories, fall apart, and generally produce surprises. And defense attorneys will rattle witnesses, color stories, and muddy waters that will need to be resettled.

For the jury in *State v. Gorman*, Monday, January 13, began with opening statements from the attorneys representing the state and the defendant. But long before the judge greeted the jury, the behind-the-scenes skirmishing about how to handle Tammy Westbrook's convenient amnesia had begun. In midmorning during this first day of the trial, the attorneys held a conference within the judge's chambers in which Bill Stokes told Justice Mills that during the morning break Attorney Lilley had handed him an affidavit detailing Westbrook's lack of memory and asking that her subpoena to testify be quashed and she be allowed to remain in the courtroom during her son's trial.[4]

The week of the trial I would wear a suit and tie so I could run across the street to the courthouse when my regular duties would allow. I also spoke with Diane, Lucille, Tommy, and Danny each night to obtain details. Sometimes, sitting there listening to the maddening variety of interpretations, I would wonder what the jury could possibly be thinking. I missed the first morning, but everyone reported that Fern had done a wonderful job in his opening remarks as he urged the jury to use common sense in putting the pieces of evidence together. It's a difficult undertaking for them since the evidence comes in in broken fragments from a handful of witnesses gleaned from the many we've interviewed.

The defense, of course, argues reasonable doubt. No murder weapon, no physical evidence, it's a purely circumstantial case, and the witnesses are mixed up in their accounts and memories of events. I'm so cynical about reasonable doubt that I believe I could convince the reader that there is reasonable doubt that you are "reading" this right now.

Gorman's lawyer, Clifford Strike, is an ethical and honorable individual who is doing his job. But when everyone does their job, the result is a process that is perplexing and complex for the jury, the public, and the family. Sometimes, to those of us who know the story, it seems almost ridiculous.

At lunch, Tom tells me to get over to the courtroom. Lilley has filed a motion seeking to prevent Tammy Westbrook from taking the stand.

Around 1300 I meet the family in the hallway outside the old Superior Court room. It's a room I've been in many times over the years—an old-fashioned, formal, judicial-looking room with polished marble floors and beautiful dark wood detailing. Tension is high as we wait outside on a long wooden bench.

Diane is angry that Gorman is paraded within feet of them as he takes his place with his attorney. She is also upset that court security is limiting the number of people inside according to the seats. I try to explain the process to Diane and Julie as I study their tired, strained faces. I have very limited authority in the courtroom, I explain, and these things are out of my control.

The court officer announces that court will be in session and we shuffle into the room's audience area, a small, boxlike section of uncomfortable wooden benches that we're squeezed into like sardines. Gorman is escorted in from our left, only a few feet away. Once again I feel that visceral revulsion toward him I am trained to keep off my face.

Gorman has morphed again. No longer the blond pretty boy or the shaved-headed young tough. He's much heavier now, paunchy, sloppy, and tired. No more Mister Charming with that innocent young "who me?" look that fooled so many girls. This is much better for the jury, I think. I am surprised that they haven't done more to polish him up. Maybe he refused. He's arrogant enough *to think he knows best. Hey, Jeffrey, how about a mea culpa when you get up there before the judge.*

Around me, I feel the family's tension as Dan Lilley appears and the attorneys begin to deal with Tammy Westbrook's move to avoid testifying and to be allowed to stay in the courtroom with her son. It's difficult to watch Lilley parade around discussing Tammy's memory loss.

I'm relieved when Justice Mills quickly shuts it down. The trial will not be delayed, she says; the motion will be heard in the morning before the jury comes in. "It's not up to me to judge the credibility of this witness in advance. That is for the twelve members of the jury to decide."

At least it's not a slam dunk for Lilley and the defense. The family half-relaxes. At least for now, the trial is going forward. But the decision is only delayed. We will all carry the uncertainty home tonight.

After discussion, the judge took the firm position that Ms. Westbrook was still under subpoena, was still sequestered, and the matter would be heard the following morning before the jury returned to begin the second day of the trial. The trial then went on with the succession of the roommates at 230 Brighton Avenue stumbling through their incoherent versions of what had taken place the night Amy disappeared, an inconsistent jumble of times and assertions that Gorman was or wasn't in the apartment and had or hadn't discussed the time of his return with his roommates before they were interviewed by the police, interspersed with the chillingly banal testimony of three witnesses that Gorman had casually discussed with them his intention to bring Amy back to the apartment for sex.

These witnesses were followed by Westbrook police officer Tim Gardner, who testified about stopping Gorman for a high-beam violation at 3:14 a.m. on the morning of October 21, 2001. Gardner described the routine of a traffic stop, said that he had observed Gorman to see if he was intoxicated, and said that Gorman had been visibly nervous and was the sole occupant of the vehicle. He then located the traffic stop on a map.

In the courtroom, watching all this unfold, were the family and friends who had now waited more than a year to see some kind of closure to the brutal death of a beloved girl: Amy's mother, Diane Jenkins; Amy's father, Dennis St. Laurent, and her "second mother," Kathy Emery; Amy's sister, Julie; Amy's last boyfriend, Richard Sparrow; and Diane's friend Lucille Holt, all accompanied by the Victim Witness Advocates from both the Portland Police Department and the attorney general's office, Janice Hackett and Suzie Miller. These courageous and fearful people would need all the support they could get as they listened to the last witness of the day, Dr. Margaret Greenwald, the state's chief medical examiner, describe the exhumation and autopsy of Amy's body.

Along with her description of the gunshot wound and other injuries, Dr. Greenwald gave a detailed description of the appropriate methods for collection of insect larvae found with the body. Those larvae would play a crucial evidentiary role in establishing a time frame for Amy's death and subsequent burial.

LaRochelle: At any point during the examination, were insect larvae collected?

Greenwald: Yes, they were . . . as we were removing the clothes, we could see that there were some larger larvae and pupae, which was sort of large black eggs that the larvae—pupae are in until they become adults and there was some of the larvae over the right arm and shoulder area and as we were looking through the dirt, we saw some smaller larvae which were over the lower extremities.

LaRochelle: These were collected?

Greenwald: Yes.

LaRochelle: What was done with them?

Greenwald: Um, some of them were placed in a container that had a paper towel and was moist and had some vermiculite to allow them to survive, to live. Some of them were placed in a solution of alcohol and glycerin which would kill them and preserve them at the state in which we found them.

LaRochelle: All right. What's the point of treating them differently?

Greenwald: . . . the entomologist examining them can see them at the exact state that we did if they are killed so they know what size or age they are and then having a live larvae, it allows them to grow the larvae so they can see how long it takes them to reach adulthood.[5]

In a world where people are fed a steady diet of fictional and true crime on television and in the movies, it is difficult to shift from such riveting yet rather clinically emotionless entertainment to imagine how it must feel to be a parent in a courtroom listening to someone describe your child's state of undress, decomposition, and the necessity to reassemble that child's skull in order to determine the cause of her death. Hearing about the removal of her fingernails. The evidence of a freshly chipped tooth, bruised lips, and broken facial bones telling of premortem blows to her face. The back-and-forth interrogation about the presence or absence of stippling in an effort to determine whether a handgun was used. The inability to get meaningful toxicity results because of the advanced state of decomposition.

It was grueling for Amy's family to sit in the courtroom, dedicated and stoic as her earthly representatives, and hear such things associated with a person they loved, while Gorman, so very much alive, slouched in front of them, turning from time to time to stare and smirk.

At the end of day one, the jurors and the family went home exhausted. The cops and prosecutors went back to work.

18

The second day of the trial began without the jury in attendance. It began with arguments about Tammy Westbrook's claim that she had no memory of her phone call with her son or her appearance before the grand jury. Although the state had anticipated some maneuver by Westbrook, they had been uncertain how she would approach her pending testimony or what her claims would be when she arrived at the courthouse. Attorney Lilley's delivery of the affidavit and motion to quash had clarified her position.

Out of the jury's hearing, the attorneys debated whether Westbrook's subpoena to testify should be quashed, enabling Westbrook to be present in the courtroom during her son's trial rather than being sequestered like the other witnesses. Westbrook's attorney argued that, as the affidavit stated, she had no memory of events surrounding the death of the victim and therefore it would be fruitless to call her. Gorman's attorney took no position.

The prosecuting attorneys contested the fact that Westbrook lacked a reasonable ability to remember, asserting that it was a matter for the court to determine after examining the witness. With Westbrook's evidence as a centerpiece of their case, they were prepared to fight long and hard to get it before the jury. It was dramatic, it was damning, and it would explain to the jury what had really happened the night Gorman claimed he'd dropped Amy off, gone home, and stayed in for the rest of the night.

Based on her reading of the rules, the judge decided to conduct an examination of Westbrook to determine whether or not she had any ability to recall the time of the events in question. Westbrook's attorney countered that because the state contended her claim of memory loss was untruthful, Westbrook might be subject to sanctions such as perjury or contempt of court and therefore arguably had a Fifth Amendment right to decline to answer questions that the judge might pose.

Justice Mills refused to decide the issue of Westbrook's memory, or lack thereof, solely on the strength of a sworn statement claiming memory loss. Instead, she stated that she intended to conduct a voir dire, questioning the witness about her memory in general and, in particular, her memory of events around the time and events at issue.[1] The attorneys would be allowed to question her as well.

Justice Mills and the attorneys went on to discuss the pressing question of whether Westbrook's grand jury testimony would be used only to impeach her credibility as a witness or whether, despite the traditionally secret and one-sided nature of grand jury testimony, it could be offered as substantive evidence. It was an important distinction. If the testimony was admitted as substantive, as a confession by Jeffrey Gorman of what he had done, it could be used as part of the factual basis for a conviction.

Bill Stokes argued that if Westbrook persisted in her claim of a lack of memory, her prior testimony before the grand jury *was* admissible as substantive evidence. He reminded the court that Westbrook had already tried to avoid testifying before the grand jury, appearing in response to her subpoena and stating she wouldn't testify. She had then been sworn in, had appeared before the grand jury, had been asked some preliminary questions, and had refused to answer. She had been taken before Superior Court justice Humphrey, advised of her duty to give her testimony, and offered the opportunity to consult an attorney. She had returned the following day with an attorney and been told by Justice Humphrey she had no basis for refusal and that she must testify. Only then had she gone forward and given her testimony.

Now, with Westbrook finally on the stand in open court on this second morning of the trial, Stokes questioned her about some of her grand jury testimony. In response to the question "Nevertheless, are you prepared to come here this morning and tell the truth?" Westbrook had stated to the grand jury: "I have always wanted to tell the truth, I just never wanted to talk. I just wanted the justice system to do their job and let justice be served and leave me out of it. Because I certainly don't want to testify at any trial." She had also told the grand jury, with respect to the phone call in which her son confessed: "I will never forget it as long as I live."

Queried now, during the trial, about that testimony and those statements made to the grand jury, she studied the transcript and responded: "This is like reading a book. I do not remember this, sir."

By the conclusion of her examination, Stokes, Strike, and the judge had all had a turn to question Westbrook. She had exhibited knowledge of where she presently lived, where she was living at the time Amy St. Laurent disappeared, who her family members were, and details of her medical condition caused by the stress of having her son accused of murder. She had also described numerous contacts with the police during the investigation in which she complained that they had accused her son, and she had described being annoyed by search helicopters flying overhead.

The attorneys then argued the issue of quashing the subpoena. After argument, the judge found that Westbrook could, as the rules required, "recall the matter" and that the jury was entitled to hear her and make up its own mind. The motion to quash the subpoena was denied, and Westbrook was ordered to remain sequestered.

I am able to see parts of Tammy Westbrook's testimony. No doubt this woman is in anguish and it is difficult for her, to say the least. But to sit there and listen to "I don't remember. I do not remember, sir," is ludicrous. She has only lost her memory of the damaging statements.

Stringy red hair wraps around a crazy face with thick eyeliner as Tammy swings in her chair in the box. I must admit it is difficult to sit in that box on a creaky swing chair—a chair designed to enable the witness to move either way to face the attorneys, judge, or jury—I've been in that chair many times myself. But Tammy is swinging in more ways than one.

Stokes is doing the inquiry and he's good at demonstrating to the court in a calm and respectful way that this is bullshit. Tammy Westbrook has a memory of convenience.

"How is it that you remember the police telling you that your son killed Amy St. Laurent but you don't remember what you testified to?"

"I wish I had the answer."

Lilley is heralding that she is suffering from PTSD. I really believe her, he says. It is ridiculous, I think. An insult to everyone listening.

What about the PTSD of Julie and Diane? Of Dennis? I think, sitting there, containing myself. What about that, Mr. Lilley? But that, of course, is not your problem.

At 9:35, an hour later than they had expected, the jury entered the court-room and the second day of testimony began with Detective Danny Young. Young was on the stand for three hours, being examined and cross-examined on the basics of the case, including Gorman's meeting with Amy St. Laurent, his subsequent admission that his intentions for the evening were to take Amy back to 230 Brighton Avenue to score with her, and the fact that police had asked to look at Gorman's vehicle but were unable to. Young testified about the intensive search effort and the ulti-mate location of Amy's body. He served as the vehicle through whom the maps and photographs of the grave site, its location relative to Gorman's mother's house, and the routes from there to the location of the 3:14 a.m. traffic stop and the apartment at 230 Brighton Avenue were introduced.

Young testified about the wooden form for pouring concrete found in the grave, which had been used to cover Amy's body, and about other such forms in the area. Some were located in an unused chicken coop and others were beyond the end of the tote road through some trees by an old abandoned truck, testimony designed to show that whoever had bur-ied Amy St. Laurent was sufficiently familiar with the area to look some distance away or inside buildings for one of the forms. Young confirmed that at the time the grave site was found, the tote road was impassable after the first twenty-five feet.

Young testified that he had driven the route from the 230 Brighton Avenue apartment to the burial site at 2:00 a.m., and that it would take anywhere from eight to twelve minutes, depending on the vehicle's speed. He also testified to the detectives' interview with Gorman in Troy, Alabama, on December 14, 2001, in which Gorman reiterated his earlier statement that he had dropped Amy at the Pavilion, returned directly to 230 Brighton Avenue, and had not left the house again that night.

On cross-examination, Clifford Strike tried to suggest that, according to the maps and the place where the traffic stop had taken place, Gorman might have been coming from the Game Room, one of his favorite hang-outs. He hammered on the fact that investigators hadn't found anything

Aerial photograph showing Route 22, the tote road, and the black ponds. *Dot* indicates where the body was found.

in their search of Gorman's vehicle, Gorman's mother's house, or Ryan Campbell's room to link Gorman to the crime. Nor had they ever found the gun.

Young was followed by Eric Rubright, through whom the state established the events of the evening up to the point where Amy, unable to find Rubright, had left the club with Sharma and Gorman while Rubright, according to his statement, had returned to his rented vehicle and driven back to Amy's house in South Berwick. To demonstrate that police had considered and, on the basis of their investigation, rejected Rubright as a credible suspect, they also questioned him about his time-stamped receipts for food and gas, the fact that when he had reached the turnpike he had no change and the toll taker let him on for free, and that he had written a note for Amy and left it with some of her things inside her house.

After Rubright, a toll collector on the Maine Turnpike testified about

Rubright's coming through the tolls early on the Sunday morning that Amy disappeared, and his searching repeatedly for change until she finally waved him through and he headed toward the southbound entrance to the turnpike.

Next to testify was Robin MacKenzie, a friend of Gorman's who had visited him in jail and corresponded with him. In response to the question "Did you have occasion to talk to Mr. Gorman about whether or not he had ever carried a gun?" she stated, "He said he had had one with him all the time . . . I asked him why and he said just in case, you never know if something is going to happen."

MacKenzie was followed by Travis Gilbert, a gentleman with a rather extensive criminal record, who testified that during October 2001 he had accidentally been released for a week when he was supposed to be in jail, and during that week (a few days before Amy St. Laurent disappeared) he was visiting some friends on Main Street in Westbrook when Gorman arrived and started showing people a gun that he had. Gilbert said he believed it was a 9 mm, but he didn't know much about guns.

Mr. Gilbert was followed by Warden Roger Guay. Sergeant Guay had at that time been a game warden for seventeen years; he was a canine handler and a Maine Criminal Justice Academy certified canine trainer. Guay described the various types of training canines receive, depending on the types of evidence they are trying to recover. Dogs trained to smell human scent and search for lost people. Dogs trained to scent gunpowder. And dogs trained to recover people who are dead. These last are cadaver dogs.

On the day of the search for the body of Amy St. Laurent, December 8, 2001, Guay testified he was working with his ten-year-old chocolate Lab, Reba, a cadaver dog, and was called to a site off Route 22, County Road, in Scarborough. When he arrived, he watched another handler with his canine working the area. The other dog went immediately to a location under a series of small pine trees, showed a lot of interest there, and then broke from there and began to case, searching. Eventually it hit on the area of the grave site. Guay then moved in with his dog, and Reba exhibited the same reactions. First hitting on the area underneath the pine trees, then breaking from there, and relocating the scent at the grave site, six to eight feet away.

Asked to interpret this behavior for the jury, Guay explained that the dogs' stronger reaction to the area under the trees, then a period of searching, and then locating a second scent at the grave site suggested that there were two pools of scent: the stronger pool of scent was under the pine trees, suggesting that the body had first lain there and was only later placed into the grave. He said that for the dogs to have a strong reaction to the first site suggested that the body must have remained there for some time. The fact that the dogs didn't trace the line from the place under the trees to the grave suggested that at some point the body was picked up and moved.

Toward the end of the afternoon, the state called Justin Canney, who worked at Route 112 Auto Sales, where Gorman's mother's boyfriend worked and where Gorman sometimes did pickup work detailing used cars for resale. Canney told the jury that on the Tuesday evening after Amy St. Laurent disappeared Gorman had arrived just as they were closing and began cleaning his car. Gorman had said he was cleaning his car because he had a date. He had also brought up the missing girl, asked if Canney had heard about her, and stated that he might be implicated but he had nothing to do with it.

The next witness was Adam Deveau, nephew of Tammy Westbrook's boyfriend, Rick Deveau, who lived the length of a football field from Westbrook's residence in Scarborough. Adam Deveau testified that when Gorman moved up from Florida, he had shown Gorman around the woods and ponds area behind their houses. That they had fished in those ponds and that Gorman later went there on his own. He also testified that Gorman had told him that if he found stereo equipment down there, not to touch it. (To avoid prejudicing the jury, Deveau was not allowed to testify about Gorman's offering to sell him equipment he'd stolen from customers' cars at work.)

Court adjourned for the day, with the attorneys anticipating that on Wednesday they would finally get to examine Tammy Westbrook before the jury.

I would periodically stop in at the trial for an hour or so in the morning or afternoon, all I could manage with the demands of my new job. I have long been aware of Diane's pain throughout this process. We have stayed very close. What hits—and hurts—me now is how hard this is for Julie.

It is so important for a family to be present in the courtroom, to remind the jury that the victim, the person who was killed, the subject of the trial who otherwise has such a limited presence, was a loved and valuable human being. To be a visible witness to loss. But sitting through such a trial does not come without pain. Poor Julie, sitting on that hard bench in a room full of reporters, Gorman only a few feet away, having to listen to the strange and morbid rendition of the medical examiner's findings. Much as I wanted to protect her, I couldn't fully prepare her for that. What does one say?

I'd like to show the jury photos of the scene and of the autopsy so they could see what Gorman did. I'd like to show them my favorite picture of Amy, and then the soil-coated mummy that we exhumed, and yell right in their faces, "See what her family got back? See what happens to a girl who says no to Russ Gorman?" But that, of course, would be too prejudicial. It would shock the conscience of the jury and thus offend the Fourteenth Amendment due process clause. It should shock the conscience. What about the shocked conscience of Julie?

And then, the coup de grâce of evil. Gorman turns, stares, and smiles at Julie. Did I just see that? Julie is aghast and a strange sound—a groan, a cry—lurches out of her throat.

I couldn't believe what I'd just seen. Then, a short while later, when we stood as the judge left the courtroom, he turned and mouthed "I'm sorry" directly at Julie.

Julie's hand flew to her mouth in horror as Diane glared at me, her eyes blazing, and said, "Do something!"

As Gorman was led quickly past us, it was all I could do not to reach out and throttle him. The gall. The arrogance.

Julie rushed out of the courtroom in tears, Diane and Lucille following. I explained that if I attempted anything verbally there would be a mistrial. That what I would have to do would be to report the incident to the prosecution, who could bring it to the attention of the judge.

It was another of those things the jury never saw. Would never even hear about until sentencing. If we ever got that far. It was one of the most disturbing parts of the trial. His face. His expression. And Julie's devastation. It was monstrous.

While the newspaper ran stories that questioned whether Gorman's mother would testify about his phone call,[2] she took the stand so judge and jury could assess her competency and nattered on about her diarrhea, her stress, her meds, her weight loss, and how her lovely long hair had broken, Amy's mother sat in dignified silence and prayed for justice for her child.

That evening I would travel to Cape Elizabeth, a bedroom community outside Portland, where Lucille was making dinner for me and Diane. Diane was tired and seemed to be in a haze, but also peaceful and accepting of fate. She has such solid faith it truly does sustain her. We gather around a warm fire and sip wine, trying to avoid the case. It's like pretending there isn't an elephant in the room. There's the ridiculousness of Dan Lilley and Tammy claiming to remember nothing.

I let out some of my anger while Diane stifles hers. Unable to contain myself, I get up and start pacing, blurting out a few unprintable comments about the system. I've lived with it for over twenty years, but sometimes experience doesn't help. It's maddening to watch these people continue to suffer so much.

Eventually we push it all away and return to our oasis of peace—a lovely home, the warmth of the fire. It's nothing we can control. At least the trial is moving fast. A few more days could yield the end of a long road.

We clink our glasses and toast to Amy, justice, and peace in our hearts.

19

After a lengthy fight about the rules and procedure that would apply to Tammy Westbrook's testimony and how the trial would proceed if her memory could not be refreshed, day three commenced for the jury at 9:48 a.m. with some good old Court TV forensics. Dr. John Burger, a zoologist from the University of New Hampshire specializing in the biology of insects, took the stand to explain the significance of the insect larvae found with Amy's body. Dr. Burger testified that he had received two sets of samples from the medical examiner's office, one preserved in alcohol and the other in vermiculite.

LaRochelle: And what types of insects are these, sir?

Burger: The two types of insects that were . . . present were a species of blowfly and a species of coffin fly.

LaRochelle: As to the blowflies, what was the significance of finding a blowfly on a cadaver?

Burger: Blowflies tend to be the first insects that are attracted to an animal after it dies and these insects, blowflies in particular, are important in determining the nature of death, time of death and so forth because many studies have demonstrated for particular species the time that it takes for particular species to develop in a cadaver over time based on different temperatures, different humidity and so forth.

LaRochelle: How long would it take . . . for a blowfly to be attracted to a cadaver and deposit, I guess, the eggs which would result in what you received in this case?

BURGER: I would estimate that given appropriate temperatures for development and for blowfly activity, that this process could very well have occurred within 12 to 24 hours of the death.

LaROCHELLE: Now are blowflies active at night?

BURGER: Generally speaking, they are not active at night.

In response to Fern LaRochelle's questions, Dr. Burger stated that generally speaking, in a case such as Amy's, where there were injuries, it would take a postmortem interval of at least twelve to twenty-four hours for a blowfly to arrive at the body and to lay eggs. He further stated that the body must be exposed for there to be blowfly activity. Blowflies, unlike the coffin flies that were also present, do not burrow into the ground and would not be found on a buried body unless it had been exposed for the requisite period of time.

Dr. Burger was followed on the stand by Tammy Westbrook. At this point, Bill Stokes took over the questioning. Stokes's plan was to examine Westbrook before the jury so that they could assess the credibility of her claim of lost memory. He would then question her about her grand jury testimony. If her recollection could not be refreshed either by referring to the transcript or by hearing her own voice as it had been recorded during her grand jury testimony, he would offer the transcript as past recollection recorded and have it read to the jury.

Stokes walked Westbrook through questions about her current residence, where she was living prior to that, how long she'd lived there, with whom she was living at her home in Scarborough, and if her son, Jeffrey Gorman, lived there with her. Westbrook testified that her son sometimes lived with them and sometimes somewhere else. She recalled when they had moved up from Florida. That she had a kennel license to show dogs and breed dogs.

He asked her if she remembered hearing about the disappearance of Amy St. Laurent, which she did, and whether she had had discussions about Ms. St. Laurent with her son. Westbrook answered that she was aware he'd been questioned by the police and that his car had been searched. That she knew the police seemed to be pinning it on him. Stokes asked her if her son had told her what he had done the night Amy St. Laurent disappeared. Westbrook responded that he had told her he'd dropped Amy off at the Pavilion nightclub.

When Stokes moved into the area of Gorman's first altered version of the events of that night, in which he admitted not taking her back to the Pavilion but said Jason and Kush had killed Amy and asked for a place to hide the body, Westbrook couldn't remember discussing it with her son. She did remember something going on in the woods behind her house on December 8. That police had blocked off the road and she had seen police cars. But in response to Stokes's questions, she could not recall receiving a phone call from her son the following day. Nor going before the grand jury.

STOKES: Ma'am, do you believe that if you heard your voice on tape, do you think that might refresh your recollection of testifying before the Grand Jury?

WESTBROOK: I don't know.

The Grand Jury tape was then authenticated by Donald Mitchell, the court reporter who had been present at the grand jury hearing to record the testimony and who subsequently prepared a transcript of that testimony. Mitchell described the way that the testimony had been recorded—that he had made a shorthand version and also recorded the actual proceedings as a check on the accuracy of his transcription. Tammy Westbrook was identified as the witness who had appeared in the grand jury courtroom and given that testimony.

Then the unexpected happened. Questioning Donald Mitchell about the transcript of the grand jury testimony, Gorman's attorney established that the reporter's certification, in which he attested that it was a true and accurate record of the proceedings, stated that it had been prepared on the sixth day of February 2002. The date of her testimony was February 8.

It was a reasonable attempt by the defense to exclude the damning grand jury testimony from the trial, and one the prosecution had anticipated. Challenging that typo, however, led to a decision that couldn't have worked better for the prosecution. The judge determined that Westbrook's memory was not refreshed by hearing the tape. (When the tape was played for her out of hearing of the jury, Westbrook claimed she couldn't recognize her own voice.) Having decided that the grand jury testimony should come before the trial jury, and with the validity of the transcript under attack, the judge decided that the tape itself was the most reliable record of the proceedings. Therefore it, rather than the typed version of her testimony, should be used.

Once again, the jury's chance to hear the evidence of Gorman's confession, which was the centerpiece of the state's case, was delayed. With the defense's objections to the admissibility of the tape firmly on record, the jury went to lunch while the judge and the attorneys bent over the transcript, deciding which portions of Westbrook's testimony the trial jury would be allowed to hear. Following a tensely debated line-by-line editing session, Bill Stokes left the courthouse to get the tape edited, having asked Danny Young to call ahead to the state's audio agency and tell them not to leave before he got there. Stokes was aware, as Scott Harakles drove him back to Augusta on slick winter roads, that he was carrying the only existing copy of the tape.

While Stokes was getting the tape edited, Fern LaRochelle continued, like a goldsmith creating the perfect setting for a jewel, to craft the testimonial foundation into which Westbrook's information about Gorman's confession would nest. Testimony resumed at 2:00 p.m. with Robert Milton, manager of the Game Room, the pool hall in Westbrook where Gorman was a regular.

Milton described an evening at Denny's, about two weeks after Amy St. Laurent had disappeared, when Gorman told him that he had been questioned several times by the police. Milton said he had responded, "If you have been questioned, what's the deal?" and Gorman said, "Well, they think I did it." Milton asked "Well, did you?" And Gorman said, "No, I didn't." So Milton said, "Well, don't worry, if that's the case. When they find the body, they'll be able to tell exactly what happened," and Gorman said, "They're not going to find the body, they don't have any evidence."

Later in the afternoon, the state called Richard Deveau, the boyfriend of Tammy Westbrook and father of her two youngest children. Deveau told about a Tuesday night near the end of October when Gorman had shown up at Route 112 Auto Sales, where Deveau worked, at closing time wanting to clean his car. In response to Deveau's protest that it was closing time and his question of why the car had to be cleaned that night, Gorman told him that he was letting a friend borrow the car. Deveau stated Gorman spent twenty minutes cleaning the car and then left. Deveau stated that it was uncommon for Gorman to clean his car.

Asked about a time when Gorman had wanted to borrow a shovel, Deveau backtracked from his earlier statements to police, became fuzzy-minded about the details, and told an incoherent story about Gorman's borrowing the shovel to put in some fence in exchange for a piece of fencing. When pressed, he claimed that the words in the recorded interview transcript were not his, that he couldn't recall his earlier statements; finally he admitted that Tammy Westbrook had been so upset that he'd talked to the police she had made him sleep on the couch.

On cross-examination, Gorman's attorney asked for and got confirmation of the difficult relationship between Gorman and his mother. Clifford Strike also established that the witness, Richard Deveau, was no fan of Gorman.

To clarify Deveau's testimony, LaRochelle recalled Danny Young to the stand and asked him about his interviews with Richard Deveau during the investigation into Amy St. Laurent's disappearance. Young stated that on December 5 he had interviewed Deveau at Route 112 Auto Sales. In that interview, Deveau had said that around the time Amy St. Laurent went missing, Gorman had asked to borrow a shovel. When he was re-interviewed in January 2002, by Young and Harakles, Deveau had stated that the request was a couple days before or after Amy St. Laurent's disappearance.

The day ended with another conference in the judge's chambers. Fern LaRochelle, responding to Clifford Strike's line of questioning about Gorman's acrimonious relationship with his mother, argued that if Strike was suggesting to the jury that Gorman's mother had a motive to manufacture evidence against her son, he wanted another portion of the grand jury tape included in the testimony played for the jury: the part in which Westbrook, recalling the day after Gorman's confession, talks about sending her son money. Danny Young was sent to put the video editing on hold while the information about the newly added material was conveyed to Bill Stokes. Then all the weary parties went home to prepare for day four.

Day four led off with the judge informing the attorneys that the deputy had just observed Tammy Westbrook taking some kind of prescription drug. Then came the moment everyone had been waiting for. Westbrook was sworn in by the clerk, and while she was on the stand, the audiotape of her grand jury testimony was played. Hearing the testimony in her own words, her reluctance, her pain, and the trembling anguish in her voice had a power and impact a dry transcript of the same words could never have had. You could have heard a pin drop in the courtroom as the jury listened to the voices of Fern LaRochelle and Tammy Westbrook.

LaRochelle: Miss Westbrook, yesterday when we were talking I was asking you about conversations that you had with your son, Russ, about the disappearance and death of Amy St. Laurent. I understand that you're here this morning very reluctantly, is that right?

Westbrook: Well, I've never dreamed, dreamed isn't the word. I never imagined being in this situation . . . So I'm shocked. I'm traumatized. I'm scared. So if that seems reluctant than [*sic*] I'm sorry. I'm dealing with this as best as possible.

LaRochelle: I understand.

Westbrook: With all due respect to Amy and her family and her mother, you know, this has been very hard. It's the hardest thing I've ever had to do.

LaRochelle: Let me direct your attention to the conversations that you had with Russ about the disappearance and death of Amy St. Laurent. Following her disappearance, you spoke with him on several occasions; is that right?

Westbrook: Yes.

LaRochelle: And some of those conversations had to do with the fact that he was with her the night that she disappeared?

Westbrook: Yes.

LaRochelle: And he described to you what happened when he was with her on that particular night?

Westbrook: Yes . . . the day after they found her body I started having a terrible feeling that maybe he knew something more. I was on my way to the Mall around 2:30 in the afternoon on Sunday December 9th and my cell phone rang. And I was horrified. I think I had been up all night thinking about poor Amy in those woods. They found her the night before . . . And I kept asking him. He had told me that two other guys had left with her that night. And they didn't search the guy's truck. It was the only car they didn't impound and search. So in my mind I'm thinking, oh, my God, these two guys they did something horrible to Amy and they buried her next to my house to make it look like my son did it. But I thought, you know, something's wrong because he's changing his story. And I just had this gut feeling there was something else to it. And so I said, Russ, is there something else? Is there something you want to tell me? And he said, no. I said, Tell me, Russ. Tell me. Tell me. And he said, okay. Mom, I did it. He said, I'll tell you what happened. He says I was, I was walking, we were walking by the lake. And he says he had done 4 hits of acid that night. I guess he had been out drinking. I don't know. But he said we were walking by the lake and she said something to me. He said, I don't even remember what it was.

He said he looked at her and he saw my face. And he said he doesn't know what happened. I don't know if he blacked out or if he just, he doesn't know. He snapped. He doesn't remember.

But he said he pulled out a gun. And I shot her in the head. And he said, he goes I woke up the next morning and I kept, I can't believe it happened. I thought it was a nightmare. It was a real bad dream, mom.

I'm sorry it happened. I don't know what happened. And he said, but I saw your face. And he said, you ruined my life. He said, excuse my language, he said you fucked up my life.

And I started screaming. I said, Why? Why? I said, why? I said, I love you, Russ. I've always loved you. He was my first child. I have always loved him. And he said, I love you, too, mom.

The last few years I love you. But you ought to be glad it wasn't you, mom. You ought to be glad you're not dead. He says, I'm sorry. But you ought to be glad it wasn't you. This is almost word for word too.

I'll never forget it as long as I live. And he said, he use to lay in bed at night from the time I was 13 and think of ways to kill you.

LaRochelle: Did he say anything to you about how he buried Amy?

Westbrook: I'm sorry. I did leave that out. He told me that I, I can't even say it again. When he killed her, he told me he left her there for three days and then he went back and buried her.

LaRochelle: And did he mention anything about where he got a shovel?

Westbrook: Yes. He was screaming. Sobbing is more like it. Because I was in my mind, I'm thinking I was remembering his face sitting in that chair that day holding his head about half a day with the look of shock on his face. So I started, I was just realizing this was maybe true but still denying it. And telling him no, no, no. He told me that he says, I did it, mom. He told, do you remember, I asked if I could borrow the shovel?

LaRochelle: And that's when it sort of came back to you. Did you remember him asking about the shovel?

Westbrook: Yes. I can't remember when it was but I do remember him asking to use a shovel. And they were just sitting outside by the gate outside the house. The shovel. I don't know why he would ask but he did.

You know, I can't even walk out in my own yard without seeing those horrible woods where she was. Or looking out my window or going outside and play with my kids.

I hate it. People ride by and slow down and look like we're monsters. And you may think I'm a horrible person by not coming forward with this sooner. But I knew good and well my son would pay for what he did. I just didn't want to be the one.

Tammy Westbrook looks like Linda Blair in The Exorcist. Possessed as she struggles to respond to questions while maintaining her story of not remembering. Torn between two worlds as Stokes pleads to her soul to let the truth come out. She's up there on the stand, shifting, swinging, stopping, sliding, her outward movements mimicking her inward swings. And then that moment we've waited for—Gorman's confession. Dangling like a carrot on a stick since day one, it's been offered and jerked away so many times we're exhausted from the waiting. But now it's coming. The tape.

God, what a moment. It's going to be the actual tape. Bill Stokes slowly introduces and sets up the process and then, at last, we hear it. The jury. The family. Actually hear Tammy's voice on the tape. Actually hear the truth. The whole courtroom practically holding its breath as the tape is played.

Tammy dabs at her tears. Trying not to testify has been a contest between her soul and her will. In spite of my anger and bias, I feel pity for the woman until my eyes rest on the product of her poor parenthood, alive and well at the front of the room. Anger again, then sadness, as I observe this courtroom drama and reflect on our night at Amy's grave.

Then through the silence of the courtroom, I hear Tammy's voice on that tape, reporting, "Okay, Mom, I did it." Her voice goes on but I stop listening, suspended in time, the tape in the background as I think, God, the jury heard that! I am aware of Diane and Julie, of Dennis and Kathy, Richard Sparrow, and the others in a courtroom so silent except for that scratchy tape.

I stare at the textures of the warm wood in front of me, at its striations and contours, as I listen to the truth. Lilley must be going crazy. It is so good that we can finally hear the truth.

Gorman's attorney, Strike, speaks of the drug Tammy took in the courtroom. It was Seroquel, an antipsychotic. I see where this is going. Create reasonable doubt in the minds of the jury regarding her testimony.

On cross-examination, Strike questioned Westbrook about the prescription drugs she was taking. He then argued to the judge that it was unfair to his client to have to question such an important witness when she was affected by powerful drugs. The jury was excused, and Westbrook was asked what drugs she was taking. After she reported that she was taking Seroquel, Celexa, and Klonopin, Strike argued that she should be excused from testifying and ordered to come to court without taking her medications so he could deal with the unmedicated Tammy Westbrook. It was finally decided Westbrook would be excused, would remain in the courtroom, and would be recalled after a few other witnesses had been called. The jury reentered, and the next witness was called.

Jamie Baillargeon was Gorman's ex-girlfriend. She testified that she had dated him for about a year and broken up with him around the beginning of September 2001. She testified to several conversations with Gorman about the disappearance of Amy St. Laurent. On the day after Amy disappeared, Gorman called Jamie, told her he'd met a girl downtown, gone to an after-hours party with her, and taken her back downtown at the end of the night. Subsequently, he called her again after he had gone to Alabama, and Jamie said that his story didn't make sense. At that point, Gorman told her that he hadn't dropped Amy off. That Jason and Kush had dropped her off, that they were gone for approximately three hours and returned with blood on their hands and asked him how much he loved his mother, his sisters, and Jamie. Jamie testified that Gorman told her his roommates made him go to the police.

She testified that she then had a third phone conversation with Gorman after Amy St. Laurent's body was found, because she was troubled by Gorman's earlier conversation. It wasn't like him, she said, to take a threat and not do anything about it. In this last conversation, she asked him why Amy's body had been found in his backyard, and he told her that Jason and Kush had asked where a good place would be to put her.

LaRochelle: Did he tell you how long after Amy had died that they had decided that they had to find a place to put Amy?

Baillargeon: A couple of days.

LaRochelle: Now when he said this to you, did you believe it?

Baillargeon: I wanted to. I didn't.

LaRochelle: What occurred to you when he told you that he had told them where they could put her body behind his house . . . ?

Baillargeon: It made me sick that he had known where she was. How he could not say anything, that she had a family and all.

LaRochelle: Did you ask him about that?

BAILLARGEON: I asked him if he felt bad and he said he didn't really
care.

On cross, Strike asked her if she had broken up with Russ because he
had been cheating on her. When she answered yes, he asked, And it's also
true that shortly after you broke up, you discovered you were carrying his
baby, yes? Are you mad at Russell? At that point, Jamie collapsed in tears,
the court recessed, and the jury was excused.

Pending the recall of Tammy Westbrook, the state's final witness was
Sergeant Jon Goodman, who had picked up Gorman, Jason Cook, and
Kush Sharma in the Old Port and brought them to the police station the
night the police first learned of Amy's disappearance. Goodman reported
that Gorman had told him he had given Amy a ride to the Pavilion on
Middle Street and that he had done that all by himself and that he had
dropped her off there at 1:45 a.m.

LaROCHELLE: And how did that strike you?

GOODMAN: It struck me—and I asked well, where did she go when
you dropped her off? He said that she—actually first I asked if there
were people around when he dropped her off and he said there were
people around and I said well, did she go with them or where did she
go? And he said oh, she just went inside of the club, and it struck me
immediately because he said 1:45 and the bar closes at 1:00 o'clock
and really quarter of, but usually by 1:15 or 1:20 at night, there is
nobody around there at all. The doors are locked and if there are
employees there, there is no one to be seen, so I asked him to confirm that it was 1:45 and that she went into the club and he said yes,
that she walked in and it was about 1:45.

Following Sgt. Goodman's testimony, Tammy Westbrook was again
called to the stand, and Strike began the cross-examination that had been
postponed earlier.

*When Strike examines her, she actually giggles as she testifies to urinating
on a cell phone once while talking to her son. What does this tell the jury?
What effect will it have on how they analyze Gorman's confession? Another
courtroom moment when I really feel my revulsion for these people.*

Dan and Scott, Amy's constant guardians, maintain their composure like centurions.

I am relieved when Stokes comes back with fire. "How would you know that Amy St. Laurent was shot in the head on December 9 when the autopsy had not even been conducted yet?" The police didn't even know that!

Frustrated, she blasts out at the police and others. "I am not a complete lunatic." Okay, Tammy, how about half a lunatic? In regard to her son, she delivers the calling card of the guilty nationwide. "He is being persecuted. I am being persecuted. By the police. By the press."

It was an intense, electric, yet deeply sad day.

At the end of the afternoon, following a lengthy examination of Tammy Westbrook calling into question her stability and paranoid state of mind, examinations of Ryan Campbell's flaky, ever changing story of his lost gun, and Matt Despins's attempts to assist the police, the defense rested. The jury was excused one more time, sent home with the knowledge that in the morning they would receive their instructions and begin debating the fate of Jeffrey "Russ" Gorman.

After a long and exhausting week, detectives, attorneys, and families headed out in the dark of a January afternoon, full of restlessness and unease. Prosecution and defense went home to prepare their final arguments. Detectives went home veering between "We've got him" and "Is it enough? Is there something more we could have done?" Amy's family went home full of trepidation and prayers for a conviction and closure.

20

Friday, January 17, 2003. Trial day number five. No one had slept well. Meeting with the lawyers before court began, Amy's family was frayed with tension and taut with anxiety. This was the day the police and the prosecutors had been working toward for more than a year. The day that the family had longed for and dreaded. The very air had an electric intensity as people gathered and filed into the courtroom.

Once the prosecution and the defense made their closing arguments, the jury would be charged and would begin debating Gorman's fate.

The *Portland Press Herald* reported that Tammy Westbrook had been the star witness for both the prosecution and the defense. A woman who painfully testified about her son's confession or a troubled, delusional, and vindictive mother. A mother whose doubts about her son's story had led her to demand, and get, the truth, or a paranoid and unstable woman who believed the phones were tapped, had once urinated on one to extinguish a call she didn't like, and who took a phalanx of powerful drugs including antipyschotics to get through her days.

Justice Nancy Mills, a tough and formal judge who ran a tight courtroom, addressed the jury, beginning to give them the instructions that would guide them in reaching their verdict. She was careful, thorough, thoughtful, and precise. "Your job," she told them, "is to find the facts, which means you're going to decide what happened in this case back in October and November and December of 2001 and the beginning of 2002. You're going to do that by analyzing the evidence and by determining what evidence you find believable. You will reach your verdict by applying the law that I'll now give to you to the facts that you find and you should not be concerned about the consequences of any verdict you may reach."

To guide the jury in analyzing the case, she explained what they might consider—the sworn testimony of all the witnesses, including the grand jury testimony they had heard by tape, all the exhibits in the case, and the stipulation of the attorneys. If the jury found that certain facts had been proved beyond a reasonable doubt, the evidence might also consist of any reasonable inferences that could be drawn from those proven facts.

The term "reasonable inference," she told them, was another term for circumstantial evidence. "Circumstantial evidence is indirect evidence, proof of a chain of facts from which you can find that another fact exists even though it has not been proved directly." Explaining that making reasonable inferences was a process they used every day, she gave them the following example:

"If you go to bed at night and just before you go to bed you look out the window and you see green grass. That's a fact that you have seen, that's a direct fact that the grass is green. You go to bed, you sleep all night and you wake up in the morning and you look out that same window and instead of grass, you see snow everywhere . . . the reasonable inference that you can make . . . is that during the night it snowed."

Justice Mills instructed the jury about judging the credibility of witnesses and how to analyze discrepancies and inconsistencies. She told them that the defendant had an absolute right not to testify and that no inferences could be drawn from that. That they could believe some portions of a witness's testimony and not others. She told them that in addition to determining what evidence was credible, they must determine whether sufficient credible evidence had been introduced to prove the state's case beyond a reasonable doubt. Proof beyond a reasonable doubt, she told them, was proof of guilt sufficient to give them a conscientious belief that the charge against the defendant was almost certainly true.

It was the state's duty to prove that the defendant had acted knowingly or intentionally, but the state had no obligation to prove motive. In the event that the state failed to prove that Gorman had acted knowingly or intentionally, Justice Mills also gave the jury an instruction about manslaughter. "A person is guilty of manslaughter if he recklessly or with criminal negligence causes the death of another human being."

They were excellent instructions, yet every word that raised the pos-sibility of reasonable doubt or uncertainty, or suggested the jury could find Gorman guilty of manslaughter rather than murder, or not guilty, reverberated painfully with the detectives and Amy's family. With the de-tectives, in particular, because they had all been there before. They had sat through trials and had juries in other cases come back with bad verdicts. They knew that even in a strong, well-tried case, no matter how hard they'd worked or how thorough and careful they'd been, there were still elements of a crapshoot in sending a case to a jury. And this wasn't just any case. This was Amy's case.

The collective sense of everyone holding their breath continued as the attorneys began their final arguments. Fern LaRochelle went first, leading the jury step by step through the evidence. On the night Amy St. Laurent disappeared, Gorman told at least two people, and later told the police, that it was his intention to have sex with her. Her body was found without pants and with her underwear rolled down, suggesting at least an attempted sexual assault. He was the last person seen with her. She was shot through the head, and several people had testified that Gor-man had access to a gun.

Continuing in his calm and careful way, Fern LaRochelle reminded the jury of Gorman's lie about the timeline and the facts that showed he was lying. The Westbrook traffic stop showed that he was out on the road alone at 3:14 a.m. and back in the apartment by between 4:00 and 4:30, not out in the woods burying her. The delay in burial was confirmed by the forensic entomologist and by the warden's testimony about the behav-ior of the cadaver dogs.

He asked the jury who would want to bury a body so it wouldn't be found? A person who could be connected with her, that's who. A person concerned about concealing evidence. And why was she buried at that lo-cation? Because that was where she was killed. Practically in his backyard, in an area that he knew very well. How likely would it be that a random killer would choose that small portion of Scarborough to bury his victim?

He invited them to look at the testimony of Gorman's mother. She says that, on December 9 at 2:30 in the afternoon, he told her that he had shot Amy in the head. At 2:30 in the afternoon on December 9, the medical examiner was just finishing the autopsy and hadn't yet concluded that it *was* a gunshot wound. His mother knew before Dr. Greenwald, the medical examiner, and the police how Amy St. Laurent had died. How did the mother know that the body wasn't immediately buried, that it was buried three days later? Not because she had the services of a forensic entomologist or a game warden with a trained cadaver dog. She was told by the defendant. By her son.

LaRochelle reminded them of Gorman's conversation with Robert Milton, manager of the Game Room. Gorman told Milton they would not find the body. They've got no evidence. How would he know? The police can talk to Gorman until the cows come home and if there is no body, there is no crime. LaRochelle told the jury that the location of the body was so significant with respect to the identity of the person who had killed Amy St. Laurent that when Amy was found, Gorman changed his story. He told his ex-girlfriend Jamie that Kush and Jason had killed Amy and threatened him unless he told them of a good place to put her. He told Jamie that he had known all along where Amy's body was.

Gorman's own mother testified that it was her son's changing stories that aroused her suspicions. He'd told her the Pavilion story. He'd told her the Kush and Jason story. When she pressed him for the truth, he confessed to her that he killed Amy. He shot her in the head and went back three days later to bury her. Succinctly, methodically, and in an extremely believable way, LaRochelle summed up for the jury what they had heard. He showed them maps demonstrating the proximity of the grave site to Gorman's mother's house.

After a short break, Clifford Strike began his closing argument. The family and the detectives listened, if anything, more closely than they had to Fern LaRochelle. Strike began by reminding the jury that the standard of proof was "beyond a reasonable doubt," repeating the words "reasonable doubt," and that they, as jurors, were the keepers of that standard. He then began to show the jury how the state's weak case wouldn't get them beyond a reasonable doubt.

"The case that the state has presented for you this week is a strictly circumstantial case," Strike told them. "We have no murder weapon, we have no ballistics, no bullet, there is no DNA evidence. We don't know what time she was killed, we don't know where she killed, we don't know what date she was killed.

"We do know that Ms. St. Laurent died of a gunshot wound to the head. That's a fact." Strike spoke about the traffic stop in Westbrook. He said that at 3:14 in the morning, Mr. Gorman was in Westbrook, and he was alone. That the officer who stopped him noticed nothing unusual except that Gorman was a little nervous. He used the map to support his statement that the burial site was not in Tammy Westbrook's "backyard."

Strike reminded the jury that Gorman and his roommates all told the police that he had been gone only fifteen or twenty minutes and suggested there was nothing to say that Mr. Gorman didn't drive over to Westbrook afterward to see if anything was happening at the Game Room. Pointing out the inconsistencies in the various stories given, Strike told the jury that just about every witness testified to multiple stories or multiple pieces of the story of what happened that night. He reminded the jury that the tote road was six hundred feet long and that it was pitch black on the night the investigators dug up Amy St. Laurent's body. That the tote road was choked with debris. He argued that Gorman couldn't have taken Amy down that road for a walk, killed her, and still been stopped in his car by Officer Gardiner at the time he was. Nor would Gorman have appeared calm.

About Gorman cleaning his car, Strike told the jury, everyone cleans cars, and fifteen to twenty minutes isn't detailing. He pointed out that the police tore Gorman's car apart and didn't find any evidence of a crime. That other than the testimony of Travis Gilbert, a thief, no one ever saw Gorman with a gun. That the police never found any evidence on the shovel.

With respect to Tammy Westbrook, Strike pointed out that she was delusional, taking powerful medicines, and under a doctor's care. She believed that her phones were tapped and helicopters were flying over her house spying on her and her children. As for the statements she made to the grand jury, she could have created them from rumors that she'd heard. Look at what Westbrook said—that her son had taken four hits of acid and had been drinking—and yet when the police officer stopped Gorman there was no evidence of intoxication. Even if you were to believe Westbrook's testimony, Strike went on, if Gorman snapped, blacked out, was on acid and drinking, then your verdict has to be manslaughter.

Strike also suggested that Westbrook could have believed the story she told because of her mental problems and her long-term history of a love/ hate relationship with her son. Alternating throwing things at him, exploding at him, and kicking him out of the house with inviting him back and sending him money. Finally, Strike told the jury that the fact that the body was buried didn't signify anything. Whoever shot Amy St. Laurent would not want her found.

After a brief rebuttal by LaRochelle, the judge dismissed the three alternate jurors and continued with her instructions. She told the jury that it was her job to decide the law that applied, their job to decide credibility and the facts. That they must not allow their emotions or any feelings of prejudice or sympathy to play any part in their verdict. That they had a duty to be businesslike.

As everyone stood and the jury filed out, Danny Young looked over at Diane and Lucille and he almost started to cry. He realized that after nearly a year and a half of intense, day-to-day involvement, he no longer had any control over what was happening with the case. Even when it was going to trial, and control had passed from the detectives to the prosecutors, he had still worked closely with Fern and Bill and had been very much a part of it. Now control had passed from all their hands into the hands of those twelve people.

I am worried based on my experience with juries. You just never know. I look over at Danny, at Scott, at Fern and Bill. Everyone is tired. It has been a long, difficult week and we are still clenched with tension as Fern gets up to make his closing argument. He is great—calm, patient, brilliant, his inflection perfect as he makes his points about the testimony—the map, the timeline of events, the grand jury testimony, the location of the body. I want to scream out, "Well done, Fern, well done!"

We listen nervously to Strike. Reasonable doubt, no evidence, no DNA, timeline is off because of roommates and other witnesses. He attacks the grand jury testimony as illegal and tells them they must find reasonable doubt. The pressure on the jury is tremendous. I can see it in their faces.

Justice Mills instructs the jury with poise and skill and a professional directness. Please God give us justice, I think, as they slowly file out, moving together like a caterpillar.

We stumble out of the courtroom to wait in a newer courtroom set aside for us down the hall. This is the hardest time of all. Diane's brow is furrowed with worry. Julie's face is a study in pain and weariness. Everyone else shuffles around awkwardly, not knowing what to do. It is just too hard to be in the room. The air is dense with feelings, with trepidation.

I leave them in their individual solitudes of pain and worry and return to the mass of details that await me. It feels surreal walking into 109 through walls of cops and questions. I know better, but it feels like all this other stuff should stop while we wait for the verdict. Danny, Scott, and Tommy are conversing, worrying, predicting, projecting. Matt Stewart isn't with us today. His son is graduating from the army at Fort Sill, Oklahoma, and he left last night to attend.

No one lets the family into their real fears. Danny looks at me and says, "What is taking them so long? This is so easy."

We discuss the hows and whys to occupy our nervous minds. "Well, shit, Dan, at least he goes to jail even if it is a bullshit manslaughter."

I look at Dan and Scott. "You guys did your best." Scott is biting his nails again. "Scott, you did great. It's up to them, now."

So hard to leave it up to them. As if we had any choice.

To ease the tension, the detectives start a betting pool on when the jury will return. From 1300 to 1900. I go with 1520. It's an incredibly anxious time and I know I'm not the only one who's praying.

At 11:10 a.m., the jury was excused to begin deliberations.

An hour later, the jury asked to hear the grand jury tape again.

The lawyers, the detectives, and the families waited in the small courtroom assigned to Amy's family. For the next four hours, everyone hovered, slumped, and paced, waiting in an agony of indecision.

1425. I'm in the hallway outside the old courtroom, listening to Danny's heels strike the marble as he paces. Like decades of cops before him, Scott is leaning against an historic marble pillar. Danny looks at me and says, "Manslaughter. I know that's what it will be. They are struggling with murder/manslaughter. I cannot even think 'not guilty.' I can't, Captain."

"It's Joe, Dan. Joe. And I can't think that either. We've gotta pray that they will see the truth."

Tommy is in and out, in and out, full of energy, pacing like a parakeet, his shoes shuffling and clicking. Eyeing me with the thrill and anxiety of the wait.

I go in and out of the room where the family is waiting. Everyone does. It's awkward. There's not much more we can say. There's nothing to do in this stark room except wait. No one dares to leave in case the jury comes back. No one knows what to do with themselves. So we pace. Shuffle. Every now and then there is a funny word, an injection of humor into the awful tension. Then we return to a somber silence and our shuffling, pacing, and waiting.

1520 passes and I've lost my ten dollars. What's the holdup? God, please help them. Amy?

Danny's still pacing the hall, a nervous nelly. "It's gotta be manslaughter. They'll think he was on acid, believe his version, and . . ."

"Danny, as long as he's guilty of something . . . and goes to jail! Did you see that prick turn around and look at Julie? Sometimes I wish Dennis would snap and jump on him." Dennis has done an impressive job of holding himself together. He has told us he'd like to kill Gorman for what that bastard did to his daughter.

Bruce Coffin comes over from 109. Still out? He feels the tension, then quietly grabs me and says, "There's a grasshopper at a bar, you see, and the grasshopper says to the bartender . . ."

"Bruce!"

Around four, the jury sent word that they had reached a verdict. Hastily, everyone entered the courtroom and took their seats.

Before the jury returned, the judge spoke to those who were waiting. "Before we bring the jury in, I just want to say that I know this is a difficult—has been a difficult trial for many in this courtroom and I know this is a difficult moment.

"Regardless of what the verdict is, there would be people who would be pleased and there would be people who will not be pleased, but I am telling you and I am instructing you that I will not tolerate any sort of outbursts from anyone in this courtroom when the verdict is given by the jury for two reasons.

"The first reason is that would be disrespectful to the Court and I don't mean by the Court myself, I mean what we are doing in this room. And second of all, it would be disrespectful to the members of the jury. We have asked these twelve people to do a very difficult job and they have done it and so I would ask that everyone show the respect that they deserve and that the Court deserves as well."

At 4:08 p.m., as Amy's family held hands and held their breath, the jury entered. Danny Young and Scott Harakles were waiting side by side, and they saw that none of the jurors looked at Gorman.

THE CLERK: Madame Forelady and members of the jury, have you reached a verdict?

THE FOREMAN: We have.

It's 1600. The jury is back. My stomach flips. Everyone moves quickly toward the hall leading to the courtroom. The tension in the air so tangible a cloud of it seems to move with us. We file into the wooden spectator area. Danny, Scott, Fern, and Bill are up in front. It seems so right that these four men should be aligned for this.

Gorman is led past us. He's got an air of indifference, cavalier as he comes to learn his fate.

Everyone is in their places, standing, bending, swaying with the weight of the moment.

Justice Mills looks at us for a moment. It is very intense. Then she speaks, taking charge of her courtroom. The decision is in. There will be no outbursts in this court. She continues to warn everyone about respect for the process. You could hear a pin drop as she reminds us of the sacredness of what is happening.

"Remain standing for the jury," the bailiff announces. They file in from the right side of the courtroom. Ordinary people.

The room is surreally quiet. Danny and Scott practically reek of tension and concern. They have put so much into this. Eyes closed, I pray as I listen to the jury move into their positions.

I have no reservations. No doubt. I know that Gorman is guilty. But I have no idea what we will hear. Please, God. Please.

Justice Mills announces the protocol to the court as the jury remains standing. Then her clerk turns to the forelady. "How do you read to the charge of murder?

THE CLERK: As to the indictment charging murder, do you find the
    defendant Jeffrey Gorman guilty or not guilty?

THE FOREMAN: Guilty.

THE CLERK: So say you madame forelady?

THE FOREMAN: Yes.

THE CLERK: So say you all?

THE JURY PANEL: Yes.

Justice Mills continues, thanking the jury and addressing the attorneys, but many in the room aren't listening. They're hearing the word "guilty" echoing in their ears. Danny Young and Scott Harakles grab each other's arms and murmur, "Yeah! We did it!" They're feeling incredible jubilation and trying not to let it show. The air in the room is filled with murmurs and suppressed sobs. Rising above them is a piercing cry from the back.

I hear the foreman returning with other words, and then the word "guilty."

A collective gasp from the crowd in many frequencies. I still can't believe my ears. Like it was an echo chamber, there are whispers of the word. "Guilty."

I look up and thank God. Danny's head is bowed. Scott is looking up at the ceiling. Both emotional. The judge is still speaking, giving instructions, but I don't hear what is being said. It is drowned by the muted mews, strange, stifled cries and sobs from where the family is seated. In the back, Gorman's mother howls like a wounded animal.

My eyes are wet as I look to the ceiling, trying to stop tears I don't want anyone to see. The jury files out. The judge leaves. Danny's eyes are wet as I grab him, Bruce, and Scott. After the seemingly endless wait, everything has happened so quickly.

Now that court is dismissed, the sound of crying grows louder as people stop holding back. Diane, Julie, Lucille, Dennis, and Kathy and Richard are all hugging, choking, holding back emotions and cries.

Tammy Westbrook's grief is unnerving. A steady, muted howl punctuated by tragic wails.

We stumble and shuffle out of the courtroom, bumping into each other, as

Gorman is led away. I watch his face for a reaction and there is nothing there. Nothing. I heard later that he leaned over to Bill Stokes and said, "Watch your back, bitch."

We move out into the hallway. I shake Fern's hand. Bill's hand. Well done. Well done. I don't feel happy. This is not triumph but closure. It will take time to sink in, to penetrate the barriers we've erected to brace ourselves against the possibility of a "not guilty" and Gorman going free.

I hold back tears as I walk, but one runs off my right cheek and ski jumps onto my shirt. First time I ever cried in court.

Tommy, Danny, and I grab hands, soft-punch each other, and offer awkward backslaps. Hundreds of images come flashing back from the case as we move toward the room reserved for us. As we leave the courtroom behind, the crying begins in earnest.

I hold my breath to control my own tears as I hug a few people. Making the rounds. Eventually, I approach Diane, following a line of others. I will not cry. Her slight body heaving as she sobs out a muffled thank-you.

"Don't thank me. Thank Danny. Thank Scott. They're the ones who made this happen."

We part. She goes to Dan and it starts all over again. The scene is repeated over and over with different people as everyone tries to absorb it and to comfort each other.

I call the chief and Deputy Chief Burton. Listening to their "Congratulations" and "Great job!" I think, funny, it doesn't feel like congratulations. Nothing like a celebration. It just feels sad, as though part of everyone's grief was suspended, awaiting this verdict, and now it has all come rolling back.

We all just sit there in awkward silence. Finally, Lucille's friend Louie blurts out, "So what do we do now?" It breaks the tension and a few of us laugh.

Eventually, Fern and Bill come in, finished with their legal obligations, and talk to the family. Dennis and Kathy hug and listen, while Fern gives us an overview and Bill even makes us laugh.

I speak of how we wouldn't be here if it wasn't for Danny Young starting all this. About his passion for solving this case. I continue, speaking about Scott and the two agencies and how Amy brought us all together. I tell everyone that I have no doubt Amy influenced all of us, and many lives, through this horrible tragedy. Let us think of the good that has come from this.

Finally, we all embrace and hug again and shuffle out of the room.

When he could finally get away, Danny Young ducked into an empty courtroom just to be alone for a while. He had spoken with his wife, Linda, several times during the day, keeping her posted on the progress of the jury deliberations. Now he called her again to tell her about the verdict. This was when the fact that Gorman had been convicted of murder—that the good guys had won justice for Amy—finally hit home, and he broke down.

Outside, the news converges on all of us as we exit the courthouse. We've lost all track of time and are surprised to find it's dark. Diane, Julie, and Lucille form a covey as bright lights and colorful microphones identifying the stations invade their sphere. Dennis and Kathy slowly slip away.

Diane is flooded with questions and, as courageous as always, fields them with grace. Julie stares at the ground. She's not ready for this. She needs to do her processing in private. Bill and Fern are there, and Bill speaks.

Danny slides away into the dark. Tommy slides away, then Bruce. They leave the bright lights of the news as Stokes's words lift on the night air, walking out of the circle of light and into the dark.

I am reminded of the night we found Amy. How people would disappear from the glow of the spotlights, fading like ghosts into the gloom.

I can hear Stokes's voice trailing off. "From the very beginning we realized . . ." I head through the parking garage to 109. "Hey, Danny! . . . wait up."

We walk through the lot, shoes clicking, coats and ties flying. I put my arm around Danny. "It's great, Danny. Great," I say.

"Captain," he says, raising his red eyes and shifting his wide shoulders wearily, "I gotta work tonight. My regular shift . . ."

"That's crazy, Dan, I'll get you out of your shift," I tell him. "Go home."

As we approach the station, I realize we don't know what to feel. It's such an anticlimax after waiting so long. I just feel numb. I think I need a beer, but I need to go home more.

Cops are moving in and out of the building, congratulating and asking questions. News vans circle the station and the courthouse like sharks. At my desk, I try to explain it to other cops and find I can't and that I don't want to.

Danny, relieved of his shift, leaves 109. "I'm going home," he says.

I see Tommy and Bruce in the hall. "Hey," I ask, "feel like a beer?" "Naw, let's just go home," Tom says. "We're all kinda wasted."

Neither Tom nor Bruce give up a Guinness easily. But I know how they feel. No beer. No celebration. Just a strange, drained feeling. The victory is not what we all imagined.

I drive away in silence. A patrol car, sirens blazing, runs up Pearl Street, another east on Congress, headed toward Smith for a "10-45," another domestic.

I snap off the radio, sick of police shit, and drive home in silence, the defroster blowing warm air into my face. Almost there, stopped at a red light, tears slowly fill my eyes, turning the traffic light and waiting cars into a kaleidoscope of colors.

Later, alone in my hot tub outside, it's about fourteen degrees. So cold. So crisp. I sit in the gathering warmth, more peaceful now. Stars are twinkling blue white through the branches.

Images from the case are rushing through my head. I see her corpse in the dirt. I'm sorry, Amy, so sorry. For you, for everyone. Those stifled sobs in the courtroom are back with me, all that blurting out of pain. As images flash, I wonder, What it is really all about? I look up at the heavens and get no answer.

I rest in the water, so tired I'm half dozing in the silence. Then wind whispers through the trees and my buoy bell chimes. I have not heard that sound in a while. My tears pour down, hot in the cold air. Suddenly, I feel peace as the wind shifts and the chimes sound again.

I know it's Amy, telling me, telling us, that it's okay.

I reflect on Amy's diary entry on September 10th. "Surely goodness and mercy will follow me all the days of my life, and I will dwell in the house of the Lord forever." Forever. FOREVER.

Epilogue

Amy's Legacy

And can it be that in a world so full and busy the loss
of one weak creature makes a void in any heart, so
wide and deep nothing but the width and depth of vast
eternity can fill it up!"
—Charles Dickens, *Dombey and Son*

Amy St. Laurent's family had to wait a long time for the closure that would finally let them begin their grieving process without repeatedly having to sit in courtrooms rehearing the details of her death. It would not be until six months after the verdict, at the sentencing phase of Gorman's trial, that the family would finally have a chance to tell the court what Gorman's violent act had done to them, and what the world had lost when Amy St. Laurent was killed.

Amy's younger sister, Julie, spoke of the pain of spending seven weeks with the missing person posters everywhere she went, downtown, in her favorite stores, and all over the USM campus. How she'd be out putting up posters and expecting that Amy would come around the corner and start laughing at her. But it went on and on. There was no place she could go where she could get away from them.

She told of driving down the road past the spot where Amy had been buried, a place she passed several times daily on her way to school and work, and how, since Amy was found, the knowledge that Amy had been there the whole time made her physically ill. She had never been able to travel that route again.

She told the court that when she lost her big sister, she also lost her best friend and her sense that the world was a safe place: "when that day happened, everything in my life came to a stop. My family was walking around like zombies . . . the look in their eyes of not celebrating her birthdays. You should see the hurt on their faces. Even now, after it's been two years, I don't see things the same. The world isn't the same to me . . . everywhere I go, I am constantly . . . watching myself."

Amy's father, Dennis St. Laurent, said that he had been in a living hell for twenty months and doubted that he'd ever come out of it. He told the court that his daughters were all he had in this world, all he lived for, and Gorman had hurt both of them. He said that Amy had been a loving and caring person who did not deserve what Gorman had done to her. He reminded the court that, not only had Gorman never shown any remorse for his crime, he was so cold blooded he had tried to hide Amy from her family so that they could never find her and at least have the closure of a funeral.

Last to speak on Amy's behalf was her mother, Diane Jenkins. After thanking the court for the opportunity to finally be heard, she said:

> I wanted to start out by saying that there are two kinds of people in this world. One who makes the world a better place for having been a part of it and those who leave it with destruction in their path.
>
> I want everyone to know who Amy was because up until now, she has only been the victim's face on the posters. I also want everyone to really understand the impact that this has had on my family, friends, and me. Amy was a pretty remarkable young woman for only being twenty-five. She loved her family and friends and was extremely caring and loyal to them. She understood what it meant to care and give from the heart.
>
> You see, people genuinely loved Amy because she knew how to love and care about them. Amy was also a very hard worker, a contributing member to society. She had the opportunity to go to college and she didn't take it, so she worked very hard to finally get where she was. She had a very good job with a lot of responsibility.
>
> The words her boss wrote in a note to me were "Amy was the best" and she was.

So this is what her friends and colleagues have left—photographs and memories of a young woman who touched their hearts.

My personal loss is beyond words. A piece of me died that day also. Pain does not end, it only changes and pain really doesn't care when it rears its ugly head and what it is that triggers it to come back at you one more time.

I want people to understand what this has done to us and me. Imagine getting the call that is a parent's worst nightmare, being told that your child can't be found. After the initial shock, can you imagine how traumatic that is? Then having to pull yourself together because you have another child and you need to be there for them.

Imagine having to tell your parents and trying to explain that their grandchild is missing and then just two days later, having to go back into the same nightclub you know your daughter was in last and asking everyone if they have seen this young woman and having to explain to them that this is your daughter and she is missing. Then going back out two days later for the next two nights and doing it all over again in hopes that someone will remember something.

Imagine days turning into weeks, imagine walking railroad tracks, construction sites, woods, marshes, truck yards, fields, and vacant buildings. Nothing. Nothing. By that time, you're not looking for your daughter, what it is you're looking for is a body. Not the vibrant, beautiful daughter.

Imagine doing this until you emotionally and physically can't anymore. That is pain and trauma. Imagine for seven weeks seeing your daughter looking back at you from the reward posters, those beautiful blue eyes piercing your heart, but you know how important those posters are.

Imagine having to maintain a career during all of this. Imagine having to send your other child back to school. Imagine having to deal with the missing child's finances, try explaining to someone why you're canceling someone else's phone service, cable, or why the bills now have to be put in your name. Imagine seven weeks of this.

Imagine finally getting the call that you are hoping for and dreading, the call that they found her and they are waiting for positive ID and then waiting to learn how she died. Then imagine being told that she was found partially clothed and died of a gunshot wound to the head. Then imagine telling her sister how she died and imagine what you would say when you were asked the question by this child who has lost her only sibling, "Why her? Why did she have to die?"

Imagine having a funeral service just a little over a week before Christmas and what would you do with the gifts you already bought her?

Now imagine having to pack up your child's apartment, boxing up a young life. Imagine going through her clothes and holding them next to you because they smell like her and you know you will never hold that person again. So you keep going back and holding the sweater and inhaling the remains of the person you loved very much, but eventually the scent goes away.

So what are we left with? Memories, possessions, pain, the ring she wore when she was murdered.

I'll never see her children, my grandchildren. A funeral for a friend's young sister brings all of the painful memories back to the surface like it was yesterday. Even simple everyday things like listening to the rain bring pain.

For the duration Amy was missing, each time it rained, my heart ached thinking she was out there somewhere cold, wet, afraid and wondered why someone hasn't come to save her yet. I can't stand listening to the rain now.

When I allow myself to go there, I can imagine what the last moments of her life must have been like. The fear, pain, and horror and I am also almost ashamed to tell you that I don't allow this to happen often, it hurts too much. This I want you to know is real. I live with this every day and it invades my thoughts, breaks my sleep, and breaks my heart over and over again and I'll never forget it as long as I live.

Our family and friends were not the only ones who lost when we lost Amy. Society did as well. If she had this much caring, understanding, and compassion for the human spirit at twenty-five, just imagine what she could have done if she lived.

Jeffrey Russell Gorman was sentenced to sixty years in the Department of Corrections custody for the murder of Amy St. Laurent.

Subsequently, Gorman appealed his conviction to the Maine Supreme Judicial Court (the Law Court), arguing that allowing his mother's grand jury testimony violated both the Maine rules of evidence and the Confrontation Clause of the United States Constitution. Legal matters move slowly. The case was argued before the Law Court in February of 2004. In March of 2004, the United States Supreme Court decided a landmark Confrontation Clause case, *Crawford v. Washington*. Because the Gorman case involved potential *Crawford* issues, both sides had to rebrief and rear-

Gorman and his attorney, Clifford Strike, listen as he is sentenced for the murder of Amy St. Laurent. (*Portland Press Herald*)

gue the case. A final decision, denying the appeal and affirming Gorman's conviction, was issued by the Law Court on July 22, 2004, two years and nine months after the night Amy St. Laurent disappeared.[1]

While the sentencing phase of the trial was the family's first opportunity to speak for their daughter in a legal forum, and while their anxiety that the conviction might not be affirmed and they might have to face Gorman again through the ordeal of a second trial was not laid to rest for another year, Amy's mother, Diane Jenkins, did not wait for finality to begin taking steps to ensure that other young women would have a better chance to be protected than her daughter had.

When a loved one dies, survivors often have a powerful desire to perform some memorial act to ensure that the value of that person's life does not simply fade away. When you've loved someone, you want the world to

Dennis St. Laurent, Julie St. Laurent, and Diane Jenkins speak with the press after Jeffrey "Russ" Gorman is sentenced to 60 years in prison. (*Portland Press Herald*)

understand something of who they were. You want to create a legacy that will confirm that the person who is gone lived a meaningful life. Most important, you want to carry on the meaning of that life into the future.

Within months of her daughter's death, as the facts concerning the circumstances of Amy's death came to light, Diane Jenkins, from the depths of her own personal pain, was already looking for ways to prevent the same thing from happening to someone else's child. In Amy's memory, she created the Amy St. Laurent Foundation to encourage the avoidance of violence, to provide help for victims, and to help arrest and convict violent offenders.

The first project undertaken by the foundation was to bring RAD[2] (Rape Aggression Defense systems) courses to the area by underwriting the training of a group of Portland police officers as instructors,[3] and providing the equipment necessary to teach RAD classes. The RAD system is a basic self-defense program for women, taught in a series of three or four sessions, that involves awareness, risk reduction and avoidance, and basic physical defense systems. It is designed first of all to make women safer by enhancing their awareness of their surroundings, teaching them strategies to make their environments safer, and teaching them to recognize and avoid risks. Second, the course teaches assertiveness and verbal confrontation skills to help women avoid the appearance that they are victims and to stop aggressors. Finally, the course teaches realistically employable tactics to women who are serious about defending themselves in situations where their life is in jeopardy, allowing them a chance to escape.

Diane Jenkins also began speaking to high school students, beginning at a "Give Back the Night" safety forum at Falmouth High School, sponsored by the Junior League. She joined Chief Chitwood and community policing officers to deliver the message that violence and danger are real and can happen in the lives of ordinary people. No speaker, however well prepared or sincere, could possibly have matched the eloquence of someone who had been through it. Seeing Jenkins's small, upright figure holding her daughter's picture, and hearing the deep vibrations of sorrow in her voice as she told about who her daughter Amy was and the impact of her disappearance on the family, was the most vivid reminder possible of the real-world effects of violence on a family.

The audience was absolutely silent as Jenkins, who never imagined herself as a public speaker, described the last conversation they ever had, ending with Amy's last words: "I love you, too, Mom." Jenkins's willingness to share her personal story had a powerful impact on adolescents who imagined that bad things happened in other places and to other people, and that their lives couldn't be touched.

In an interview after that first event, Jenkins said, "It could have been either of my kids sitting in that audience, any one of our children . . . It's important that they don't think they're invincible and that nothing bad is ever going to happen to them."[4]

While Diane Jenkins honors her daughter's memory and carries out Amy's caring and compassion for others by working to make other people's children safer, Amy St. Laurent's memory lives on in another arena as well, and the bonds forged by her spirit linger. Ask public safety officers involved in the Amy St. Laurent case what was special about the case and they will come back, again and again, to the unusual working relationship forged among their different agencies.

On January 22, 2003, Deputy Attorney General William Stokes wrote the following in a letter to Captain Loughlin:

> In my 25 years of service to the State of Maine, I have seldom seen a case involving such a wonderful collaboration and level of cooperation between law enforcement agencies as in this case. The Portland Police Department and the Maine State Police, together with the Maine Warden Service, did themselves proud by their cooperation and their single-minded focus in first, finding Amy's body and second, bringing her killer to justice. I want to thank you for your wonderful support and for assigning such terrific people, such as Danny Young, to work on this case.
>
> His relationship with the Maine State Police, and in particular with Scott Harakles, is an example to all of the law enforcement agencies to follow.

As Bill Stokes recognized, it had been an unusual case for everyone. Without the collaboration, and an extraordinary willingness to put personal differences aside, combined with the passionate desire they all shared to secure justice for Amy, the case might never have been resolved and Gorman might not have been convicted.

Cooperation happened at every level and at every phase of the investigation. Despite radically different personal styles and command structures, Sergeant Tommy Joyce and Sergeant Matt Stewart, both used to deference to their status as CID sergeants and both used to calling the shots, were able to work out or put aside their differences in order to ensure that their primary detectives were able to work, unimpeded, on Amy's case. Both recognized the importance of smoothing the path and providing staff support and moral support throughout a long and difficult investigation. Matt Stewart said that even if there were differences of opinion regarding the case higher up, on the ground, the detectives just kept things rolling and worked it out.

Sergeant Stewart summed up the relationship between the agencies in this way:

> This case showed the reality of having two experienced and capable homicide units, both staffed with a bunch of "alpha dogs," go after a case together. Add to that some fairly blurred jurisdictional lines and an outspoken and media-savvy Chief of Police whose press philosophy is basically opposed to

that of the MSP and AG, and you've got quite a challenging situation. There was always mutual respect between the investigators and supervisors on both sides because we all knew we were dealing with fellow homicide detectives who had been "there." So maybe the real story is how this bunch of cops rose above all of the distractions and confusions of this kind of blended investigation and prevailed to successfully bring a killer to justice.

Scott Harakles gives the credit for their positive working relationship to Amy, to the goodness of her spirit and to the way she got under their skins and made them *need* to solve her case. The situation with Amy was so important that everyone focused on getting justice for her. He also talks about the unusual nature of his reception at the Portland Police Department. In many situations, when the state police come into an investigation where they have superior authority, the welcome may not be very warm. People often don't greet him or make eye contact. In Portland, where he had to go every day, he was treated like one of the guys, welcomed and made a member of the team.

Danny Young now has Tommy Joyce's job, as CID sergeant, while Joyce has left the department to teach criminal justice. Danny Young and Scott Harakles continue to be good friends, maintaining the bridge between the two agencies that was built while solving Amy St. Laurent's murder. Recently, they have begun to work together on some of Young's cold cases, the cases he would never give up.

Another significant, and in many ways even more surprising, legacy of the Amy St. Laurent case was the involvement of the Maine Warden Service. When Lieutenant Patrick Dorian made his initial phone call, asking if the warden service might offer its search and rescue expertise in helping to find Amy St. Laurent's body, he knew it was a long shot. It was unheard of at that point for the warden service to get involved in what was essentially an urban murder case.

Every police investigator went into that initial meeting skeptical about the possibility that the wardens would have anything to offer, and came out of it convinced that it was a chance worth taking. On the Saturday of the massive search operation, even as some of the detectives rolled their eyes in cynical disbelief about the possibilities of finding a needle in a haystack or, as one of them put it, a buried needle in a buried haystack, Danny Young and Scott Harakles woke with the firm belief that they would find Amy before the day was over. They ended that day grateful that Amy had been found and firm in their conviction that Amy's spirit had guided them.

It is also part of Amy's legacy that, having succeeded in that initial effort, the Maine Warden Service emerged more willing to offer its search expertise to other law enforcement agencies, and its success encouraged other agencies to call on them.

Warden Kevin Adam says that these days, when there is a high-profile missing person case in Maine, the state police or local police will get the call and they, in turn, will call the warden service. Wardens have assisted in finding the body of David Langley, in Glenburne, where the police, following up a tip, had located the skull but couldn't find the rest of the remains. They searched the site with dogs and MASAR volunteers, and on the last pass a warden spotted an out-of-place piece of dirt in the woods the size of three silver dollars. The dogs were brought back in, and they found the dismembered remains. Wardens also located the crime site in the disappearance of a Colby College student. And they used their dogs to find the body of Cody Greene in Brunswick, camouflaged with brush in the yard of the house where she was last seen.

In the spring of 2003, the wardens and MESARD (Maine Search and Rescue Dogs) went north to Miramichi, New Brunswick, to assist in locating the body of a homicide victim. The first effort failed, but a second effort, in June, eventually led investigators to the body after one of the wardens noticed, from their mapping, a gap in the area initially searched.

In the summer of 2004, a teenage girl named Crystal Higgins went missing. The warden service was called in and searched hundreds of miles of roads. Finally the wardens sat down and had a meeting, applied their training and experience, and said that either she had left the area or she was in the water. Based on what they knew about the missing teenager, it seemed unlikely she'd left the area. They got the Marine Patrol out and found that her car had gone off a pier.

As with all areas of expertise, the more searches the wardens do, the more experienced and better at it they get. And the impetus came from Lieutenant Dorian and Amy St. Laurent.

In Fort Williams Park in Cape Elizabeth, facing the ocean, is a granite memorial bench donated in Amy's memory. Here, in a place of quiet

The memorial bench in Ft. William Park in Cape Elizabeth.

beauty, those who loved her can sit and remember the lovely, vibrant girl Amy St. Laurent was. It is a fitting memorial to the thoughtful, wistful young woman who wanted to be more attuned to the beauty of the world. She touched many lives with her warmth and generosity in the brief twenty-five years of her life. She has touched many more through the actions of those who strove to bring her killer to justice. And she continues to reach forward into the future through the efforts she has inspired to bring closure, justice, and safety to others.

✳

A portion of the proceeds from this book is being donated to the Amy St. Laurent Foundation, to continue the work being done in Amy's name. Readers wishing to send contributions to the foundation should send them to:

The Amy St. Laurent Foundation
P.O. Box 664
Yarmouth, ME 04096

Notes

1. Edgar Allen Beem, "Teflon Tough Guy," *Boston Globe Sunday Magazine*, July 28, 2002.
2. In his preface to *Practical Homicide Investigation*, 3rd ed. (CRC Press, 1996), Vernon Geberth writes, "Homicide investigation is an aggressive business. Not everyone is qualified for the mission-oriented commitment of death investigation. *Your* homicide case is *yours* forever." Detective Young keeps the files from unsolved cases that he hasn't given up on, and has families he has stayed in touch with for years.
3. Under the SOP (standard operating procedure) in place at the time, unless extenuating circumstances such as suicide, an elderly person, a mentally handicapped person, etc., existed, reports were not taken on adults until they had been missing for twenty-four hours. In Portland, 99.5 percent of missing persons cases are resolved within a few days.

Chapter 3 (pp. 24–33)

1. A background check on a suspect begins in-house, with a check of the internal database for criminal history. Detectives also check with the Department of Motor Vehicles and the SBI (State Bureau of Investigation) for a record of all state convictions. For criminal history beyond state borders, detectives use the NCIC computer, which can supply a national printout of arrests and convictions. Once one of these checks reveals a criminal record, detectives often call the police department where the arrest took place to get the inside story on the suspect.
2. The "homicidal triad," or triangle, is bed-wetting at an inappropriate age, starting fires, and cruelty to small animals or children. At least two of these three characteristics are frequently found in the histories of serial killers. See John Douglas and Mark Olshaker, *Journey into Darkness* (Scribner, 1997).
3. At this point, police had no grounds on which to arrest Eric Rubright. His presence at the police station, as well as his decision to take a polygraph exam, were purely voluntary. One of the constant challenges to detectives is to create an

environment in which suspects will speak with them willingly. As Lieutenant Albert Joseph, Jr. says in his book, *We Get Confessions* (A. J. Book, 1997): "Treat them with respect + bullshit them a little + get them to like you = sell them that vacuum cleaner or get that confession."

4. Although suspects and witnesses may view polygraphs as a trap, and defense attorneys reflexively counsel their clients not to take them, police routinely use the polygraph as a way of eliminating suspects. As with Rubright, observing an individual take a polygraph provides valuable information, not simply through the person's words or the polygraph results, but through the body language.

5. It is a fact that anyone has the right to refuse to speak with the police after the initial phase of stopping if requested and identifying oneself. There is usually no legal obligation to cooperate. The obligation to cooperate stems from the moral obligations of membership in a civilized society and the simple recognition that there are many citizens and few police, and citizen cooperation is essential for an orderly society (known as the Thin Blue Line argument).

Chapter 4 (pp. 34–44)

1. *Practical Homicide Investigation*, p. 719.

Chapter 6 (pp. 55–67)

1. *Portland Press Herald*, Tuesday, November 11, 2003.

Chapter 7 (pp. 68–83)

1. Locard's Exchange Principle, a cornerstone of forensic science, states that when an offender comes into contact with a location or another person an exchange of evidence occurs.

2. Except for Gorman's own call to the police, reporting the thirdhand information that someone had told him that someone had seen Amy outside the Industry at 2:30 a.m. on the morning she disappeared.

3. Among the things the evidence techs found in Gorman's car was a stolen library copy of *The Boston Strangler*. Inside the back cover was written: "Get fucked up. Stay fucked up." Signed: Jeffrey Gorman.

4. The FBI description of post-offense behavior includes altered physical appearance, pronounced anxiety, atypical media interest, noticeable mood swings, withdrawn behavior, unusual level of preoccupation, unusual absenteeism, and altered sleeping and/or eating habits.

5. Over the next few months, he would offer varying explanations for this. He told one person he was cleaning it because he had a date, a second that he was loaning the car to someone, a third that Amy had been sick in the car.

6. Learning to listen to instinct, one of those hardwired, primitive senses designed to keep us safe, is especially difficult for women who've been socialized to "be nice." Still, this small thing, not divulged at earlier interviews, would stay in the detectives' minds, rising to haunt them again and again throughout the case. If Sharma had told the truth—no, he's not okay—might Amy have been saved?

7. A reserve police officer is an officer with partial police training, in Campbell's case, a hundred hours, who serves on an on-call basis when needed. Many departments do not subscribe to this expediency and require much more training. Portland, for example, does not have reserve officers. A person seeking to become an officer must attend the 16-week police academy, spend sixteen weeks with a field-training officer and then undergo a two-year probation period.

8. As an example of the way detectives check and recheck facts, the girls from Munjoy Hill were located, and one of them later confirmed, in an interview, the incident when Gorman took Campbell's gun out of the car and showed it to her.

9. Campbell's behavior regarding the loss of his gun ultimately lost him his job as a part-time police officer and his bid to become full time.

10. At one point, Westbrook police went to interview Campbell about his missing-gun report and Gorman was there, standing outside. As they were leaving to take Campbell down to the station, Gorman banged on the side of the police van, yelling, "You found the gun, right?"

Chapter 8 (pp. 84–92)

1. From an investigative point of view, anything that has proven to be successful in one investigation should certainly be considered in other cases, especially in cases where there is limited information. The use of a psychic can be considered as an additional investigative aid. Geberth, *Practical Homicide Investigation,* pp. 665–666.

2. Marie's drawing, which had roads and bodies of water but no street or town names, later turned out to be uncannily correct.

Chapter 10 (pp. 102–112)

1. A part of the Department of Inland Fisheries and Wildlife, under Maine statutes, 12 M.R.S.A. sec. 10105(4), the search and rescue arm of the warden service, upon "notification that any person has gone into the woodlands or onto the

inland waters of the State on a hunting, fishing or other trip and has become lost, stranded or drowned, the commissioner shall exercise the authority to take reasonable steps to ensure the safe and timely recovery of that person." Maine is unusual in having search and rescue in a conservation agency. In many states, the state police do it.

2. DOJ study: "Case Management for Missing Children Homicide Investigation, May 1997." Kenneth Hanfland, Robert Keppel, and Joseph Weis, Grant No. 93-MC-CX-K006, Office of Juvenile Justice.

3. In 2002, Guay and Reba received the Search and Rescue Canine Case of the Year award at the Maine Warden Service Awards Banquet.

4. Detectives knew it was crucial to keep this discovery from the public. Subsequently, Sergeant Stewart would get a heads-up call that a curious reporter was enroute to the Westbrook Police Department to look at records and had to persuade the reporter that revealing the traffic stop would seriously damage the state's case.

5. The next most dangerous are domestic calls.

Chapter 12 (pp. 124–140)

1. "Under ordinary circumstances an outdoor scene should not be searched during nighttime hours. Weather changes the rules. Under no circumstances should the crime scene and/or body be left unguarded and unprotected until daylight hours." Geberth, *Practical Homicide Investigation*, p. 807.

2. Crime scene response instructors teach that "the amount of destruction to a crime scene is proportionate to the number of people having access to that scene . . . non-essential persons must be kept out if the criminal investigation is to proceed in an effective and efficient manner." Training bulletin developed by the Portland Police Department.

3. "The ultimate goal is to recreate as accurately as possible the circumstances of the crime committed, identify and apprehend the perpetrator(s), and successfully guide the case through the criminal justice system." Robert M. Boyd, "Buried Body Cases," *FBI Law Enforcement Bulletin*, February 1979.

Chapter 13 (pp. 141–154)

1. There is endless cop lore about how to deal with death smells, which linger in the clothes and sometimes in the nose, for days. Often an officer returning from a death scene will strip down in the laundry room and throw the clothes into the washer with ammonia or bleach, leaving shoes outside the door to be dealt with later with water and ammonia. Some bury their clothes in the yard for a few

days. Sometimes the odor gets so bad the officers simply find a dumpster and throw their clothes away. Often there will be "phantom" smells the next day or in response to events that recall the death scene. Cops also use other smells to mask the odor—Vicks, piña colada, or mint. The risk is that, later, those scents will be associated with the death scent and become unpalatable as well.

2. Danny Young, who in part of his detective career was a rape and sex crimes investigator, said that based on the condition of the body and on his experience, he felt certain that a sexual assault or attempted sexual assault had taken place. Although Gorman was never charged with a sexual assault, Young said the medical examiner, based on her experience, concurred with his opinion.

3. Later, Tammy Westbrook would send her teenage daughter, Britney, to stay with Mary Young in Florida to get her away from all the turmoil and stress surrounding the investigation.

4. This was in a probation officer's notes in connection with the Probation and Parole Department's request to issue an arrest warrant for Gorman as a result of his probation violation.

5. Gorman's grandmother would later tell police that she didn't ask her grandson to leave because of his Uncle's expected return but because he had a gun.

6. Police would subsequently obtain phone records from Dot Gorman's house and Tammy Westbrook's cell phone that confirmed a twenty-two-minute call from there to Tammy Westbrook's cell phone on 12/9/01 at 2:27 p.m. EST.

7. As with so many of the tests that were conducted on Amy St. Laurent's body, the search for gunshot residue had been complicated by the decomposition process. Amy's body was taken from Augusta to the University of Maine in Orono, where Dr. Sorg conducted X-ray procedures. It was then returned to the medical examiner's office where subsequent testing was able to identify lead in the area of the exit wound, allowing the examiners to confirm that it was a gunshot wound.

Chapter 14 (pp. 155–169)

1. In retrospect, different players would remember this evening differently, but Harakles would say, of himself, "I certainly am a team player, but on this issue, I was a little pigheaded." And Sergeant Stewart, acknowledging this, would agree that, "Scott can be a handful."

2. This girl never voluntarily contacted the police. As Tommy Joyce says, "no one ever thinks to pick up the phone." She eventually mentioned knowing about the case in earshot of a security guard at a Marshalls store where she was working. The security guard contacted police. In a subsequent interview, she reported meeting Gorman the Sunday morning after Amy St. Laurent disappeared and seeing his pants and shoes covered with blood. He explained the blood was

the result of his mother's dog having puppies. Investigation showed the puppy story to be a lie.

3. It is a fact of human nature that most people are deeply troubled by knowledge of a crime. As in so many other aspects of police procedure—it's a peculiar balance. Cops are cynical about the level of citizen cooperation, often with good reason, and yet the system relies on the existence of a conscience and the witnesses' willingness to exercise it. Often the detective's biggest challenge is to appeal to that conscience in a way that will cause the person to do the right thing. Some willingly come forward, while others have to be found and talked into talking. Frequently, though, once they are found, they are relieved to have a chance to talk.

4. Scott Harakles notes that, in Gorman's confession to his mother, part of his motivation was clearly to hurt her and blame her for what had happened. In his confession to Mamma E, he was more frank, but he still tried to put an innocent gloss on things. He still made the abduction a moonlight walk by the pond and tried to blame his behavior on drugs and alcohol, even as he was describing a cold and calculated effort to get rid of evidence and cover up a crime. Even to himself, he was unable to admit that he was a sexual predator.

5. Gorman and his uncle, Daniel Gorman (Dot's son), had been involved in many criminal incidents during Gorman's adolescence, including stealing Dot's car.

Chapter 16 (pp. 177–194)

1. The decision to use divers to do the search brought out one of the occasional conflicts between Portland and state police. Once Sergeant Joyce and Detective Young decided the search was necessary, they wanted to do it right away; Sergeant Stewart and the MSP wanted to have a meeting to discuss and plan it before proceeding. Sergeant Joyce just said, "Well, we're doing it tomorrow." As with most such conflicts, this wasn't a conflict of purpose or a disagreement about the value of the proposed event; it was a question of command structure and internal process.

2. The ten most common characteristics of a sexual predator: refusal to take responsibility, sense of entitlement, low self-esteem, need for power and control, lack of empathy, inability to form intimate relationships with adults, history of abuse, troubled childhood, deviant sexual behaviors and attitudes, drug and/or alcohol abuse. Leigh Baker, *Protecting Your Children from Sexual Predators* (St. Martin's, 2002).

3. "When you talk about rapists, you need to understand, a large proportion of the male population will engage in coercive sex. As a male, there is a belief that getting to have sex is a birthright." From a talk by Robert Prentky, Ph.D. to Sisters in Crime, December 2003.

4. According to Robert Prentky, Ph.D., director of assessment and training at the

Justice Resource Institute in Massachusetts, and a specialist in evaluating sex offenders, those who come into a rape essentially misogynistic are going to react with rage and violence when a woman resists. Many of the witnesses interviewed described Gorman's toxic relationship with his mother and his negative attitudes toward women.

5. On October 21, 2001, the moon was only a waning crescent and the temperature around 36 degrees.

6. It is a common misunderstanding that men who rape must lack access to consensual sex. Another that coercive or acquaintance sex is not rape. However, researcher David Lisak, a professor at UMass Boston, has identified an entire population of so-called unindicted rapists who are off the radar screen. These men stake out their victims, stalk their prey, create opportunities through drugs and alcohol, and regularly engage in coercive sex, using whatever level of force is necessary to secure the cooperation of their victims and accomplish their acts, without considering themselves rapists or their behaviors criminal acts. Lisak identifies the characteristics of rapists as being: angry at women, need to dominate women, seeing women as objects to be conquered, seeing violence as normal in relationships, believing in rape myths (i.e., don't see what they are doing as rape), adopting hypermasculine attitudes, and having deficits in empathy. David Lisak, Ph.D., at a conference, "Stalking: Innovative Approaches to Investigation and Response," January 2004, sponsored by the Massachusetts Office of Public Safety and the National Center for Victims of Crime/Stalking Resource Center.

7. Increasingly, prosecutors coming before juries without forensic evidence fear what is sometimes called the "*CSI* effect," named for the television show, worrying that the TV crime shows "taint the jury pools with impossibly high expectations of how easily and conclusively criminal cases can be solved using DNA analysis and other forensic science." *Entertainment News*, December 19, 2002. There is a growing public expectation that police labs can do what TV labs can. "How Science Solves Crimes," *Time*, October 21, 2002. The public doesn't necessarily understand that this is fiction. A Florida medical examiner who teaches crime scene technique used to assign his students to watch *CSI* programs and record the errors. One episode alone had sixty-four errors. And most state and city crime labs are so understaffed and saturated with evidence that only the most serious crimes can be accepted. Even then, it may be many months before results are available. Nor do they necessarily have the latest and best equipment.

Chapter 17 (pp. 195–210)

1. On March 18, 2002, in recognition of his work on the Amy St. Laurent case, as well as his other outstanding work on the force, Danny Young was honored

by the Portland City Council as the Portland Police Department's Officer of the Year. Diane Jenkins threw a party for him at her real estate offices.

2. This was one good reason for the police policy of getting to witnesses early on and locking up their stories, so that their fuzzy recollections could be refreshed at trial.

3. Despite her unwillingness to cooperate with the prosecuting attorneys, during the eleven months between the grand jury hearings and the trial, Tammy Westbrook called Bill Stokes a few times, trying to get him to help her with legal issues involved in trying to get her daughter, Britney, back from Florida where she had gone to stay with Mary Young. Stokes had to explain that he was on the opposing side in a criminal matter, that hers was a civil matter, and that he wasn't able to help her.

4. "Quashed" is a legal term meaning suppressed or overruled. As a potential witness, Tammy Westbrook was subject to a sequestration order just like all the other witnesses. This meant she could not be present in the courtroom except during the time that she was testifying.

5. A more detailed account of the use of forensic entomology can be found in M. Lee Goff's book *A Fly for the Prosecution* (Harvard University Press, 2000).

Chapter 18 (pp. 211–219)

1. In law, a voir dire is a preliminary examination, outside the presence of the jury, of prospective jurors or witnesses under oath to determine their competence or suitability.

2. *Portland Press Herald*, January 15, 2003: "Judge Orders Suspect's Mom to Take Stand against Her Son." *Portland Press Herald*, January 16: "Gorman Jury to Hear about Telephone Call."

Epilogue (pp. 245–255)

1. Assistant Attorney General Donald Macomber described the appeals and postappeals process in a criminal case. First there is the appeal to the state supreme court, which may take up to a year for argument and months more for a decision. Then a motion for reconsideration, followed by a petition claiming ineffective representation of counsel, which could take another year or two, followed by further appeals to federal court.

2. The RAD system was developed in 1989 by Larry Nadeau, a Virginia police officer, who was looking for an accessible course that would meet the specific needs of women. Since then, over 250,000 women have taken the course, which is offered on many college campuses, as well as in communities, through their local police departments.

3. Richard Sparrow, Amy's longtime boyfriend, who, like her mother, had spent countless hours searching for Amy, took the training to become a RAD instructor. An exception to the training rules, which normally allow only men who are police officers to be trained as RAD instructors, was necessary to allow Sparrow to participate. Along with Sparrow, the police officers who trained included Mary Sauschuck, Lucas Porter, and Coreena Behnke.

4. David Hench, "From Anguish, Comes Urgency," *Portland Press Herald*, March 21, 2002.